THE
ENDLESS
CREATIVE

A. P. LAMBERT

HOUSE
PUBLISHING

HEARTS UNLEASHED HOUSE PUBLISHING

The Endless Creative
Copyright © 2023 Hearts Unleashed House Publishing

Copyright © 2023 by A. P. Lambert
Cover design by Susan Harring
Front cover illustration by Robert Clear
Author illustration by Andrew Bosley
Interior illustrations by Andrew Bosley
Interior book design by Susan Harring

For information about special discounts for bulk purchases contact:
hearts@heartsunleashed.com

Manufactured in the United States of America
Library of Congress Cataloging-in-Publication Data Lambert, A. P.

First edition 2023

ISBN: 978-1-7376063-7-6

[1. Art. 2. Crafts & Hobbies. 3. Language Arts & Disciplines. 4. Story Telling. 5. Self-Help. 6. Fiction.]

*For my kids, who continue to teach me how to be my
most creative self and how to have fun.
I'll always love you, no matter what—you goofballs!*

CONTENTS

ACT II – The Process

ACT III – The Pursuit

PROLOGUE

In the beginning, the world was formless and empty.

Doesn't sound too exciting, does it? But don't worry—it gets better.

Whatever your beliefs, I hope you can appreciate how our world—once a barren gray-brown rock—is now a dazzling place full of sound, color, and life. It has its troubles (some ugly, awful ones), but there is also wonder, beauty, and goodness to behold.

And we—you and I—are an inseparable part of such a wonderful world. We are inheritors of an incredible creation.

As residents of this world, we have a call upon our lives to take part in it, to mold and shape it, to leave a mark.

We were made to create. You, my friend, were made to create.

But there's a problem. Many of us have allowed our creative drive to go dormant. We've let our lives fall into the ruts of mindless routine—we've given in to the siren's call of normalcy.

We've forgotten our story.

Have you ever felt that way? Like you were made for something more? Like life has some truly great things in store for you, but you're not sure how to grab ahold of them? I get it, I've been there too.

It's easy to stray from the path of our true calling. And let's face it, just wandering around can be much more comfortable—and less scary. But if you want to make something that impacts, something that lasts, and something that really matters, then I'm here to help show you the way back to your true story—the story of the *endless creative*.

Just as the ghost of Mufasa in *The Lion King* instructed a reluctant Simba, you too can "remember who you are."

Make no mistake about it: *you are a creative.*

It's in your blood, in your very being. You have a purpose, a reason to use the gift of creativity that dwells within—perhaps deep and hidden, but still present.

No matter who you are or what you do for a living—whether you're a stay-at-home parent, a preschool teacher, a construction worker, a politician, a beach bum, a shoe-shiner, the CEO of a global corporation, or anything up, down, and in between—the creative power lives in you. It's just waiting to emerge again, to awaken you, to renew the wonder within.

Rediscovering it starts with small, simple steps. And it can begin right here, right now, wherever you are, whomever you are, and whatever you're going through in this moment.

"Now, hold on," you might say. "Can't I live a perfectly happy and well-adjusted life without one ounce of creativity?"

Maybe, if you call that living. But there's a world of difference between surviving and thriving. There's a great chasm between happy and fulfilled. A creative does so much more than take the steps necessary for continued existence. He or she does more than live for their own personal pleasure. A creative lives with meaning, with determination, and with purpose.

In the act of creating, we lose ourselves, and, in doing so, we become ourselves.

This invitation is for you: to answer the call, to embrace the power of creativity in every area of your life—to the benefit of yourself and those around you.

To be an endless creative is to be a world-changer. But not in the way you might at first expect. Sure, your work could touch thousands or even millions, but it's not likely. Either way, that sort of outcome is largely outside of your control.

However, the "little" creative thing you do this very day can still have an immeasurable impact. You can change a life, even a community. You can create something that lasts—something that matters.

So, are you ready to get started?

Now hold up one moment. There's something you should know before we go one step further. I may have misled you, and I need to set the record straight.

This isn't a self-help book.

You heard me right.

These days, self-help books are a dollar a dozen (used to be a dime, but, you know, inflation).

This is an invitation to be part of something more, something grand, something beyond you. Why? Because creativity ultimately requires an audience. It's a key ingredient in creating community. To be creative is to be part of something bigger, something with a life of its own: a movement.

Will you discover some helpful practices and principles of creative living here? Undoubtedly. But there's so much more to it than merely bettering yourself.

Self-help is too narrow. It's all about you.
Creativity requires a broader view.

What you'll find here is a call to be part of that big, wild, impossible something—to make a lasting mark.

I'll let you in on a secret: when we focus only on ourselves, the world misses out and we never find true satisfaction. However, when we work to improve the world at large, we also improve our own lives in the process.

Then what's all this endless creative stuff really about?

Put simply: we're going to cover some practical steps to living a creative lifestyle—one that produces positive change, both in you and around you. Because the specific methods that are useful for one person may prove a hindrance to another, our main focus will be on the overriding principles that anyone, anywhere can apply.

Ultimately, it's about an inward journey with outward results. It's about living the greatest story—one where you discover and fulfill your purpose.

And what is that, exactly?

Well, you'll just have to walk with me and find out. As with any journey, we'll take it one step at a time.

And this journey begins with a story…

ACT I

The Approach

Section 1 - The Creative

Creative (n)

One who sees the world differently, who asks questions and discovers new solutions; one who, through inspiration, imagination, and innovation, both embraces change in their own life and causes change in the lives of others.

Plateau

The weather this afternoon, warm and humid, rests upon the residents of Plateau Town like a damp fleece. It causes the dust, kicked up by bustling passersby, to cling to your skin and clothes. You're in no hurry today, but neither are you slow. You wander what seems an aimless path through cramped alleys filled with rubbish, under the shade of purple and yellow patches of stretched-out canvas, past storefront after busy storefront.

You brush past other shoppers, the hum of their talk blending into one dull cacophony, like the buzzing of bees. And yet you do pause from time to time to pick out a word or two. You recognize a familiar topic among the crowd: talk of unusual happenings—people mysteriously turning into stone, sometimes a limb or two, sometimes the whole person. You've heard this before, nearly a month ago, and dismissed it as a tall tale, but as more secondhand reports come in, you accept there must be something to these stories. It's something to investigate.

Later.

Despite the hushed tales, those who spread the gossip do not seem too bothered. Others are more interested in what is on sale today, caught up in the endless hunt for the things they most desire—things that never quite satisfy. The shops with their aromas, shiny wares, and enticing sounds seem to go on forever until, at last, you arrive at your intended destination: the Marketplace of Ideas.

It is there I notice you, standing on the other side of the street between some merchant of healthy eating habits and another who promises to teach you the twelve meditational secrets for great happiness. But their words are lost in the din. Those morsels, which once tickled your ears, do so no more. Such things have their place, but today you're looking for something else, something new, something real. You turn, and our eyes meet. In your eyes, I, too, find the very thing I've been seeking.

You cross the dirt road, deftly avoiding a reckless horse-driven cart, and arrive at my storefront—little more than a wooden desk and chair in front of a faded yellow tent covered in green patches. As you approach, you inhale…*what is that—peppermint?* You pause in silence to consider me: tall and thin, leaning forward with both palms pressed against the desk like a general studying battle plans. I wear a worn gray duster over a teal vest. Around my neck hangs a blue-and-red-striped bandana necktie. The whole get-up clashes noticeably. Under the unusually wide brim of my hat, you see eyes with a familiar gleam, one that calls to memory a place—ancient but somehow known. I welcome you with a wry grin, then shift in my chair, glance side to side, and lean in toward you.

On the desk beneath me lies a rusty compass and a weathered map made of animal skin. The map is hardly bigger than a napkin, with just a few simple lines and the occasional word to mark geographic locations— you do not recognize any of them. Then again, it has been some time since you've left town. On the edge of the table, closest to me, is a simple box made of chestnut, just big enough to hold a pocket watch.

I lean in a little closer and speak in hoarse tones, not quite a whisper, "Storm's brewin'."

You look up at the cloudless sky, then down again.

I pause for a moment, and we study one another. I tug on my bandana and clear my throat. "And just what brings you here today? What is it you seek? Another shiny object of distraction? Sorry, don't sell those. But no, you wouldn't have come to my little booth for that. You can find those anywhere. So what do I offer here? Well, it's something a little …

different. Something intangible, something of great—dare I say, immeasurable—value. Intrigued? Today I'm offering—waaaaait for it—a new perspective. Or is it an old perspective made new? You're confused. Let me explain—"

My speech stops short, and my eyes dart like startled squirrels. You look behind and see two rugged men in long black coats strolling down the street, casual yet watchful—hyenas looking for a meal. You spy the glint of metal in their holsters.

I pull back my sleeve and glance at an empty spot on my wrist. "I apologize, but it seems I've got some business I must attend to. I think it wise to continue our discussion elsewhere, more removed from the din and dither of the crowd. If you're still interested, you'll find me at The Outlook on the edge of town. I'll be there in two hours' time. Don't delay, mind you. I aim to leave soon."

I offer a sharp nod and then pull the collar up on my coat, scoop my belongings from off the table, and crouch into the low tent behind me.

My head emerges once more. "Oh, and be sure to bring your horse and an open mind. In reverse order. See you shortly."

I tip the wide brim of my hat and vanish behind the tent flap. You hear a sound like a rubber duck squeaking, and the tent shakes as if a miniature explosion had just gone off inside. Purple smoke curls up from under the tent.

The two black-coated men are talking with some merchants across the street, holding what looks like sketched portraits in their hands. You decide it's high time you slipped back into the crowd. You're soon glad you did—the merchants point in the direction of my tent.

From a distance, you observe the two men approaching the tent. They search the table, then kick it over in disgust. One of them peels back the tent flap—the only entrance—and you notice the inside is completely empty.

When the men turn back to scan the crowd, you decide it's best you disappear as well.

Creativity is inventing, experimenting, growing, taking risks, breaking rules, making mistakes and having fun.

~Mary Lou Cook

CHAPTER 1

Creative

When I first recognized *creative* being used as a noun, something sparked inside me. Everything about it felt right. The person using it was author and entrepreneur Joanna Penn, in reference to herself and one of the many guests she interviews on her podcast. She said it boldly, without a sniff of hesitation. And that's how it should be said, as if you're standing high atop the Swiss Alps like some Ricola commercial, shouting "I'm a creative!" for all of God's green earth to hear.

There's something so freeing, so revitalizing about knowing you are a creative—someone who wholeheartedly and unabashedly lives a life of creativity. It's a badge of honor, a password to a secret club, a ticket to the chocolate factory, an edict from the king, one that gives you permission to be who you are.

But I want to set the record straight: being a creative is not an emblem for only a privileged few to strut around with—it's an invitation to a party, and anyone may join. I wouldn't have bothered writing this book if I didn't believe that with all my heart.

Back when my family and I moved from Los Angeles, California to northern Arizona, I felt obligated to buy a pair of leather cowboy boots—partly to fit in, partly for their practicality. Boots offer great outdoor protection against a host of foot enemies such as (but not limited to) snakes, cacti, other pokey plants, biting insects, and biting children.

After purchasing said boots, I kept the tags on and walked around the house in them for a while. You see, I've had foot issues ever since I went on a weeklong backpacking trip in Yosemite and then lost feeling in one of my toes for six months. I blame the hiking shoes.

Now, when I buy shoes, I give them a good long test run before they can be feet approved. I keep the tags on and wear them only inside the house until I'm as sure as can be that they're just right.

Sadly, a lot of people treat creativity this way. They try it out, maybe wear it around the house where it's safe and free of judgment, but they don't really own it or take it out on the town. They keep the tags on so it can be returned if it turns out to not be so great a fit.

You'd be surprised at how many highly creative (including artistically talented) people I've talked to who will not admit their own creativity. It's shocking.

I'm here to tell you, it's time to tear those tags off. It's time to go to the rodeo.

When you do, you'll realize that being a creative is something special—something no one and nothing can take from you. It's yours, and you've earned it by right. When you're a creative, you know that you're not a hack or a fake. You stop caring what the critics say, because you know, deep down inside, you're the real deal.

That's how it should feel, but it isn't always the case. Not everyone accepts the invitation to the party. Some think it came to the wrong address. Others believe that the title must first be earned. Yet others have more than earned that title but still feel like frauds, imposters, kids who tricked a few adults into letting them sit at the big table, only to be found out.

There is a sort of truth to that last one. Being a creative is more than saying the right words and tapping your heels together. It's a process, a journey—if you will. And that journey involves struggle.

There is a temptation to live an ordinary and uncreative life, to take the safe route. This temptation comes even for those who deeply desire the life of the creative. Just when we think we've got it figured out, we fall back into old habits again. We get discouraged. We lose heart.

Sometimes, we give up.

I wish I could tell you it's easy to be a creative, but that would be misleading. So, to avoid the circumstance where my nose grows unnaturally long or my pants spontaneously catch fire, let me tell you the truth:

Creativity takes effort. Creativity comes at a cost.

Yes, creativity may come easier to some, but every person reaches a point where it is difficult to take the creative approach, where it's the last thing they want to do.

Sometimes creativity demands a great deal of effort. Sometimes the cost is high. The Statue of Liberty didn't build itself. That song you can't stop thinking about writing might require some deep soul searching, it could bring back painful memories or reveal something that you'd rather keep hidden. Developing that nonprofit organization will cost you significant time and money, will be emotionally draining, and could even lead to the end of a close relationship.

Don't misunderstand me—being creative doesn't have to be complicated. In fact, it can be as simple as opening your eyes. What's more, the reward for creativity greatly outweighs the cost. I don't think it's possible to measure the impact the Statue of Liberty has had on American and even global culture. Your song may be the one thing a person on the edge of suicide needs to pull them back. That nonprofit you built up could save the lives of an entire village by eradicating the disease or hunger that has plagued them.

Even if the benefits aren't immediately obvious, true creativity—*endless creativity*—changes the creator for good and is advantageous to those who experience it. Besides all that, if I didn't make it clear, you need creativity to live. I mean *really* live.

But I'm getting ahead of myself.

You might be wondering why I've bothered to write a big book about creativity. It's a fair question.

Having worked as a creative professional (meaning some sucker actually paid me for my work) for roughly twenty years now, I've learned a few things. Some of these lessons have come from my own experiences—both successes and failures—and some have come from the many other creative people I've had the distinct privilege of knowing and working alongside.

At some point, things began to coalesce into one unified collection of ideas that any sort of person who values creativity could benefit from. And voilà, the book you're now reading was born.

Now, I make no claims to perfection. I'm still a work in progress (as is any creative, no matter how successful or established they might be). Take anything I say with a grain of salt (and throw in some pepper for good measure). I'm simply and honestly conveying to you the very same concepts that have helped me greatly. I hope they help you just as much, if not more.

That's more than enough about me for now (if you care to know more, check out my website, creativeandbeyond.com, where I post regularly).

Where were we? Oh yes, *really* living. Right. But first, the stories.

CHAPTER 2

Stories

Hey, let's talk about stories!

Who doesn't like a good story? You, in the back there? Oh, c'mon, don't kid yourself. I know you love 'em too! We all do.

Stories have been around for a while. They're one of the oldest forms of entertainment. They're an essential part of our culture, our makeup (no blush or eyeshadow, but definitely foundation), our heritage as human beings. While the manner of presentation has changed over the years (verbal, pictorial, written, audio, audio visual, etc.) stories still share the same basic elements.

Storytelling has been around for a while, but how much do we really need it? Some, indeed, dismiss fictional stories as mere escapism. The general idea is that the characters and events are not real and, therefore, not important. Some even go so far as to say that fictional stories are lies and, therefore, are harmful. I beg to differ.

Works of fiction can lead us to the deeper truths of life, wrapped in a cleverly decorated package. They allow us a window through which to recognize the fantastic among the familiar. They catch us off guard, and, by doing so, reach the guarded places in our hearts and minds that we prefer to keep hidden and unmoved.

Consider what Allen Arnold has to say from his book, *The Story of With*:

"Just as explorers travel to fantastical places in search of the unknown, stories can transport us to places where we can then see our own stories more clearly. They invite us into other worlds and, in the process, offer a new way of seeing our own world.

Stories speak to our hearts in ways that facts alone fall short. Like when tears come unexpectedly while watching a movie. Or when a song you haven't heard in a decade provokes a forgotten longing.

We underestimate stories when we see them as just an escape from reality or a vehicle to teach a lesson. We don't need to escape our lives—nor do we need more lessons. We need our hearts awakened. And nothing reaches the heart faster than story."

Stories have the power to move us in a way few other things can. They can open us to new ways of thinking and living or remind us of what we value. Even though stories vary widely, they're all fundamentally about one thing: change.

Change happens all around us—it's unavoidable. We can choose to resist it, ignore it, or become part of it.

To be a creative is to be a force for change, to stand at the helm, steering the wheel, riding high on the waves (and making a few of your own).

Many of us want the world to change for the better, but before that can happen, we must be willing to be changed—in a big way. Why's that?

To offer something to the world, you first need something to offer.

You must undergo change. This is the journey of the creative: to follow the path from ordinary to extraordinary, from mundane to magnificent, from common to creative. Something great resides within you: the seeds of change. As you allow the power of story to mold and shape you into something amazing, your own life becomes a story to others, changing them in turn.

Just how does all that work? We're going to look into that as we examine some of the widely accepted aspects of fiction story-craft, including structure, and how they're tied to the journey of the creative. As a side note: while this book covers the elements of story as a metaphor for the creative's journey, it isn't specifically about creative storytelling.

On this journey, you'll meet new people and hear new stories. You'll encounter challenges and trials (though not without a little fun). When you emerge on the other side, will you be unscathed? I can't promise that, but you *will* come out more alive than ever. You *will* be changed. How much? That's entirely up to you.

CHAPTER 3

Structure

It all begins with the concept of the story.

If you agree that stories are important, then it's worth taking some time to see what they're made of and how they're structured.

According to Jamie Cat Callan, "Whether or not we're aware of it, we long to tell stories, because stories take the chaos of our lives and give our days and hours a shape, a sense of order, meaning, and even artfulness."

If stories help us turn chaos into order, then it would be useful to understand the way stories themselves are ordered. Time for a little history!

Today, the Three-Act Structure is widely used in novels and films. It dates back to Aristotle, who used the Dramatic Structure, also called Freytag's pyramid. In this structure, there is a beginning exposition, a middle rising action, a climax, and a falling action leading to the resolution.

There's a bit more to it now, and Aristotle himself didn't break it down into thirds, but essentially, both his version and our modern one have three parts: a beginning, middle, and end—three acts.

You will discover a similar grouping of threes in the following chapters: approach, process, and pursuit. Each of those are, in themselves, broken down into three parts.

Back to the story on stories. Along comes Joseph Campbell, a mythologist, writer, and lecturer who took a good look at the mythical stories of the past and saw a pattern. He realized they shared many of the same elements, which he identified as the Hero's Journey in his book *The Hero with A Thousand Faces* (that's a lot of faces—just imagine brushing all those teeth every day).

We will also examine parallels between the Hero's Journey and the journey of the creative.

Because the Hero's Journey is so prevalent today in storytelling, we will also examine some parallels between it and the journey of the creative. However, there are many other archetypal character arcs, of which The Hero's Journey is only one, so we won't focus on it exclusively.

Now, the three-act structure, while not the only story structure by any stretch, is arguably the most widely used form today—certainly in Western society. If you want to learn more, check out Syd Field's book *Screenplay: The Foundations of Screenwriting*.

There are many other resources that build upon and break down both the Three-Act Structure and the Hero's Journey as they relate to story structure and story theory in literature and film. One modern author I've enjoyed is K. M. Weiland, who wrote *Structuring Your Novel*, along with some other books on the subject. She even has a story structure database on her website helpingwritersbecomeauthors.com, which breaks down many popular books and movies into their basic structural elements.

These are the main parts of the Three-Act Structure, which we will examine in order:

Act 1
Hook
Inciting Event
Key Event
First Plot Point

Act 2
First Pinch Point
Midpoint/Second Plot Point
Second Pinch Point
Renewed Push

Act 3
Third Plot Point
Climax Begins

Climactic Moment
Resolution

I've given you a little background. Now the big question. What makes a story? Even more importantly—what makes a *good* story, the kind we care about most?

A good story begins with a character—the protagonist—and that character has a problem. Not just any problem—the biggest problem of their life. Sometimes they have a lot of problems, but there is one central problem at the heart of it all. This big problem is a lie, deeply held by the protagonist or the protagonist's world at large.

So, in the most basic terms, a story begins with a *person* and a *problem*—but none of it matters unless there is a change.

This is where things pick up. As the story progresses, we see a transformation in the protagonist or in their world. Either way, something must change for there to be a story: it's called an *arc*.

A character arc happens when the character goes from believing and living one way to believing and living another way. Keep this in mind—the character must move from just believing it in their mind to actually living it.

Think of Ebenezer Scrooge in Charles Dickens' classic, *A Christmas Carol*. His life and character at the end are very different from the beginning of the tale. He doesn't just think in a different way—his actions are almost the exact opposite of what we find at the start.

Alright, so you didn't pick this book up to learn how to write a story. Fine, but tell me this—how much have you considered your own personal character arc? What does your own story look like?

An excellent example of taking a step back and examining life in the context of story can be found in Donald Miller's book *A Million Miles in a Thousand Years*, in which Miller shares his experience of making a movie out of his life and the valuable lesson he learned through the process.

Miller discovered that the elements of a great story also make a great life. He set out on a journey and decided to radically change his lifestyle by taking risks and making sacrifices in order to live a good story.

As we said, every story is about a character with a problem—one that's rooted in a lie. Miller was determined to change by confronting the lies in his own life, ones that had previously convinced him the best kind of life was one of safety and security.

Have you ever considered the lies you might be holding on to and the part they play in your daily life? Oh, so you're a perfectly realized human being and have never been deceived in any way? Right. Well then, what about the lies affecting the world around you?

With that in mind, here are a few commonly held lies I'd like you to consider:

Change is bad.
Creativity isn't important.
Creativity isn't worth the effort.
Only artists can be or need to be creative.
I (you) don't need to change.
I can't be creative.

Whether you outright accept or reject the above statements (or aren't yet sure), have you noticed we live in a world that often fears change, takes the easy path of conformity, relegates creativity to a select few, and looks down upon those who do not conform to these views?

We will address many lies in this book and their corresponding truths, but first, let's get the big question out of the way: Can you be creative?

The answer, of course, is yes.

You already are.

Look at it this way: to create is to make something new. It doesn't get any simpler. A creative does just that. Can you think of any time in your life when you've come up with something new, regardless of how significant it seemed? (Big hint: the answer, again, is yes.) If so, then you have been and are creative.

Looking at it this way, you needn't be an artist to be a creative. You don't have to possess a certain set of skills or even one of those fancy French painter hats. You just have to be bold enough to make new things in new ways. Elizabeth Gilbert puts it this way in *Big Magic*:

When I talk about "creative living" here, please understand that I am not necessarily talking about pursuing a life that is professionally or exclusively devoted to the arts. When I refer to "creative living," I am speaking more broadly. I'm talking about living a life that is driven more strongly by curiosity than by fear.

And while the paths and outcomes of creative living will vary widely from person to person, I can guarantee you this: A creative life is an amplified life. It's a bigger life, a happier life, an expanded life and a hell of a lot more interesting life. Living in this manner is a fine art, in and of itself.

Everyone is creative to some degree, but not everyone takes time to develop it, to exercise their creative ability.

As Steven Pressfield discusses in his book *The War of Art*, there is a natural resistance to creativity—an opposition from within. One form of this resistance is *tension*.

CHAPTER 4

Tension

You've probably heard the term *creative tension* before, but what does it really mean? In an article on the subject, Cath Duncan describes it this way, "Creative tension is essentially a structure that helps to facilitate creativity and change."

Tension leads to change, and the more tension there is, the greater the likelihood is that a change will occur. Imagine two poles with a rubber band connecting them. The bigger the gap between those two, the greater the tension. To resolve this tension, the poles must either come back together or the band will break.

Creative tension occurs when there is a difference between the thing you want (your dream) and where you are now (your reality).

To look at it another way: creative tension builds when you embrace the challenge of creativity, when you do something different from the norm. The phrase "go against the flow" describes it well. Think of a fish not only swimming against the movement of water, but also against all the other fish who are following the water's course. That little guy (or girl, I can never tell with fish) is bound to get bumped up and knocked around by all the other fish. This is how tension can feel, and it's a big reason why many choose to forgo creative living and instead let the tide and the crowd dictate their direction.

Don't get me wrong. Tension is not a bad thing, nor is conformity wrong itself, but it can lead to some pretty terrible stuff. Tension is necessary—it's what holds up bridges; allows us to make music on pianos, guitars and drums; and even permits athletes to pull off some remarkable feats.

Tension exists on an atomic and molecular level in the form of potential energy. Potential—that's another source of tension: when you aren't yet what you could be. Tension is all around us, and it's not just necessary, it's useful. So, if tension is so important, why do we resist it?

Here's a difficult question: What is the opposite of creative? Think about it for a moment. Done? Oh, not yet? Go ahead, take your time…

Good? Okay, so if we look at the root word, *create*, its opposite is *destroy*. Then the opposite of creative would be destructive.

Destruction is certainly an act in direct opposition to creation, but let's look at it another way.

If being creative means bringing about something new, then what would its opposite be? Not bringing about something new. In this sense, the opposite of creative is normative: keeping things the same or accepting sameness.

This is why I often encourage readers on my website to "never be normal."

The very act of being creative means standing out from the norm, not being like water, which takes the path of least resistance. It means going against the flow of normalcy. This resistance creates a drag: a natural pull to bring you back into normative living, a.k.a. creative tension.

Things that aren't normal get noticed. As a creative, this could work in your favor or to your detriment. Most people don't want to be thought of as the weird one. But, like it or not, creativity is weird. It's nonstandard. It's unusual. It's strange.

This is what makes the pull of the well-traveled road so strong. It's familiar, normal, and safe. Tension is the tightrope creatives must walk daily.

But if being creative is so stinking hard, how and why does anyone do it? The key is finding a healthy balance.

There is a balance—a natural center between two or more extremes—to be found in everything. When opposing forces tug against one another, with a center of gravity between them, tension happens.

We can have an unhealthy concept of balance. There is the idealistic mindset that tells us our lives will be whole when we set aside equal time for everything important to us. One little problem: this is impossible. The harder you focus on giving everything equal weight, the more frustrated you will become. Not everything has the same weight, nor should it.

Instead, think of balance as giving the most attention to the things that weigh (or matter) the most at the time, without completely neglecting everything else. Picture a scale like the one Lady Justice holds: you can have one heavy object dipping lower than the other, and balance is still maintained, but if you put too much weight on one side, or remove all the weight from the other side, everything falls.

**If we are to practice creativity and accept creative tension,
we must learn healthy creative balance.**

You can't be totally creative all the time, nor would I suggest you try. Even the most creative people still do completely normal things.

As a perfect example, while I was writing this, one of my kids started complaining that their undies were too tight. I soon discovered they had put their whole body through one leg hole. They had not followed the normal way to get dressed and knew something was off.

If you did everything creatively, you would not only be mentally exhausted from constantly having to invent new methods, you'd also be a total weirdo. It's better to eat your food one bite at a time with the proper utensils like a normal person (and not by shoveling it down the hatch with a keyboard while hanging upside down wearing a canary suit). I'd even say the majority of your life may be spent doing perfectly normal things—that's just fine. The problem arises when you do everything normally and allow no space for the creative.

Furthermore, there is a balance between the left and right sides of our brains, between our rational, logical, structured sides and our irrational, emotional, creative sides (there's debate about whether that is an accurate model of our brain, but the general concept still holds). Both are important and necessary. Both must be held in balance, keeping the other in check. Yet in any given activity, one will dominate.

Let me be frank (no, silly, it's not my name)—we can't go totally hog wild with creativity, because if we did, our lives would quickly devolve into a chaotic mess. Nor should we neglect creativity and live bland, unfulfilled lives where we never take risks or try new things.

We must strike a balance. We must discover a healthy level of creative living. This will look different for every person. The tendency is to be unbalanced in favor of normative living (the safer way). It's time to tip the scales back. It's time to apply the creative approach to the most important parts of our lives.

But before we do that, let's take a look at what it means to be creative in the first place.

CHAPTER 5

Creativity

Stories begin with a *hook*—something to grab the audience's attention, to pique their interest and get them to read on, or sit and listen awhile. Creativity seems to come out of nowhere, but it also starts with a hook, something of interest, something that draws you—the creator—into the act of creating. And your creativity will, in turn, hook others.

But even before that point, the instant of creation, there is one big honking question we must ask—What exactly *is* creativity?

Maybe that seems like a senseless question, like asking *what is the sky?* All you have to do is point up and there it is. Creativity can feel the same—obvious.

Creative is an easy word to use and is quickly understood without much thought.

"Her lectures are so creative, I've never heard anyone teach like that."

"What a creative way to play the national anthem on rubber bands!"

"Oh, that's a very creative use of paper towel rolls—a complex Rube Goldberg machine just so you can push a button and receive a mint fifteen minutes later."

Those are all examples, but not creativity itself, just as pointing out the sky is not defining what the sky is.

Creativity is not everything—it has borders. But not everyone agrees on where they are. The question "What makes one thing creative and another not?" can lead to some highly subjective answers.

In some ways, creativity can seem indefinite, intangible, and mysterious. Other times, it's obvious, tactile, and apparent. Tomes have been written on the subject, but rather than go on all day about the definition, how about we keep it broad and simple:

Creativity is the ability to make something new by use of one's imagination.

Perfect? Hardly. But it'll do.

Instead of getting tied down by a definition, let's look at some defining characteristics—marks of creativity, if you will.

Creativity is…

- *fresh*
- *surprising*
- *unique*
- *unexpected*
- *eye catching*
- *inquisitive*
- *interesting*
- *suggestive*
- *unusual*
- *expressive*
- *provocative*
- *insightful*
- *fun*

A list such as the one above does not tell the complete story, nor does everything creative always have all those marks. You may have heard the well-known fable from India about the blind men and the elephant, each trying to describe something while only getting it partly right. Like that elephant, it can be difficult to take in all of creativity at once. We're used to looking at specific parts.

It seems we have to get creative just to define creativity. Even a person with clear vision who has seen an elephant for the first time would still not understand what an elephant is. Like the elephant, creativity is more than just what it looks or feels like on the outside.

We've listed some of the characteristics. Now let's also look at a few of its results, or the products of creativity:

Creativity…
- *produces something new*
- *combines two unrelated things or compares two different things*
- *transforms one thing into something else*
- *challenges the norm*
- *offers a different view*
- *adds distinction*
- *adds variation*
- *causes excitement*
- *enlightens*
- *leads to solutions*

Again, lists can only take us so far, but even a rough sketch is more useful than nothing. The more we delve into it, the clearer the picture becomes, like adding layers of paint to a canvas—little details here and there, while still leaving unfinished bits.

There are many lenses through which we can examine creativity and what it accomplishes. However, based on the above lists, I would make the case that the ultimate purpose of creativity is to bring order from chaos, and in doing so, infuse meaning and value into life—or, depending on how you look at it, reveal the meaning and value inherent in life.

Discussions on creativity will always continue because, in many ways, we're still discovering it. That hardly keeps us from practicing it. And practice it we must if we ever want to improve.

Creative ability is like a muscle. It grows stronger the more you use it. Just as some people are more naturally strong than others physically, so some are more inclined to be creative than others. But every person, with effort, can strengthen their muscles over time.

Looking at it another way, creativity is like a pet you keep around the house. It's not always predictable, but you can train it to do things you want. If you feed your pet regularly and attend to its needs, you will have a strong, healthy pet. If you fail to train your pet, it will do what it wants and grow difficult to control. Worse, if you neglect the pet, it will languish, growing weaker until it's just skin and bones. For many, that's what their creative ability has become: malnourished, mistreated, neglected.

I recall when my dad got his first color printer. I was thrilled by the possibilities and soon I'd printed out pages and pages of clip-art collages, mostly featuring flaming eyeballs. Yeah, I was a weird kid. I have no idea what I intended to do with all those pictures, but—wow—did that color sure look stunning. Turns out Dad was not so thrilled about all the expensive ink I had just wasted. As a reward for my efforts, I was given some new printer restrictions.

You could say I had a lot to learn back then, but at least I was practicing, testing the waters.

While my ability to firmly nail down creativity (or print decent art) may be lacking, I'll address the other burning question: what is a creative? Again, let's keep it simple:

A creative is someone who commits to the regular practice of creativity.

Have you heard this saying: a tree is known by its fruit? In the same branch, a creative is known by their creativity. When we begin to recognize what creativity looks like, and what it produces, we can learn to nurture it, to cultivate it, and to create an environment where it can grow in a healthy way.

Make no mistake, being a creative isn't about getting results, it's all about putting forward the effort. And what's the point of all this effort? The goal isn't getting to call yourself a creative or even obtaining a firm grasp on creativity. The purpose of the creative and the purpose of creativity are one and the same:

The creative's goal is to bring order from chaos—
to reveal meaning and value in life.

This is nothing less and nothing more than the creative journey itself—the natural path of the creative. In case you're curious about where we're headed, we're going to cover the three aspects of this journey:

The Creative Approach
The Creative Process
The Creative Pursuit

And just how do we feed our creativity to give it that nice, sleek coat once more? How do we exercise our creativity, accept the tension, and let it become a strong, muscle-bound agent of change? How do we pick up the little droppings it leaves all over the yard? Sorry, went too far on that analogy. Let's use a plant-based one. How do we nourish our creativity, give it the water and sunlight it requires to produce green leaves and delicious, juicy mouth-watering fruit—the kind you'd want to bake in a pie and bring on over. Sorry, I got carried away there too.

Ahem, what I'm trying to say is:

The first step to creative growth is the creative approach.

I bid you, ladies and gentlefolk, step right up and follow me onward. There are yet many wonders to behold on the other side of this here curtain.

Fantasy is hardly an escape from reality.
It's a way of understanding it.

~Lloyd Alexander

SECTION 1 REVIEW

Before we leave this section, let me break it down once more:

- There are many parallels to be drawn between the Three-Act Structure, the Hero's Journey, and the Journey of the Creative.
- Both stories and creativity are rooted in change.
- Being creative isn't always easy; it causes tension.
- There is a balance to be found: you don't have to be creative every blinking moment, and creativity doesn't have to feel like banging your head on a cinderblock wall.
- By studying the distinguishing marks and natural products of creativity, we can learn to nurture it, to cultivate it, to strengthen and help it grow (like fertilizer, but less stinky).

Interview with a Creative

JANE HANCE

Tell us about yourself.

I work in the sewn-products industry helping designers make their concepts and ideas become actual products. I also spend my spare time creating and producing a wide variety of things from fun to functional. Oh, and I'm a dance teacher, primarily West Coast swing.

When do you find it easiest to be creative?

Time-wise, that would be late afternoon into late night. Thought-wise, while I'm working on a project that is repetitive, I will usually be designing something or working out a design problem in my head.

Where do you look for inspiration?

In the case of my own creative ideas and projects, I don't look, ideas just come to me, frequently while I'm working on something else. For instance, if I need a baby shower gift, my mind will be continuously working in the background on what I could make that would be fun, useful, and different. In the case of my design clients, they bring me their concepts and I get to develop them. Every time I see something that catches my attention I immediately start thinking about how I could/ would make it.

What forms of creativity do you most appreciate or enjoy?

I love all forms of fiber art. I love glass art. And dance. Dancing frees the soul.

What is one practice you would recommend to help someone be more creative?

Get a hobby. It can be anything that requires focus, has a continuous learning curve, and requires "this or that" decisions, either choice being correct. And have an "and then what" approach to decision-making.

Where can people find you or your work?

janehance.com

Section 2 - Observe

Outlook

You arrive at the outlook and find me standing on the edge of a steep cliff. You approach slowly from behind.

I speak without turning to look. "They say nothing changes in Plateau Town. They said that about Lake Town too. But change comes whether you see it or not. Sometimes it's slow and steady like the way you're walking now. Sometimes it pounces on you without warning." I step back from the cliff's edge and turn to you. "I'm glad you came. In fact, I knew you would. You're wondering why I brought you here. And I'll tell you. But first, look out on the big country laid out before us. What do you see?" As I say this, I stretch my hand out in a broad gesture.

You step out carefully, place a hand over your brow to block the late-morning sun. Far below, a valley drapes across the landscape like a patchwork blanket made of plains, canyons, waterways, and forests. If you imagine yourself at the foot of this landscape bed, then at the head rises a mighty mountain. It's odd, you realize: you've never taken much time to notice it before, but now it dominates the landscape. You feel strangely drawn to it.

A dusty wind whips up from the valley below and blasts past us. I only just manage to grab my wide-brimmed hat from being carried away. "Do you know what you're looking at?" I ask.

You shake your head.

"A journey."

What is that expression on your face? Surprise? Amusement? No, I see it now. You hadn't intended on taking a trip anytime soon. You've begun to reconsider whether coming here was such a good idea in the first place.

"I reckon you've heard the stories about people being turned to stone. They're true: I saw someone two days ago—legs made of solid rock from the knees down. There's something big going on, bigger than you and me, bigger even than this here town. I'm on a path to a solution, and it leads to the top of Mount Dread."

You clear your throat and look back at your horse. Your shoes scrape the dirt as you take a step backward.

"Going so soon?" I ask. "Will you kindly allow me to show you one thing? I'd at least like to make the trip out here worth your while."

I pull out a little wooden box—the one you saw on the table—and hold it in my open palm. You examine its smooth dark wood. Its curved edges make for a simple yet elegant design. You see no hinge or latch, but when I tap the top of it, you hear a click and a cluck, then the box slowly opens. Inside is a disk with black and white slices radiating from the center, like a zebra pinwheel.

"Have you seen one of these before? They are very rare. This is a createamobile. Would you like to see how it works?"

You nod.

"Here, give the wheel a little puff. No, don't touch. Just blow a little over it. There you have it."

The disc begins to spin, slowly at first, then faster and faster. The black and white blurs turn into colors: red, yellow, and blue. As the speed increases, you can see every color of the rainbow all at once. There is a sharp squeak, and you can no longer tell if the wheel has stopped or continues to spin, but it has taken on an unusual silver glow.

"Impressed, I see. Wait until you hear this: the createamobile runs off imagination. You heard right."

As I speak, globular, spectral shapes begin to rise from the little disc, unrecognizable at first. You notice a strong smell of oregano. The nebulous shapes drift upward and grow in size. They take form, familiar but strange: a tree with star-shaped fruits and human-faced fishes darting in and out of the branches.

"Neat, huh? But there's more. Here, you try."

I hand you the createamobile. The colorful shapes again swirl around faster and faster like a miniature tornado until at last they resolve into an unrecognizable brown lump.

"Hmm, well, it's … something. Takes practice you know." I pause and look up. "Uh, it appears we've got company."

From behind a nearby building, the same black-coated men from the market appear, high on their horses. They stare right at us. There are five of them now.

I lean over and whisper, "Those Black Coats are trouble. Don't know how they found us, but let's just say they aren't my biggest fans."

You begin to hand the createamobile back to me, when one of them, a flint-faced man with a pointed beard and tall black hat, lifts his gun from its holster.

"Hold it right there," the man says. "We've been tracking you awhile, stranger. We know you're the cause of these unnatural 'incidents' round here. You're a curse upon this town, and we've come to end it. Drop the contraption and come easy, if you know what's best."

You freeze in the middle of the exchange. Both our hands touch the createamobile, and it lets off a whistle like a locomotive, then shoots out white beams of light. There is a smell of burnt cinnamon, and after a blink, the lawmen's horses have been transformed into yellow-and-purple spotted armadillos with butterfly wings.

I nod in appreciation. "Nice work. Those wings were all you, pal." I pull my hat down tight. "Now, I think it's past time we skedaddle."

I pocket the createamobile as we jump on our mounts and hightail it down a path to the valley below.

The Black Coats manage to fire off a few rounds, but we're far enough away that the shots whiz harmlessly past—if you call a new hole in my hat harmless.

"Don't look back," I call out, "you'll need your eyes on the trail ahead. The path gets mighty steep here—just follow my lead and I'll steer you right."

Creativity is not simply a property of exceptional people but an exceptional property of all people.

~Ron Carter

CHAPTER 6

Approach

It is time, my Padawan—time to spell out exactly what this is all about. What is the creative approach? What does it look like? How do I get there? And what's with the stories at the start of each section? And while I'm at it—all right already, enough questions!

Strap in and hold on tight, cause the ride's about to begin. Oh, right, it already has. In that case, just throw your hands in the air, have fun, and let gravity do its thing.

Let us begin! The exclamation mark is to let you know this will be fun. A boring book would never have put one there.

To approach requires movement. When you approach, you move away from one thing and toward another. My hope is that by the end of this book, you will have begun to move away from a plain old ordinary life toward one of purpose and excitement. More on that later.

By taking a creative approach, you are allowing something to come to life: an idea, a thought, an inkling. It's more than just a shift. It's a move from nonexistence to existence, and that's no small step, even for Neil Armstrong.

It all begins in the mind—your imagination. But how do you get there, from nothing to an idea, from a dead standstill to a sure-fire approach? Rocket boosters and two thousand tons of fuel would help, but let's say you don't have those on hand.

First, let's take a step back to take two steps forward. Again, we examine the story.

In storytelling terms, the tale really starts to pick up with the inciting event: it sets the story in motion (the start of World War II, for example), soon followed by the key event, which gets the protagonist personally involved (such as getting drafted into the army at the start of the war). In both cases, there is movement.

Without motion, nothing happens.

Creativity often comes to us while we are actively doing something. There is a connection between mind and body. Movement and breath help the mind think more clearly. It's one of the reasons I (and many others) will pace around a room while deep in thought.

Sitting around slack jawed, hunched over, and staring at a screen does not promote mental engagement. However, this doesn't mean you need to constantly be "doing something" in order to be creative.

In her podcast series *Bored and Brilliant* (and book by the same title), Manoush Zomorodi presents strong evidence to suggest that our minds are most creative when we unplug, tune out the distractions, and allow ourselves to be bored. I couldn't agree more.

Rather than spending all your time fussing over to-do lists or trancing out in a cat GIF–induced coma, I suggest creating a space for your mind and body to roam freely—physical and mental movement. Go places where you don't feel pressured to be productive and where you're safe from the deluge of distractions. It could be a larger room (one that is empty of digital devices), a park, a museum, a hiking trail, a coffee shop, or an outdoor amphitheater. What's important is that it's a place where you feel unrestricted and able to move about the cabin, to engage with the space, or at least with your own inner thoughts.

The creative approach is not just about movement toward something, but also away from something. We move from distraction toward focus, from inaction toward action.

Newton knew well enough that objects without motion tend to stay that way, while moving things keep on a-movin'! But distraction can often feel like a magnet, pulling you back into the siren's call of app notifications and the like.

This is why starting can often feel like the hardest part: it takes focused effort to turn everything else off and get from stationary to mobile—to fire up those jets and move with increasing force in a single direction.

A story doesn't begin until something happens—something that matters to the plot and character. Your creativity won't kick in until you get your groove on and move on.

So how do you do it? How do you transition from still to loco-motion? How do you get the ball rolling, the crank turning, and the hopper hopping—just how do you generate creative motion? Easy—you move.

The creative approach is a three-step dance. The first step in the creative approach is to observe, to take in the world around you. Next, ask yourself questions based on your observations. Questions get the gears turning, which get you thinking in new ways. They'll lead you to the third and final step: respond. Again, the three parts of creative approach are: *observe*, *question*, and *respond*. We'll cover each one in detail.

Let me repeat that, but with different words: you must first take a new angle or look for a new direction. After you do, questions allow you to see the matter from a different perspective, or as they say in the biz, get a new view. No, they don't actually say that in the biz. I don't even think they say "the biz" in the biz—who are we even talking about? Once you've gained your new view, you've got to do something about it: you must take action.

Example time!

A friend explained how much she disliked her job at a bakery. She had a multitude of reasons: the boss didn't have a clue about how to run a bakery, the food wasn't any good, they were in a bad location, and on and on. Now, those all may have been legitimate reasons, and it is important to recognize problem areas, but, as I pointed out to her, complaining about them won't get you anywhere. She was at a standstill.

Taking the creative approach, I asked my friend a few leading questions: Why was the food so bad? She explained they just baked from premade packages, often purchased from wholesale stores. I asked what in particular she didn't like about her boss. It seems the boss made poor business decisions, though my friend's direct manager was actually trying to turn things around. My friend claimed business was bad, no one knew where the shop was, and the few people who showed up never came back.

Finally, we made it to the most important question for my friend:

What can you do to change it? It was time to get another view, time to move in a different direction. We looked at each of the problems—the bad food, boss not helping, and poor location, and worked on ways to bring about change to make my friend's job more enjoyable and for the better of the company.

So after some discussion, we came up with a multifaceted plan: my friend would work on having a better attitude while there and help her direct manager as much as possible with improvements around the place. She could even offer to bake and bring in some of her own cookies and give some out at the guitar shop next door as an effective—and delicious— form of advertising. Using this approach, she would have the opportunity to make and bring something new that added value (the cookies) and to build up something of importance (her relationship with her manager).

When I talked to her next, things had changed. The food was better, and not only had her relationship with her manager improved, but even her boss and other coworkers had become friendlier to her. Was it perfect? No, but things were looking up.

Can you see the three steps in this interaction? First, I had my friend explain the problem. Clearly, she'd been thinking about what was wrong with the business and why she didn't like working there. You see, until we identify the problems or needs, there's no use looking for solutions. Then I asked her some leading questions to get her thinking. And last, we looked for opportunities—new and different ways to address the problems.

It sounds simple—because it is.

CHAPTER 7

Look Around

Now, let's dive into the details—the nitty and the gritty. The first step of the creative approach is *observe*.

Open your eyes. Seeing those words, I can't help but recall the very same words in the opening line of the hit song *Always*, by the band Erasure, which is obviously about the endless struggle to be creative amid a contrary society. Okay, maybe it's open to interpretation. Either way, this phrase sums up your first step in the creative approach: look around. Now that I mention it, that reminds me of Simon and Garfunkel's *A Hazy Shade of Winter*, which is clearly about seeing the world around you through creative eyes—no question there.

Where were we ... oh yes, observation.

Open your eyes and look around—there are many wonders to be found.

Where exactly should you begin? Why not start at your own front door? Go outside and take it all in. Take your headphones off for a minute and look up from whatever mobile device your eyes have been glued to.

Give your surroundings more than a passing glance. Notice all your senses—what are the sounds, smells and even tastes? Don't go licking light poles, though. People might call the authorities on you. Trust me on that one.

Tell me, how do you feel when you first step outside? Refreshed by the first breath of a new day, reluctant to join the herd of people stamping off to work, dread for an oncoming storm, hopeful for what is to come? Is it hot or cold, wet or dry, windy, or calm? What sorts of people or animals are nearby and what are they doing? What do the nearby buildings or landmarks look like? All of this may seem mundane at first, but when you pause for a moment to take in your surroundings, you will begin to notice things you haven't seen before.

**The ability to look outside oneself
is both a great gift and a greater challenge.**

My friend Joel Kling wrote and illustrated a wonderful children's book called *What Do You Notice, Otis?* It's about a goat who takes the time to take in and interact with the world around him. Some literary so-and-so criticized the book because its protagonist does not overcome any obstacles. I disagree. Intentional observation of the world around us is a constant challenge for both children and adults in today's screen-laden and advertisement-saturated world.

It's not just our devices that demand attention. We spend the vast majority of our time thinking about our own wants and needs (often ones that are not immediate), and because of it, our surroundings go unnoticed. As a creative, you should learn to recognize and appreciate your environment. We'll discuss this later, but your environment is a place from which you draw inspiration. To be forever stuck in your own head is to miss out.

As you begin to look around, you will see the world with new eyes.

After you've taken note of the world immediately outside your home, it's time to look elsewhere. Use the same observational methods on the way to work, or to the store, or whatever outing you may have planned today.

If you can, try taking a new route to jog your system from falling back into habitual modes of thought. Otherwise, plan a specific time to explore somewhere new. It doesn't have to be far. It could even be a twenty-minute drive to a nearby town you haven't had a reason to visit yet or a walk down a neighborhood street you haven't yet frequented. Make it fun. Find a new ice cream shop to check out, or some other treat you enjoy.

Notice the things taking place around you. Is there anything you could learn from them? Are there particular thoughts they bring to your mind? Is there something beautiful, sad, or ugly taking place?

Start people-watching (you have my express permission). Do you see any behaviors you find remarkable, unusual, funny, kind hearted, or mean? Bring a journal and write down what you notice and the thoughts that come to mind, even if it's just a sentence or a few words.

Not so difficult, right?

Observation isn't hard. Most of us are just out of practice.

Anyone can do it—even a distracted, oblivious guy like me. Allow me to illustrate with some notable things I've seen. First, while out on my normal morning walk with the dog, I noticed a toilet, which seemed to be in perfectly good shape, just sitting out on the street corner as if it belonged there. A few days later, I saw the same thing in front of multiple houses: toilets in varying states of repair sitting on the curb in front of houses. Now, maybe *you* see such things all the time, but they certainly raised my eyebrows.

Another thing I noted was a neighbor's house a few blocks down whose front door was completely inaccessible because it was surrounded by wrought iron railing, with no stairs to the porch. I began to wonder why anyone would build such a thing.

I spotted another house, not far from my own, with those Mother Mary candles all around—still lit at 6:00 a.m. Then I saw a picture of a boy, maybe ten years old, with a circle of flowers draped around it in their yard. I realized, with great sadness, their child had recently passed.

Each observation brought with it an entirely different emotional reaction.

On my drive to and from work, I saw a group of girls walking together, all dressed up for a night on the town even though, to my knowledge, there were no clubs or even bars within walking distance. One of them had a large black boot cast on, which gave her an unusual gait, causing her to stand out from the others. I saw a man strolling casually down the main street, going nowhere in particular, with a guitar strapped to his back. On many days I saw a nicely dressed boy standing near a traffic light, holding a sign asking for college money.

Each of these sights, these people, told a story—some more obvious than others—but all interesting in their own way.

While working out in our yard, a song's lyrics prompted my wife to ask my three-year-old daughter if she wanted to see the world someday.

My daughter, who was in the process of digging up dirt with her little shovel while searching for new bugs, looked up and said, "I already am!"

It's easy to believe our own surroundings are rather ordinary—like everything exciting is happening elsewhere. I guarantee that people living in those other exotic places you'd like to visit feel the same way you do.

Many great stories begin with the hero feeling trapped in a mundane existence, desiring to leave home in order to explore the great beyond (think of Belle in *Beauty and the Beast* or Luke Skywalker in *Star Wars*), but the truth is that wonderful and fascinating things are happening all around you, if you just look for them.

It's your turn. Take a moment to pause and observe the world around you—even better, schedule some time and find a place to do so.

Observation is something that becomes more natural with practice. Eventually, you won't even have to think about it. You'll just find yourself doing it regularly. This is an indication of creative progress.

When you take the time to look around, you'll see things you've never before seen. This will set off the sparks to ignite your creative drive and get those wheels in your head turning right round.

While it's good to keep those peepers ready for pretty much anything, let me suggest something in particular to keep a lookout for. Two things really: the unexpected and the combined.

Read on, and I'll tell you why.

CHAPTER 8

Unexpected and Combined

While you're on the hunt for inspiration, there are two common aspects of creativity I'd like you to keep your eyes peeled for. When you do, you'll notice they, like flies at a picnic, show up all the time.

1. Creativity is unexpected (yet understandable)
2. Creativity combines (the unrelated)

It's hard to say one is more important than the other. Both are essential in their own way and can often be found together.

Let's start with the first: creativity is unexpected. If you've seen the sci-fi show *Firefly*, you may remember this line from one of the early episodes: "Curse your sudden but inevitable betrayal!"

It comes during an unusual scene (the titular spaceship's pilot is playing with toy dinosaurs on the dashboard). It's comically melodramatic and a great character moment. I believe its memorability comes in large part from a truth it contains—something we inherently understand about storytelling and creativity: the need for the unexpected yet understandable.

How often have you heard of a movie receiving criticism for being too predictable? There is something about predictability we can't stand—it's uninteresting, unexciting, unimpressive and unfulfilling. To put it plainly…

The predictable is dull.

When we were young, the world was fresh and new. Everything was a surprise. But as we age and experience more, we become harder to impress, especially in this age of information oversaturation. We're hard to impress because we already know it all and have seen it all.

Predictability is not a bad thing—we'd be in big trouble if mathematical equations didn't yield predictable results. Without predictability, we'd never get a grasp on how the world works.

The problem with the predictable is that it fails to grab our attention, to make our brains think in different ways. Besides, it's not all that entertaining.

The unpredictable, however, leads to discovery and learning. We love stories with unexpected elements like plot twists and surprise endings because we didn't see them coming—they challenge our expectations. While we might not like our expectations to be wrong in real life, it can be very rewarding in someone else's story.

When it comes to humor, the unexpected is a mainstay. Jokes are often based on misdirection. For example: A man walks into a bar. He was out cold.

How about this one (my sister's favorite):

There are two muffins baking in an oven.

One of them says, "It's sure hot in here!"

The other muffin replies, "Eeek! A talking muffin!"

Even if you've heard them before, you get the point: we think things are going one way, then they take an unforeseen turn.

So it is with creativity.

The unexpected is what turns the same old thing into something new and unusual.

But there is a balance. It can't only be unexpected—it still has to make sense. Just as we complain about movies being too predictable, we'll also complain when we leave the theater scratching our heads, often due to an ending unwarranted by the rest of the movie. In a way, we feel cheated or tricked.

A good story should surprise the audience with an outcome that also makes sense—one the narrative naturally leads to with foreshadowing and the repetition of theme.

Consider the above joke about the man and the bar. What if it went this way instead?:

A man walks into a bar and the bar walks right back into him.

Unexpected? Probably. Understandable? Not unless you're on heavy drugs. Now, what if this line were to take place in a story about a world with autonomous robotic mobile restaurants. Well, then it would make more sense and probably still be unexpected. It's all about the context.

Our lead animator at work once used the phrase "clasp my jewels" in reference to something a southern belle might say. Like a replacement for "oh, my word" or "I do declare." He had us all convinced (he'd even convinced himself) it was a real thing, until we looked it up. Turns out it was a complete fabrication. We loved it all the more, especially as we imagined a shocked lady clutching her jeweled necklace in surprise. It made complete sense even if it wasn't something people in the south really said.

As Tom Fox, a writing instructor of mine, often told our class, "You need to say the same old thing in a fresh new way."

They say every story has already been told, or that there are really only a few types of stories (something like five to seven). Despite that, new and interesting stories are coming out all the time, some with massive success. Some element of the familiar is necessary, otherwise the story will be unrelatable, but there is always an opportunity to add something fresh and surprising to the mix.

Keep this in mind while you're in observation mode. When you discover something that surprises you and also resonates with you, take note of it.

Now, the second point—creativity *combines*. It's about juxtaposition—two different things placed together. For example, a sculpture, made out of discarded *Starbucks* cups, of a man walking a dog.

This juxtaposition is a hallmark of creativity. It's unmistakable and easy to identify.

It's one of the qualities that makes the work of the famous UK street artist Banksy so popular (besides his controversial nature, of course). Images like trees growing out of a barcode, a man who appears to be throwing a bomb but is actually holding flowers, the Mona Lisa with a rocket launcher, or the painting of a grim reaper in a boat painted over an actual dirty old canal—they all catch your attention because of their unusual combinations.

But don't think for a nanosecond this only applies to art. For example my brother-in-law, Jonny needed to find a place to teach his students how to read maps. He found a local *Frisbee* golf course (one with a fairly confusing layout) and printed out a satellite view from *Google Maps*, with a few discovery points he'd included for the students to chart. Mapping and Frisbee aren't two activities often found together, but the event was a big success.

It's remarkable what you'll find when you look for unusual combinations. I heard about a board game being featured at a game convention, where the board itself was actually created during the game by a programmable sewing machine. The way the game was played determined what sort of board the machine ultimately printed out. Such a game might not have mass appeal, but it's a clever idea.

You won't have to look far to find creative combinations. Start where you are right now. In my house, we have a book for babies in which the pictures are made from fingerprints combined with images of everyday objects. A page with a boy has his face made from a giant fingerprint and his hair is lettuce. A turtle has fingerprint arms and legs and a soup bowl shell. It makes the images unusual and fun to look at, even for adults.

You can even find such things during your regular old day-to-day activities. During a visit to the dentist, I noticed an informational poster about gum disease and tooth loss. It had a large picture of a pearl necklace with one pearl missing beneath the words "each one matters." The tooth of their message was not lost on me.

Like Banksy's work, some combinations are more to prove a point. Some are simply made for the novelty. Take the shoebike—a bike where the wheels are made of shoes. It sounds fun at first, but when I saw it in use, it looked like a very uneven ride and I can't imagine it's a joy tying all those laces.

Other combinations are actually useful, like a backpack that becomes a tent or a bracelet that's also a paracord, compass, whistle, and lighter. Yes, I just went on a hike. Why do you ask?

When you stop and gander (but please don't goose), you'll find creativity all around. Whether it's the unexpected, the combined, or some other aspect of creativity, you'll soon have more source material than you know what to do with.

So what do you do with all your discoveries? That's an excellent question and a wonderful segue because the fine art of the question is where we're headed next.

You weren't hoping for an answer, were you? Worry not—we'll get there too.

Everything has its beauty, but not everyone sees it.

~Andy Warhol

SECTION 2 REVIEW

Just what did we learn in this section?

- The creative approach has three parts: observe, question, and respond.
- The first part, observe, is simple enough. Open your eyes, look around, use your senses to take in your surroundings. Look for things that are unusual, remarkable, and even outstanding.
- Record what you've noticed and how it makes you feel.
- My neighborhood has some serious plumbing issues

Interview with a Creative

K. M. WEILAND

Tell us about yourself.
I write historical and speculative fiction from my home in western Nebraska and mentor authors on my website Helping Writers Become Authors.

When do you find it easiest to be creative?
It depends on the day and what else is going on, but I tend to favor either midmornings (after breakfast, etc., but before looking at email or any other distractions) or late afternoons (after I've cleared all the other distractions from my desk).

Where do you look for inspiration?
I believe inspiration is everywhere. Art is all about observing life and trying to make sense of it via creative metaphor. All we have to do to be inspired is pay attention. Still, I find my greatest inspiration in the art of others: books, movies, and particularly music.

What forms of creativity do you most appreciate or enjoy?
Definitely the forms that are blatantly about story: books, movies, music. I appreciate all art, but even in media that isn't directly a story form (paintings, dance, etc.). I'm always looking for the story!

When has a creative approach helped you accomplish something impactful?

I like to think one of the most impactful things I've done so far has been my work on character arcs, which I just recently published in book form as *Creating Character Arcs*. Although this is nonfiction, it is entirely a creative pursuit based on my own study and practice of storytelling.

What is one practice you would recommend to help someone be more creative?

Sorry, I gotta pick two things! Because, really, they go hand in hand:

1. Pay attention.
2. Be disciplined.

Immerse yourself in the world so you have something to write about, then discipline yourself to show up at your desk every day and learn how best to share the beautiful realities you find with others.

Where can people find you or your work?

HelpingWritersBecomeAuthors.com

Section 3 - Question

Valley

"What a rush!" I shout. "Why, we nearly fell off that cliff at least five times. And the look on their faces when we morphed their horses into spotted armadillos, whoo-boy!"

We reach the base of the plateau. The valley stretches out ahead. We're each out of breath—the trail was difficult and we did not take it slow, for fear the Black Coats were close behind.

"You shoulda seen your face—I thought you were about ready to faint on me. Suppose I did get a little carried away jumping that ledge back there while doing a double axel off my horse, but it just felt right in the moment, y'know?"

We bring our steeds to a trot. I can see the worry painted across your face—plenty of dirt, too.

"Listen, I didn't mean it to go like that. Thought we had more time before the Black Coats arrived, but this won't be your last brush with danger if you're going to stick with me. Oh, right, you're still making your mind up about that? I see. You think the Black Coats are right, that I'm the one turning people to stone, don't you? I promise the opposite is true, I'm trying to find a way to stop it. It's not just your town where these things are happening. If you come along with me, you'll see. Anyhow, you've got some time to think it over. Welcome to Worrisome Valley." I reach an arm out like a waiter holding a tray of food. "It rests in the shadow of Mount Dread. Pretty welcoming, huh?"

You take in the great valley ahead. It's laced with the occasional stream and sports clusters of tall, thin trees. It is carpeted in short, faded-green grass. Beyond the valley rises a crescent-shaped range of steep-pointed mountains. A shrill wind beckons us, sounding almost like a voice crying out a warning.

I trot my horse forward. "We've got a day's ride to the opposite side. Should be safe once we get there. You can decide what to do then."

We continue along at a steady pace, past sandy riverbanks and low hills. We pass the remains of huge structures, whose original function remains a mystery. As we ride, you notice sections of buried wheels reaching four stories high, a rusted mechanical arm with a claw at the end, a staircase that leads to an open platform held up by a single wall, great metal spirals, large chunks of curved glass—some as big as a rowboat. They are remnants of a time long ago, an ancient civilization of innovative prowess. But what became of them?

We're quiet until we stop to rest at a shaded pool. It is fed by a stream of water gushing out from under a pile of rocks. Short, misshapen stones are gathered around the pool—their form and positions suggest they might have once been statues. Something about the place feels safe and calm.

We dismount, drink, and fill our canteens. I pull out a map—the same one you saw sitting on my table back at Plateau Town—and study it.

As you sit and rest, an odd sensation comes over you. Could it have been the water from the pool? You realize the short stone figures are moving. In fact, they aren't stone at all, but little creatures with gleaming skin. You look around and find—to your shock—the ancient ruins have been replaced by magnificent working inventions, some that tower so high you can hardly make out their tops. And the valley is no longer deserted but instead a place filled with residents, both human and ones like the small creatures around the pool. Your eyes return again to the figures by the pool, and you're surprised to find them kneeling before you, heads bowed low.

"Hey, you all right?" I ask.

You blink, and everything is as it once was: broken and empty. You shake your head, but whatever you thought you saw is gone now.

I stare at you for a moment in puzzlement, then point to the little statue-rocks. "I bet you're wondering about those. Tales tell of creatures called Dwelfin, who lived here long ago. They were excellent builders. Some folks believe there was nothing they couldn't make, given the right resources.

"For many ages, they worked alongside human inventors, but one day they all up and left. Why they took off and where they went remains a mystery. Some say they got tired of us, others think they were scared off. But that was over a hundred years ago. All we have now is this weathered monument and some busted-up ruins.

"According to the legend, they wait for the one who will find and lead them back: the Endless Creative. It all sounds like a bunch of sow slop to me. I bet they just got tired of our ways and moved on to greener pastures. Maybe we really built all this and the Dwelfin never existed in the first place—just bedtime stories we made up for the kids."

I pull a tear-shaped vial from my pocket and fill it with spring water. "We should keep some for the road; folks claim these waters have healing properties. Don't know if it's true, but, hey, this tastes good and might pick your spirits up when you most need it." I sniff the air and look around. "Anyhow, I don't think those Black Coats will give us chase, not yet. They have more important concerns to attend to. Look at your town."

You look up to the plateau high above us and see a thick cloud of smoke rising from it.

"Probably didn't realize it, but the Black Coats have been residing there and recruiting for months now, ever since the stone curse began. Same thing at Lake Town, where I came from. What do they want? Wish I knew. Control, I'd wager. And they get it through fear and intimidation, all while pretending they came to help people. Once they have control, I'd be surprised if they let your marketplace of ideas stand another day—they don't fancy that sort of thing. It ain't just the Black Coats either. There are other...agents on the prowl."

Something rustles in the dry shrub nearby, and we start. A rabbit dashes out and sprints across the valley. A hawk swoops down, snatches the startled animal in its talons, and flies off. The shrill cry of the rabbit echoes over the valley and then cuts off sharply.

I rise and pull my hat down. "I think it's time we move on."

We are born creative and it is worked out of us.
                                                    ~Sir Ken Robinson

CHAPTER 9

Change

Everything changes. Some people don't deal with that fact very well. Some resist it with every fiber of their being.

For example, Walt, the main character in Clint Eastwood's movie *Gran Torino*, is a retired vet who is, in many ways, stuck. He's old, in bad health, has lost his wife, and despises his multiethnic neighbors. He's a man haunted by his past wrongs and who has a grim outlook on the future. He resists change tooth and nail.

But things do change, and Walt is drawn out of his self-made cocoon of beer, home repairs, and car maintenance into caring relationships with his Hmong neighbors.

By the end, Walt takes a heroic (dare I say, *creative*) action to stop a gang that has been attacking the family he has grown to love. He at last accepts and embraces change—in a powerful way. That's not to say everything is peachy, but it's a much better story than what would have happened if Walt had stayed holed up in his house until old age or sickness laid him to rest.

We've already briefly discussed change and its relation to character arcs. There are three basic arcs: positive, negative, and flat. In a positive arc, the protagonist changes from believing a lie to embracing the truth. In a negative arc, the protagonist goes from believing a lie to rejecting the truth and fully embracing the lie—no happily ever after. In a flat arc, the protagonist doesn't change (they already live the truth), but the world around them changes.

Two great examples of the positive arc versus the negative arc in classic literature are *Moby-Dick* and *The Count of Monte Cristo*. In *Moby-Dick*, Captain Ahab is driven by the lie and his need for revenge, until his ship and nearly all his crew are destroyed.

In *The Count of Monte Cristo*, Edmond Dantès, on the other hand, during his quest for revenge, eventually discovers he has taken matters too far and instead shows forgiveness to a man who wronged him, and he reunites a separated couple—a restorative action from a man who had been separated from his own bride-to-be.

A flat arc is common to what has become known as the iconic heroes. As Robin D. Law describes it, "An iconic hero re-imposes order on the world by reasserting his essential selfhood ... an iconic hero's ethos motivates and empowers him."

Some examples of iconic heroes include Miss Marple, Sherlock Holmes, Wonder Woman, Wolverine, James Bond, and Conan. There are some exceptions in which these characters do change, but because of the episodic nature of their stories, most of the time they will be essentially the same person from one tale to another.

In our personal lives, we are all following one of these arcs: moving toward the truth, moving away from the truth, or living the truth and leading others toward it.

**Before we can discover which arc we're living,
we must first ask the age-old question: What is the truth?**

Relax, we're not talking about *the truth*—the very fabric of reality itself. We're talking about something much more personal: your most important truth. The one thing you need to believe in order to live the life you were meant to live. The one thing that if you don't believe it, you will be held back in every aspect of your life.

Sometimes it's easier to start by discovering our lie.

In some stories, the lie and truth are easy to spot. Take the film *The Greatest Showman*, for example. P. T. Barnum, inventor of the circus, wants his work to be appreciated by all. Having grown up in poverty, he especially wants the social elite to accept him. This desire comes at a great cost to himself and those around him. But his wife, Charity, speaks the truth to him: "You don't need everyone to love you, just a few good people."

I'll admit, in real life, the truth can be a tough one to figure out. And it's different for every person. Stories on the silver screen are clear and concise, while our own can be confusing and complicated.

Discovering your truth could require a good deal of time and self-discovery. Many people will not even recognize the truth until they've been completely broken down, until everything that supports the lie has been taken from them. That's a hard place to be.

I can't promise this book will reveal it to you, but I believe you'll be much closer to it by the end.

Here's a good place to start: look at your wants versus your needs. We want safety, comfort, and approval. These things can be good in themselves, but we live a lie when we place them before the things we need, like growth, contentment, and joy. We want to live in comfort, but we need to be challenged beyond that comfort in order to grow.

The solution is change. I have to change and you have to change. And one way or another, we will change. The question is, for better or worse?

Normal is a temporary state. Our world is in the process of change. We live on a giant rock spinning around an enormous fireball within a galaxy on the move. Time and gravity constantly mold and shape the universe.

To desire stagnancy is to desire an illusion. To embrace creativity, however, is to embrace the reality of change, of newness. All things will be and are being made into something new.

We often resist change because it is unfamiliar, which makes it uncomfortable. We like the safe and expected. We want to relax on a tropical beach in front of an endless sunset. But even there, we are in front of a vast body of water in constant motion and no two sunsets are the same.

There isn't a place in the universe that is not in the process of change.

You yourself are changing: every aspect of who you are is shifting in one way or another. You learn. You grow (or shrink). You age (no amount of Botox, creams, or essential oils can stop it). Yes, change can be difficult, but to pretend it isn't there is to stand in front of a tsunami with your hands out—pointless.

How then do we accept and embrace inevitable change? We become part of the process. To be creative is to be part of the change, part of forming something new from something old. Although things are changing, it doesn't mean we have no control, especially when it comes to ourselves. We still get to decide what sort of people we will be—how we'll think and what we'll do.

Whether or not you know the truths and the lies that shape your life, it isn't difficult to figure out which direction you're heading.

You likely know a person or two who always complains about the way things are, comparing them to the good old days, resisting at every step, hiding in the thin safety shell of what they're used to while the world moves on.

On the other side, you've seen (or at least heard of) the innovators, people who take what they have and make the best of it, those who adopt, adapt and improve—the ones who never give up.

The second group may be few and rare, but they sure stand out from the crowd. Which kind of person are you? Maybe you fall somewhere in between. Maybe you're on your way to becoming someone who not only acknowledges change, but who brings it about themselves, someone who makes waves. This is good, and it's high tide to make a bigger splash.

Here are a few questions to ask yourself:

- Are you growing or are you stagnant?
- Do you make a positive or negative impact on the people around you?
- Do you take bold risks or do you run away in fear?
- Are you sharing your gift with the world, or hiding it?

If you're honest with yourself, you will know which direction you're going. If you still aren't sure, ask someone you trust, someone you know will tell you the truth—because they're living it.

Now, I don't want to mislead you—I'm not claiming all change is good and positive. I mentioned the negative arc in reference to an individual, but it can also take place in a whole society. Change doesn't always move us in the right direction. It's quite possible for change to lead to a place where creativity is discouraged, even forbidden.

The point is, there will always be something in our world that will change (for good or bad) whether we like it or not, and there will always be things which should change (for good) which we can take part in.

Change starts with you.

If we embrace positive personal change, we can become people who bring about change in the larger world. The sort of change we bring is up to us, but it is only through creativity that we can become world-changers.

And there are many ways to change the world for the better, both big and small. All of them matter—whether it means sending a handmade card to someone in a hard place, growing a vegetable garden to share with your neighbors, inviting a coworker over for a nacho-laden game night, or showing up at the airport with a basket of treats to welcome a refugee into the country—all these are feasible with only a little creative thought.

As Maria Goff wrote in *Love Lives Here*, "Most people I've met want to help others, but they don't know where to start. I'm right there with you. We all don't need to do big things, but we can do equally important small things."

Even a small change can be an important and life-giving one. Not only that, but we also come alive inside when we cause change. As we bring change to the world, we ourselves are changed.

As creativity changes us, it changes the world around us.

The way you change the world may seem small, but its impact is immeasurable. Think of a moving song or a stunning photograph—it's hard to tell how such things change us, yet the change is undeniable.

Our creative works may not have the same immediate audience of a big-budget movie, but every little creative act you perform causes a small splash that ripples out further and further until it's impossible to tell how much your little amount of creative effort has impacted others.

Change is powerful. It's a force to be recorded with. It is unstoppable.

Change in itself, like any natural force, is neither good nor bad—it just is. But there's no changing change. So instead of dropping anchor and sitting out in the middle of the ocean, we should set sail and let creativity be our vessel as we ride the waves and harness the winds of change until we're headed in the direction we wish to go.

Exciting, right? It can be, if you let it.

But what does all that have to do with the creative approach?

We started with observation: taking in the world around you, recognizing the changes taking place. Now it's time to use what you've noticed and start asking questions, especially the ones that lead to change.

CHAPTER 10

Questions

What if?

Yes, I said, What if?

Why, you ask?

Hey, I'm the one asking the questions here!

"What if" is one of the most powerful and open-ended questions we can ask.

What if the sky were green and the grass blue? What if we knew what would happen tomorrow? What if we could walk up walls? What if Big Rock Candy Mountain really did exist? What if we grew all our own utensils? What if the 'lunch special' was all the time every day? What if spaceships were real? I mean, like the *Enterprise* kind. What if there were a server room out there where dreams were stored? What if milk couldn't go bad and it gave you night vision? I think you get the eye-dea.

Unlike "if only," a thought connected to regret, "what if" is an opportunity to imagine, to hope—it opens a door to endless possibilities. It's not the finish line, but it's a fantastic place to start. When you ask "what if?" you open the door to more questions, and eventually you arrive at answers.

Story time!

Scott Harrison, CEO of the nonprofit Charity: Water, asked a big "what if" question. It went something like this: "What if there was a way I could help thousands of people in need?" After some thought, he asked, "What if I could build wells for people all over the world who didn't have access to clean water?" I expect he then went on to ask, "How in the heck would I do that?" which led to, "What if I used my influence and friendships to fund such an endeavor?"

Eventually he arrived at the idea of holding a giant birthday party for himself, but instead of receiving gifts, he had everyone give money toward building wells. It worked so well, he built a whole nonprofit organization, which itself answers a great question: "What if all the money people gave toward building wells actually went directly to the wells and nothing else?"

Asking "what if" can lead to some big ideas, but first it starts out small.

You've taken a good look at your surroundings, a practice I encourage you to continue for the rest of your life. Now ask questions, even the silliest, most ridiculous ones.

What if the mailman really wanted to be a psychiatrist? What if the birds outside my window started singing Elvis? What if my commute took me through a secret tunnel to a magical world made of creamed corn? All fine questions. But let them lead you somewhere more practical.

What if the mail carrier turned out to be a really interesting person? What if I spent a little time out in nature? What if there was a way to shorten my commute or make more of it?

"What if" is a great place to start, but don't stop there. There is an endless list of questions you could ask about an endless number of things.

Asking "Why?" or "How?" can lead you to the understanding of a thing or situation. It could reveal the inner workings of something you previously didn't understand. It could uncover a past history of which you were unaware.

Often, when you ask someone else a question, you provide yourself an opportunity to learn. Pretend you're an investigative journalist and it's your job to learn more about a person. Even if they don't answer your question directly, you'll still learn something—sometimes the unspoken things speak the loudest. Don't be rude, of course; recognize some topics may be sensitive or deeply personal. However, most often you'll find people are happy to talk about themselves, their occupation, and especially their hobbies.

In turn, be open to answering other people's questions to the best of your ability. You never know where the conversation will lead, and if you maintain an attitude of curiosity and helpfulness, you'll both come out the better for it.

When I was a young boy (twelve or so), with so much to learn about the world (I'll admit, I'm still there), a family member gave a particularly unkind response to a question. I have no idea what I asked, but the person responded with, "If I wanted you to know, I would have told you." Granted, they might have just been having a bad day or felt pestered by my many questions, but I found this response hurtful—why else would I still remember it after so many years?

I urge you, don't be that way, and don't accept such a response from the world. Don't shut down curiosity, either in yourself or others. It is the very fuel of creativity, the birthplace of discovery. There is so much we do not know and so much we can share with one another.

The more willing you are to share your knowledge and experience with someone else, the more opportunity you will have to grow.

Questions get your mind working in a certain way—they open it up for possibility and potential. They give purpose and direction to your musings.

If I can wonder about the possible existence of some magic city built upon creamed corn (instead of rock and roll), then finding a simple way to get my life a little more organized isn't such a stretch.

Let your questions take on more focus. Write down a few problem areas in your life (start with small ones), and begin to ask questions about them. For example, if you have a problem getting to sleep early enough, you might ask yourself, "Why do I want to get to bed earlier? What keeps me up so late? How did this become a problem? Do I know other people with this problem and what have they done? What will happen over time if I don't fix this?"

Questions lead to new thoughts, which lead to change. However, it isn't instantaneous.

Just as it takes an entire novel for a character to complete their arc (sometimes a whole series), it will take time for you to change, for you to become a change-bringer.

Questions are an important and necessary step on the yellow creamed corn–brick road to change. I'll admit, that's more than just corny—it's kinda gross.

Once you've spent enough time asking questions that lead to other questions, like any good detective, you will eventually want some answers. Stay tuned for the next chapter's gripping tale: "The Response" (I'll leave your mind to play the dramatic horn sound).

One of the most empowering moments of my life came when I real-ized that life is a question and how we live it is our answer. How we phrase the questions we ask ourselves determines the answers that eventually become our life.

~Gary Keller, coauthor of *The One Thing*

SECTION 3 REVIEW

And now, I proudly present, your review:

- Change is as inevitable as it is essential; for good or bad, everything is changing.
- Much like a fictional character's arc, we are either changing in the right ways or the wrong ways, leading us closer to the truth or closer to the lie. This is the difference between living for the things we want and the things we need.
- Questions lead to change. We begin to accept change—and be changed—when we ask them.
- "What if?" is a great question to begin with: it opens our minds to possibilities and leads down many avenues of thought.
- As you ask questions, let your mind wander, but keep asking questions that direct you toward a specific purpose.
- If all this talk about ch-ch-ch-ch-changes gets a David Bowie song stuck in your head, you can thank me later.

Interview with a Creative

WES MOLEBASH

Tell us about yourself.
By day, I'm the creative and communications director at Brookside Church in Chillicothe, Ohio. By night, I'm a cartoonist/illustrator/sketch-noter.

When do you find it easiest to be creative?
When I'm driving and I've got my music cranked up. Or when I'm mowing and I've got my music cranked up. Really, anytime I can do monotonous work while listening to loud music, I know I'll have some great creative ideas.

Where do you look for inspiration?
Books, music, and movies. There are several artists that have influenced my own artwork, and I follow them on social media so I can see more of their work and philosophy.

What forms of creativity do you most appreciate or enjoy?
Animation, graphic design, comics, music, and movies.

When has a creative approach helped you accomplish something impactful?
Over the past six years, I've been working in church ministry, both as a volunteer and a full-time employee. There have been several ministries and outreaches that I've been able to innovate and/or guide creatively.

Using my skills to share my faith with others in a unique and attractive way is extremely satisfying.

What is one practice you would recommend to help someone be more creative?
READ FICTION. You should definitely read nonfiction too. In fact, you should have a good balance of both. But it always makes me sad when I hear people say they don't read fiction. Fiction is vital to keep our imaginations properly fueled.

Where can people find you or your work?
www.wesmolebash.com

Section 4 - Respond

Archway

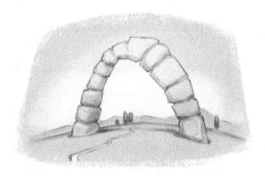

After another half hour of riding in silence, I speak. "The way I see it, you've got two options: you can come with me, or you can find another town. I doubt you'll be safe back on the plateau. If you're inclined, I know of a town near the mountain's base, not far off this path."

A shrill wind picks up. Our horses are careful to skirt around the chest-high tumbleweeds that now bounce across the trail.

"You wonder why I'm going to Mount Dread and what it holds."

You again look up at the behemoth of a mountain in front of us. It has a blanket of clouds resting like a jacket over the middle, but the peak still pokes out. At the top you spy an unusual glimmer.

"To tell the truth," I say with my eyes fixed on the mountain's peak, "I'm not sure. I believe up there we'll find a means to fight off the Black Coats and their ilk—a secret weapon of sorts. So I've been told. Don't have a lot of other options."

I hold up the createamobile and pop it open. After giving it a breath, a thin, sparkling shape arises, moving rhythmically like a charmed cobra from its basket. As the shape rises and falls, you smell a hint of basil in the air.

The shape forms into something you recognize but can't put a name to, a metal cone with thin, angled protrusions at the base. Then it dissipates. I snap the createamobile shut with a click and hold it up, examining it. "A friend gave this to me. It's saved my neck a few times. If only I could have saved her."

I pocket the createamobile, lower my eyes, and move up ahead.

After a time, you catch up to meet my gaze.

"I suppose you want to know." I sigh. "She stayed back at Lake Town to help others. People turning into fish—scales and all. We couldn't figure out why. Then the Black Coats showed up … shoulda been me that stayed."

Two hawks begin to circle overhead. The wind picks up again—a low, mournful cry.

We ride until the hot-white sun passes its zenith, and we near the base of the mountain ridge. In the baked red dirt only a sparse bush dares to grow. Gray and white stones the size of a person's head cover the land.

I hold up a hand, and we stop near a broken wooden post.

"This is the place."

You look around but see nothing out of the ordinary.

"There used to be roads here. At least there's still a flat path." I pull out the createamobile once again and blow gently over its black-and-white disk. "Observe."

You smell lilac as a translucent blue spike shoots up from the splintered old post, then splits into four sections, which peel off like a banana's skin. They stretch out into thin blue lines along the four compass directions.

You look down the blue line ahead of us and see a tall stone archway in the distance. Had it been there all along? There's a similar arch to the left as well. Another to the right has crumbled into two pieces.

"Those are gateways"—I nod to the arch ahead—"they'll give us some protection. There used to be more, long ago. The one to the left leads to Foothill Town. It's still safe there, as far as I know."

You gaze toward the town and can just make out some stone buildings camouflaged by the mountainside. It looks like a good place to hide.

"Listen, I realize this whole journey is more than you bargained for. Here's your one chance to turn back. No one will blame you for it. But, if you do, you'll also never find out what lies ahead. There's no telling how long the gateways will hold. What'll it be, partner?"

You hesitate for a moment, turning to look at the town, then back to the path ahead and the imposing mountain it leads toward. You shake your head and point to Foothill Town.

"Well, it's sure been nice knowing you. I have a friend or two over there who will—"

A shriek pierces the air high above us. It's followed by another, then more—many, many more. The sky is filled with hawks, hundreds of them.

"Night Talons! Known to tear a person's face off when they have a mind to. These ones don't look friendly. To the arch. Fast!"

The land becomes a blur of red and gray as the shrieking black cloud begins to swirl and descend upon us like a tornado ready to touch ground.

Over the cry of the birds, I shout, "There's no way we'll make it to the arch like this. Here, create a diversion." I toss the createamobile, and you barely manage to catch it without falling off your horse.

You look at me, confused.

"Just try. I know you can."

You shrug, then snort into the disk. Nothing happens.

"Come on, just—" We are now galloping through a field of bright pink and yellow balloons that had been pale round stones just a moment before. "Not what I had in mind, but it'll do."

As the hawks slash through the balloons in search of us, glitter bursts out, startling and confusing the birds.

I laugh. "Not bad by half. Still, don't expect it'll fool them for long. They're sharp—in more ways than one."

We're almost to the arch now, and you realize it's taller than you'd imagined, nearly three stories high, but how could it protect us from the birds of prey?

There is a flap of wings and a shrill cry from behind, so loud it seems to be right beside your ear. You look back to see a dark blur dive straight toward you, but I ride in fast from behind. The blur hits me square on the shoulder before tearing off again with a shriek. You hear more cries—the birds have all begun to dive in one collective attack funnel. You brace, ready for the pain of a hundred talons ripping you apart.

The shrill cry of our aviary attackers becomes deafening. Any moment now we'll be bird food.

Just then, we pass under the great stone arch. My mount rears up and whinnies as I pull it to a stop. "Close one." I pat my horse's side to settle its nerves. "We made it, thanks to you."

When you turn back, there's nothing there—no arch, no birds, just the valley and the wind behind us.

"No use thinking about it now. Even if you could find a way back, they'd be waiting on the other side."

You notice a deep, red cut in my shoulder, and you wince.

"Ah, don't worry 'bout that. I can sew the jacket. Wouldn't be the first rip it's had. And with paper-leaf and some creativity, I'll get myself patched up proper."

We turn to look at the high-walled canyon before us and Mount Dread in the distance—it seems even bigger now, reaching up to pull the orange afternoon sun out of the sky.

"Guess you're along for the ride now. Wouldn't say I'm not glad for it. No use standing around. Let's find somewhere to make camp."

Man is never truly himself except when he is actively creating something.

~Dorothy Sayers

CHAPTER 11

Respond

There comes a place early in a story where our protagonist reaches a point of no return. Think of Robert Frost's famous poem *The Road Not Taken*. The hero must make the irreversible decision between two or more paths. To sit idly by and remain uninvolved is no longer an option.

It is their response to this call to action that drives the rest of the story.

This happens smack dab in the first plot point.

Before we delve into that, let's step back for a bit. During the natural flow of a story, the protagonist goes between two states: reaction and action. In the first half of the book, they react to what occurs around them, mainly the antagonist's presence and power.

Somewhere near the middle, the protagonist shifts from reaction to action—from responding to taking charge. But before they can get to the point of being action-takers, they must first gain an understanding of the conflicts, both the internal and external ones.

The story gets interesting at the end of the first act, when the hero becomes fully engaged in the plot. At that point, they have departed from their normal world, and whether by choice or not, there is no going back.

What does all that have to do with the journey of the creative?

As the hero is confronted with the first plot point, they face a change: they move from reluctant bystander to engaged responder. They still remain at the whim of the antagonistic force, but they are finally doing something.

As you engage in a creative approach, you will move from indecisive and distracted to decisive and determined. You will still be tempted, and may even give in, to the siren's call of ease and normalcy, but you will know how to return to the true path, the path of the creative.

When at last you reach a response, you've completed the cycle of the creative approach.

To recap (to put your hat back on?), the first two steps in the creative approach are *observe* and *question*. Once you've taken a look around and seen what there is to see, once you've made some inquiries based on your discoveries, the next step is to form a response—a reaction.

Not every question has an answer and not every quest needs an answer. However,

every question seeks a response.

This is true even if the response is "I don't know." If that is your response, it's high time to figure a few things out.

There's a boy I know, practically an adult, who, when asked a question, often adopts a far-off look, then gives the same predictable response: "I honestly do not know." He says this constantly.

It seemed genuine enough the first few times, but it got old fast. I have had some good conversations with him, and I don't believe he's unintelligent, just unwilling to engage. I don't want to be too harsh on the kid—he's had his share of family problems and clearly life hasn't been a walk in the petunias for him—but it's difficult to have a conversation with such a person, to get them to think creatively, or much at all.

It is possible my friend struggles with some mental or emotional setbacks—I'm no expert in that field. They might have even become an excuse for him. However, when I ask him about anime (his favorite subject), he offers a wealth of well-articulated information.

I won't believe for a second that he isn't smart, but his excited interests in anime do not carry over to much else. Sadly, his attitude is not an unusual one. I've seen the same response in a good number of youth and young adults today: unmotivated, disinterested, disengaged—checked out. It may seem obvious, but these qualities do not open the door for creativity to come in.

My intention is not to throw blame. There are many factors that contribute to this attitude. Judgment and accusations do little to help.

What we need is a solution—an overall change from unresponsive to responsive. We need people who are responsible, or rather response-able. People who are able to respond. See what I did there?

A story where the protagonist does not respond to events is hardly a story at all. If Bilbo from *The Hobbit* stays in the Shire, we've got no adventure. If Luke stays on Tatooine, the rebellion loses and he's Jawa jerky. If Meg Ryan's character Kathleen from *You've Got Mail* doesn't stand up and fight for the survival of her little bookshop, it simply goes under, and all we have left is a pity party.

If we refuse to engage with our world, if we wall ourselves in, close the blinds, and click shut the ten locks on our doors, what will we gain? A sense of security? Possibly. But it looks more like defeat to me.

Have you ever had an ingrown hair or ingrown nail? Boy can they hurt. The problem isn't that they're not growing or changing, the problem is they're growing the wrong way—they're bent inward. They cease to be healthy for the body, just as an inward-focused life ceases to be healthy for the soul and for society.

What happens when everyone lives this way? Creativity dies, and we have no stories to share. A downright shame, I say!

In contrast, another one of my friends, Ben, whom I worked alongside for five years while he served as a youth pastor, is one of the more creative individuals I have known. It doesn't take great observational skills to recognize youth ministry has some real challenges, one of the biggest being how to engage the kids and hold their attention, many of whom are checked out and would rather be anywhere else.

Ben responded to that challenge with a number of creative activities: little games before the lesson, like ultimate hopscotch, or special events, like breaking into groups and making their own short movies.

A favorite event of mine was called Urban Man Camp. It was more than just your typical youth lock-in—it was an excellent solution to this question: What's an affordable way to entertain a room full of boys and build relationships with them? It involved cardboard, and lots of it. They competed to see who could build the tallest cardboard tower, they knocked down cardboard Goliaths by launching tennis balls at them from three-man water-balloon launchers, and at the end of it all, they built a massive cardboard shanty town to spend the night in. The whole thing was an awesome example of what one can do with a little creative response and a lot of cardboard.

To respond is to do something, to take action.

It is not enough to wish and wonder. Take a look at the information you have gathered through your observation and questions, then find creative ways to address it. Here is one question that will lead you to a response: "What now?" When you live out the answer to that question, you put your creativity to work.

I met a guy in college who discovered a unique way to potty train his boy: playing the ukulele. According to my classmate, it was the only thing he found that would work—after many other failed attempts. He had a problem (a kid who refused to be potty trained), and his response was to look around at what he had available and test it until he found a solution.

Let your response begin with what you have available.

The answer to the question "What now?" doesn't always have to be a solution to a problem. Perhaps you simply want to develop a hobby. For example, if you've learned about a local scrapbooking club, why not join and see how you like it?

When I moved to a new town, I learned of a local board game group that met twice a month at the library. After only going twice, I had already formed some lasting friendships with people who were complete strangers just a few weeks prior.

To respond is to put yourself out there.

If a group of neighborhood kids often kick cans down your street, why not go play hacky sack, show them how to yo-yo, or set up a little soccer field? Maybe invite their parents over for dinner. If you see the same homeless woman on the way to work every day, why not buy her a flower, or make one out of paper? Hey, nothing makes me feel special like a little floral origami.

If you pass by an interesting little mom and pop shop, why not pay it a visit, find out what inspired the owner to start the business, and maybe even write a little story about it? Your world is full of interesting little places containing fantastic stories, but you'll never know until you go.

Instead of just hitting the Like button the next time you see a post, why not comment how it made you feel, or even talk one on one with the person who posted it—who knows where your discussion could lead? Engage, engage, engage.

Is there someone in your life—a coworker or acquaintance—who might be able to mentor you or teach you an interesting skill, say woodworking or how to play drums? Is there someone in your life—a friend's kid perhaps—who is going through a hard time? Why not take some time to share your own experience or skills with them and offer some help through instruction? Believe me—it will change their life in a way you could never predict.

A creative response can be as big or as small as you want it to be: a fifteen-minute project or a lifelong work. However, if you haven't given much time to creativity in the past, I encourage you to start small.

Sometimes a good response just needs a few prompting questions. In Orson Scott Card's book *Characters & Viewpoint*, he lists three basic reader questions every fiction author must address:

1. So what?
2. Oh yeah?
3. Huh?

Phrased another way:

1. Why should I care?
2. How am I supposed to believe that?
3. Is this supposed to make sense?

If you strive for a creative response, one both unexpected yet understandable, you'll address at least two of the questions. The audience will care because you've given them something interesting, and they won't be confused because it makes sense within the context. If you follow those, you'll have a good shot of believability as well. It's sudden yet inevitable: the outcome we should have suspected but are delighted we hadn't.

I invite you to consider this in your daily responses. Even a work email or a text to a friend can be made more creative this way.

Change up your sentence structure or word order. Add in a phrase you don't use often, or make one up. Combine two words to make a new and more interesting one (there are many portmanteaus [two words blended in to one], like *ginormous* or *keytar*). Instead of a simple "What's up?" why not ask, "What's the word on the wind?" Instead of, "Here are the files you requested," how about, "Here, here! Your files have arrived, and just in the nick of time." You don't have to be strange or silly about it, just don't be boring—reject the easy and obvious.

Don't get too worried about what your response looks like. More importantly, don't feel pressured to come up with the perfect one. There's no such thing. Instead, start with whatever comes to mind. Then consider how it could be improved or modified next time. The more you consider your usual response and then change it up, the more natural it will become for you to begin with a creative one.

Long ago, when I was at the tender age of four, my dad sat me down to explain some difficult things to me. Because of my parents' divorce, I'd no longer get to see him as much. Our life and relationship would never be the same. Sadly, this is a story many are familiar with, yet the experience is unique to each person. After Dad had taken the time to talk it all out, feeling he'd explained it pretty clearly, considering the audience, he asked what I thought.

I turned to him and said, "Daddy, I hate giant vampire bats."

He nodded. "I do too, son."

Not every response makes sense at the time. But that doesn't make it wrong. Nor does it make it unimportant.

I have no idea what I was thinking back then. Maybe that was the only way my four-year-old mind knew how to express the way I felt inside.

It isn't easy to know which response might be best. Some require a good deal of thought. Then again, sometimes those spur-of-the-moment ones are just as good as anything else.

There are many ways to respond and just as many questions that lead to great ones, but the best kind of response is one that leads to improvement—a change for the better.

CHAPTER 12

Solutions

In your observations, I'm sure you've noticed many delights to behold on this fair planet as it spins its course among the stars. But, there's also a great amount of brokenness and pain.

Darkness lingers between the lights of space, places of shadow in our world, and if we're honest, even in our own lives. All is not as it ought to be. From the start, there has been a struggle, a tension; living hasn't come easily.

I see struggle everywhere, as I'm sure you do. People are unhappy, stressed out, depressed, addicted, unmotivated, discouraged, angry, defeated, lonely, afraid, lost—the list goes on and on. I've been all those things and more.

I'll wager you've also experienced your fair share of struggles. It's the lot we've been born into, our inheritance. To live is to struggle, to know pain and sorrow.

But hope thrives as well: a desire for change, for goodness, truth, and beauty to prevail. Change, however, requires the introduction of something new. It requires a response.

It takes a creative mind to see past what is, to envision what could be, and to have the courage to transform a vision into reality.

Creativity promotes problem solving. In fact, the bigger a problem, the more necessary a creative solution becomes.

Think about it this way: the simplest solution to any problem is one that has worked before—the go-to answer. But when the typical solution doesn't work, you're left with a bigger problem.

Unsolved problems rarely fix themselves. Once you've exhausted all the expected solutions, you have a growing problem and no choice but to look elsewhere, to discover a *creative* solution.

For a real-world example, take the Ballot Bin.

Trash on the ground is both a nasty and pervasive problem in most cities (unless you have the staff and funds of Disneyland at your disposal). One of the worst perpetrators is smokers (you know who you are). Trust me—when you volunteer with a street cleanup crew for a few months (as I have), you really notice the carpet of cigarette butts mashed into the sidewalk. It's a problem in dire need of a creative solution.

A company in Edinburgh came up with the Ballot Bin. It's a bin that encourages passersby to vote on something fun (such as which Justin you like more, Bieber or Timberlake) by dropping their butts into one of two slots in the bin. It's an invitation for community participation and a greater opportunity for people to deposit their trash into an appropriate receptacle instead of on the floor.

Seiichi Miyake invented tactile paving slab or "tenji block" with his own money after discovering a dear friend was losing their vision. The tenji blocks consist of raised patterns, such as bumps and lines, on walkways, which can be felt by walking on them or with a cane. They serve as indicators for the visually impaired, designating safe walking areas as well as upcoming changes or dangers like steps, cross-walks, and railways. And for those who can see, they've got some real aesthetic appeal.

Have you heard the history of the Band-Aid?

Earle Dickson, a cotton buyer and employee of Johnson & Johnson, was a newly married man with a problem. He had married an acci-dent-prone woman who would often cut her fingers while working in the kitchen. So, what did he do?

From the Johnson & Johnson website:

Dickson wanted a bandage his wife could easily apply herself, so he took two of the company's early products—adhesive tape and gauze—and combined them by laying out a long piece of surgical tape, and then placing a strip of gauze down the middle. To keep the adhesive from sticking, he covered it with crinoline fabric. His wife could then dress her own wounds by cutting a piece of the tape and gauze pad, and fashioning it into a bandage.

Think of just about any successful invention, and you'll find a creative solution to a common problem (like losing your keys or animal hair gathering on your clothes).

In order to find creative solutions, we need more creative people—folks like you and me.

Yes, the world is a big ol' bag o' problems, and creativity is a great path to solutions. But a response that leads to a solution isn't always easy—there is another element required.

May I present to you, not for the first time ever, determination!

CHAPTER 13

Determination

Determination may be a foreign concept to some—a language in which you know only a few common words. Sure, you know about it, but is it actually incorporated into the way you think and operate?

Much like learning a language, determination requires effort and concentration—two things that have, for many folks, fallen out of practice. It's easy to get distracted, but we have to be careful not to blame the distractions themselves. Often, we chose the distraction with more purpose than we'd like to admit. Let's face it,

it's easier to distract ourselves than it is to do difficult things and make hard decisions.

Making life decisions requires commitment. It means sticking to something, often when we aren't sure we're able to complete it. It means taking a risk. A creative response is necessary, but it can also be difficult—scary even.

You know what isn't scary? Checking your Twitter feed, posting a nice picture on Instagram, binge-watching your favorite Netflix show. That's all easy stuff.

The easy things should frighten us.

They may seem harmless at the time—we might even come up with excuses of why we *need* to distract ourselves, why we deserve it. But—be honest here—how often do you look back on those things and feel better about yourself. How often do you feel more accomplished?

I usually feel worse—a lot worse.

I've wasted the precious time I could have spent growing as a creative. None of these things are bad, but when they dominate our time, there's none left for creative pursuits, for the things that matter—the sorts of things you'll be remembered for.

We (I'll admit, I do this all the time) make excuses for doing things we know are a waste of time, claiming such activities are a reward for our hard efforts. That's a straight-up lie.

A reward is something you get for doing the right thing. A treat is something you get for no reason. Most of the time, we're treating ourselves for no good reason, claiming it as a well-earned reward.

Marketers capitalize on this. You deserve a new watch, purse, or car. You deserve an ice cream sundae. You deserve to binge-watch a nine-season show while neglecting family, career, and your own personal health.

Have you ever seen a pet that got too many treats? It becomes fat and lazy. Stop and think about it next time you're about to indulge yourself—are you rewarding or treating?

Stop "rewarding" yourself for nothing. Yes, positive encouragement is the best motivator, but only if you encourage the right thing.

There is a time for rest and enjoyment, but it's much smaller compared to the time spent working. Hey, even God worked six out of seven days.

Whew. Okay, I'm done with my rant. It was more for me than anyone.

Besides the temptation of rewards and treats, there are other distractions. As comedian and writer John Cleese (of Monty Python fame) once said in a lecture on creativity, "It's easier to do trivial things that are urgent than it is to do important things that are not urgent."

Distracted people don't take the necessary time to observe, question, and respond. They either never begin the creative approach or they lose focus along the way.

Utilizing the creative approach requires determination—a mindset that enables you to finish what you start (and start what you intend to finish). Does it help if you're actually Finnish? No idea. You'll have to ask them.

When I think about all my wasted hours, I feel like a failure. That's an incorrect assessment. A failure is someone who at least makes an attempt. Doing the easy, fun, mindless stuff isn't even trying.

When you examine your life and find most of it comprised of frivolous activities, you should be truly and utterly scared, because you will never, ever get that time back.

Think of where you could be right now if you had made the most of your time.

It's pretty depressing if you dwell on it—so don't.

Recognizing our past mistakes helps us avoid them in the future. Dwelling on them cripples us.

Spending too much time in the past keeps you from making the right decision now.

I'm reminded of *The Lion King*, when Rafiki hits Simba on the head with his stick. Simba asks why he did it, and Rafiki responds, "It doesn't matter. It's in the past." He then points out two options: run from the past or learn from it.

Rafiki takes another swing, but this time Simba dodges it, having learned a lesson and saved his noggin from another bump. The past can hit us hard sometimes, but if we're smart about it, we can escape an abusive relationship with it.

Students learning to fly an aircraft are instructed not to focus on obstacles but instead on where they want to go. Why?

When you focus on an obstacle, you end up moving toward it.

When you're fixed on the past, it's the equivalent of flying forward while looking backward. A crash is imminent.

The only way to get where you want is to keep your eyes fixed ahead, where you intend to go. It's time to shift our focus off the wrong behaviors and instead look at where we want to be.

Determination gets you where you want to go. Begin by making purposeful decisions that lead to an intended outcome.

Why is decision making so hard? A commitment narrows your options, allows potential for failure. However, as difficult as decision-making may be, it's a world better than the reverse: indecision.

As the quote goes, "I used to be indecisive. Now I'm not sure."

When you refuse to decide, you release your hold on the wheel (or whatever steering device you'd like to imagine in this analogy) and let other forces steer your life.

Indecision doesn't just take us nowhere. It doesn't just stop us in our tracks. It moves us in the opposite direction.

Imagine driving a car uphill: the moment you let your foot off the gas and begin to coast, you lose momentum and then begin to fall backward.

It's the same with a boat—if you kill the engines, it'll soon start to drift at the mercy of the wind and waves.

**Every moment we aren't progressing,
we're drifting backwards and off course.**

When in life have you ever drifted in the right direction? The people we call drifters are those who live without direction, going wherever their whims (or circumstances) take them. They may have known where they were headed at the start, but without course corrections, they soon look back at the beach to find they have floated far from the lifeguard tower into unfamiliar and shark-infested waters.

**Determination is more than just being decisive—
it requires you to stick to your decisions.**

My stepfather and my half brother hiked the Pacific Crest Trail together in one go. The PCT extends all the way from Mexico, though the United States, and into Canada—roughly 2,650 miles. Even completing it over a series of trips is quite a feat. Only a few hundred people actually hike the entire trail every year.

My mom also played a big part in helping them through the journey, by supplying food drops and occasionally making visits when they stopped into town to resupply. Without each other or my mom, it wouldn't have been as feasible. Consider it a lesson on not traveling alone or without outside support.

After my stepfather and brother's return, they shared a surprising statistic with me: fifty percent of the people who attempt the PCT quit by the third day.

It takes about five months to complete the trail. That means most of the people give up after they've just begun.

I believe the same can be said of creative endeavors. We follow the creative approach, we come up with a meaningful response, we start with high hopes, and then we turn tail and run a few days in—usually the minute the going gets tough, when we first glimpse the difficulty ahead.

It doesn't have to be that way.

Only by sticking to the trail, come what may, can you reach the end. Taking every side trail and diversion is a sure way to become hopelessly lost. This determination is what changes the reactive protagonist into a person of action.

Do any of your own abandoned creative endeavors haunt you? I still hold regret over a couple of fan-made video game missions I'd put significant work into but never finished. At this point they're as good as dead since the system is very outdated and it would be time-intensive to re-learn the software. Would completing them have made much of a difference in the grand scheme of things? There's no way to know. But I still feel a strange sense of loss over them.

While it may be necessary at times,

there is always a price for giving up.

It could be you're not the only one paying the price.

Los Angeles is known to have the worst traffic congestion in the US. No surprise there. I lived in LA for a number of years and can confirm that it's bad and only getting worse. But did you know it held an expansive subway network, which ran from 1925 to 1955?

Back then, the subway's Red Cars could shave off fifteen minutes from a trip to downtown or other places of interest like Hollywood and Glendale. Instead of being further developed, the subway ceased operation in favor of above-ground buses. Much of the subway was filled in or used for skyscrapers and hotels.

Nowadays, LA transit does include an underground section, called the Red Line in a nod to the old subway system, but it hardly compares to what once was.

Can you imagine the difference a major subway system would make on traffic today? But rebuilding it now would be a costly undertaking. Perhaps Elon Musk's cleverly named Boring Company will again make underground mass transit a viable solution to the growing traffic problem.

Whatever you may have left behind, new opportunities still await. It's better to take the next step than to be forever stuck in the past. However, once you've made a commitment it's just as important to see it though, if at all possible.

The decision to press on is what makes an ordinary person into a hero.

As you'll see, the more you take the creative approach, the more you will exercise your creative muscle and the stronger you'll become. You'll recognize and avoid the distractions in your life. You'll learn the difference between the true path and the meandering side trails.

You will undergo a remarkable transformation—a change for the better. You will go from passive, uninvolved bystander to engaged, active player.

In the immortal words of Whoopi Goldberg from the movie *Sister Act*, you will "Get up offa that thang." You will put your rear in gear and get your feet on the street.

Until the protagonist gets involved, the story is just setup—an introduction to the people, places, and situations that are important for the reader to know about. Necessary—true—but it gets boring fast.

So it is with your story. Until you get involved, it's just set dressing and prep work. And since most people don't pay to watch the dress rehearsal,

it's time to start making things happen.

The world needs creatives who are inspired, imaginative, and innovative—now more than ever. It hungers for creatives.

Take a look around. We ain't living in paradise, baby. There are more people on this planet than ever before. Many of them are lost, lonely, sick, starved, depressed, or fearful. Some are all the above. Hate crimes, terrorism, and active shootings are commonplace. Global resources are depleting faster than ever. Though we've taken some preventative measures, the world is as polluted as ever. And studios keep producing bad remakes of your favorite childhood films and shows. Dang.

Is everything getting worse? I wouldn't say that. But this much I know: you can help make it better—for yourself and the rest of us.

Hey, that's what this is all about.

So hold tight to the handrails (and grab a barf bag if you need it), because we're pulling out the stops, pushing pedal to the metal, and going full throttle into the great beyond bordering possibility.

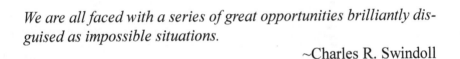

We are all faced with a series of great opportunities brilliantly disguised as impossible situations.

~Charles R. Swindoll

SECTION 4 REVIEW

Let me re-explain. No, there is no time. Let me sum up:

- All questions seek a response.
- A creative response doesn't have to be difficult or complicated—it doesn't even need to make sense—but it should matter, and it should stand out from your normal routine.
- The most persistent problems are best solved by creative solutions.
- Responses may require determination. In a world full of distractions, you must make a commitment. Use your time well and with purpose.
- Creativity demands a response. The creative approach will lead you from observation to questions and finally to response.
- Drifting never takes you where you want to go, and focusing on obstacles is a sure way to hit them. Setting sail and staying the course is what it's all a-boat.

Interview with a Creative

CHRISTOPHER HASTINGS

Tell us about yourself.

I am a writer, cartoonist, and comedian. Over the years, I'm usually more of one than the others when it comes to doing it "for a living," but so far, that's been the blend. As of this writing, I'm making most of my living writing comic books for Marvel, Boom!, and Dark Horse, and directing sketch comedy at the Magnet Theater.

When do you find it easiest to be creative?

The time of day changes depending on my schedule, but it seems like I can't really focus unless other little things are sorted: email cleared, dishes done, house tidy, that kind of thing. I recognize this could be an easy procrastination trap, but since I'm aware of it and schedule it into everything, I'm still usually doing my creative work by some point in the morning or early afternoon, with no other distractions to stop me from getting in a state of nice creative flow.

Where do you look for inspiration?

I don't really go out looking for inspiration, but I do try to notice when I really like something that someone else has done, or when I'm particularly annoyed by some other story or movie or whatever. Those are the emotions that make me want to either "do something cool like that" or "prove that I can do better than that." And that'll usually start me down some road to a project.

What forms of creativity do you most appreciate or enjoy?

I work in comic books, so I'm always interested in seeing people doing exciting things with that medium. I also direct live sketch comedy in NYC, and I like to keep an eye out for interesting ways to take advantage that the shows are performed in front of a live audience. There are certain things in comedy that are better suited to video, and certain things better suited to the stage, so I try to look for ways that excel or maybe even fail, as a warning.

When has a creative approach helped you accomplish something impactful?

I think my experience in writing stories and performing live comedy really helped me deliver a good speech for my brother's wedding, funnily enough. I approached it with the same creative vigor that I do with any job, as it's certainly as important, or more important, than the script to some random comic book. I researched and broke down the elements of successful wedding speeches (it's usually as basic as "Funny story X, story about when couple started dating Y, sentimental and sincere wrap-up Z"). Then I started writing free association thoughts about my brother and his wife. I picked some funny anecdotes, found a theme, and was able to put it all together in a way that was entertaining to the (enormous) room of wedding guests, and ultimately express a true and loving welcome to my new sister-in-law. I know writing it out this way might sound a little robotic, but I was really proud to use my professional skills to create something meaningful for my brother, his wife, and our family.

What is one practice you would recommend to help someone be more creative?

Make the time for yourself to not be bothered, to just have a space to think, to write (or draw or whatever). It's easy to go through life feeling distracted and out of control, but if you prioritize yourself, you will likely find creativity brings focus. John Cleese gives a terrific speech on this advice, and you can find the video online for a more thorough and well-stated version.

Where can people find you or your work?

You can read my webcomic, THE ADVENTURES OF DR. MCNINJA at drmcninja.com. And my general info-hub is drhastings.biz

ACT II

The Process

Section 5 - Focus

Canyon

Two days have passed since we traveled under the stone arch. We're in serious need of water and provisions.

The canyon's sheer walls curve inward, creating a curved ribbon of sky above. Patterns of sunlight wind along the ground like lost snakes. As we ride, you can't help but wonder if there is something hiding in the dark little pocks that mark the concave sides of the canyon. You hear a low gurgle sound and glance around to find its source.

"Sorry," I say, "that'd be my stomach. I wager you think we should have gone to Foothill Town instead. I've considered the same, but we just as easily could have been trapped there. Those Night Talons caught me off guard. I thought they only hunted in the dark. Something strange is happening, and I fear the strangest is yet to come."

The canyon opens to a wide, circular area with three natural stone pillars in the center. The pillars are an unusual shape, with flat tops that are wider than their bases. Many paths lead off this opening—none offer more promise than the other.

"This place is like a maze: meant to confuse and mislead—the Canyon of Indecision. A person could get stuck here for years and not realize it, but if you have company, your chances of escape are greatly improved. I hope you don't mind me saying it, but I'm glad you're here. Where next? I'm open to suggestions."

You ask to see the map, but I shake my head. "It won't do us any good here—trust me. Any other ideas?"

You shrug and offer the createamobile to me.

I hold a hand out and then stop. "Know what? How about you keep it for now. I think you could use practice."

You give it a try, but all it does is produce a smell of old spinach and a big green question mark, which inflates and then pops, squeals, and shrinks away.

"Don't blame yourself. Something about this place is odd...Hey, what's that?"

In the middle of the three stone pillars is a circular ditch with movement down inside. When we walk up and peer down, we find a frail old man pacing around.

"Hello there," I call.

"What's that?" the man asks with a shaky voice. His pacing stops, and he looks up. "Oh. Can't you see I'm busy?"

"What are you doing?" I ask.

"Deciding where to go."

"Have you tried any of the paths?"

"None yet. Too many options. I've got to make the best decision possible before I continue. No mistakes, no going back, you see."

You offer a helping hand to get him out of his round pit, but he dismisses it with a wave. "No need," he says. "I'll get myself out of here in another moment or two." He continues to pace and mutter to himself.

I turn to you. "How about you choose a path. Going anywhere is better than nowhere at all."

You head down a tunnel, which seems to lead northward, toward Mount Dread. I follow close behind.

Time passes, and though it seems we've traveled straight, we again emerge in the area with the three pillars.

I notice your concern and pat your back. "Don't worry. We're not lost, just delayed."

"See, that's what you get for making a wrong decision," you hear the man from inside the trench say.

"Ignore him. How about I give it a go?" I try another path, one to the right of where we entered. It feels a little different but eventually leads to the same area once more.

You begin to wonder if we'll ever escape, or if those Night Talons will find us first.

"Now, don't be discouraged," I reply, as if reading your mind. "We've just got to use our wits. You choose again. Don't rush. Think about it for a moment."

You think but still can't come up with a way to go.

"How about this," I offer. "Try something you haven't done before, even if it feels silly. The worst that could happen is we end up back here."

You shrug, close your eyes, and follow along the wall with your hand, pausing at each offshoot. You notice one that seems different, sounds different. You hear a faint splash of water.

"Interesting," I say. "It looks like that leads back the way we came. Still, I'll try anything."

We head that direction, and after some twists and turns, the path widens until we emerge at a riverbank with a clear view of Mount Dread, its peak now hidden above the cloud. The river is wide, and the water rushes by with a low roar.

We stoop down and refill our canteens with the cool water of the river. You take a moment to rest while I use a net lying nearby to catch a heap of silver fish with bright-blue bellies—they'll sustain us for a time. With aid from the createamobile, you create a fire to cook the fish, and I nod in approval.

Along the banks are clusters of pepperweed with bell-shaped orange and bright-green striped fruits. I mention that they're fine for eating, though sometimes a little hot.

"This must have been a fishing village at one time." I point out a group of holes in the rock wall on the other side of the river, ones that look just tall enough to walk through. Some of them have rough stairways leading up to them, carved right out of the rock. "I wonder what happened to everyone."

Just as I finish preparing the fish, I stand up and stare at the other side of the river. "Did you notice movement over there? Probably my mind playing tricks on me. Either way, we'll need to get across, and unless you know how to walk on water, I suspect it'll be a challenge."

You catch me rubbing my shoulder where the Night Talon attacked.

"Still just a little sore," I explain, "but the bleeding has stopped. It'll heal in no time. You should worry more about that river."

While we enjoy a satisfying meal under the shadow of the clouded mountain, we ponder how best to cross the rushing river.

"Something I should mention: I don't know how to swim. What? Don't look at me like that. Just because I'm from Lake Town—Mama never taught me, all right?"

I take a bite of the pepperweed and swallow with a loud gulp. "Whoa, that was a strong one!" I wipe my brow with a handkerchief from my pocket. "All right, maybe I was always afraid some big fish would come swallow me. Every man's got his fears—least I'll admit mine." I take another bite, then lift my hat and scratch my head. "We're gonna have to cross over somehow. Even if I could swim, I wouldn't take my chances with that current."

We finish eating and prepare to go. We walk to the right, following the course of the river for a time. We discover a few stone arches extending like ribs from the canyon tops over the river, but we'd have to find a way to get on top of the canyon before we could use them.

We pass a little dock—unfortunately without a boat. At last, we come to a stone arch low enough for us to walk onto, but its surface is round, and it narrows severely in the middle. Thankfully, someone has strung a rope across as a handhold.

I shake my head. "I don't like it—poor footing, and it doesn't look strong enough to hold a horse. I guess we'll have to leave our steeds behind. Don't worry. They'll know the way back. Hey—what is that?"

You also notice something small and dark scrambling among the rocks on the opposite side—a strange little creature that soon disappears around a bend.

"Trouble, that's what." I answer my own question. "Unless you've got another idea, I think this is the best we've got."

You give the createamobile a try, but the only result is a smell of burnt toast and a yellowish foam that rises to the surface of the water and then dissipates.

"It was worth a shot, but I'm not surprised. This is the River of Doubt. Besides, that contraption has never worked properly around large bodies of water, leastways not for me." I sigh, long and heavy. "I'll go first."

After we stow what we can carry from the horses into our packs, we begin to cross the slender, stone bridge. We cling to the tenuous wet rope for our lives and make our way one slow, slippery, timid step at a time.

You point out something unusual about the rock formations on the other side of the river. I pause to examine them.

The rocks are worn and weathered, but it doesn't take long to recognize their unmistakably human shape. They look like a crowd of people who had been suddenly frozen in stone while running from some unseen danger.

"Not a good sign," I admit, "but whatever happened, it was a long time ago."

The figures remind you of your fellow townsfolk back in Plateau Town. If only there were something you could do to fix it. If only you could reverse the strange curse.

Just as we cross the halfway point, I pause and turn to you. "You hear something?"

Above the constant roar of the river, you notice a deep rumble—felt more than heard. The earth shakes, and we look up to see great rocks tumbling down from the mountain, hitting the water in mighty splashes. Explosions launch more bits of rock into the sky. The arched bridge beneath us begins to crack and fall into the torrent below.

As you start digging in your pocket for the createamobile I shout, "Forget it. Grab the rope!"

The whole arch breaks in half, then drops, and we grab the rope just in time.

The mountain settles and the rocks cease to fall, but we're now dangling above the rushing river.

Amid the chaos, you notice something peculiar—those stone figures on the other riverbank have vanished. But with our lives in peril, this is no time to think about it.

We try to inch our way to the other side, but the rope is too wet to hold for long.

"C'mon partner," I shout, my voice nearly drowned out by the river. "Think up something, quick!"

But we're both at a loss and nearly out of time.

"We're in one dilly of a pick—" My words cut off as the rope snaps and we fall.

Overcome the notion that we must be regular... It robs you of the chance to be extraordinary.

~Uta Hagan

CHAPTER 14

Uncomfortable

Here's a shocking fact about me: I love bread. Especially homemade bread fresh from the oven. I could smell that stuff all day long.

Mmmmmm...

This is something I've learned about bread: heat helps it rise. Heat speeds up the metabolism of the yeast—the fungi that feed on the flour—which then causes the bread to rise. Why am I talking about bread? Hey, can you fault me for it? But there is a reason, and we'll get to it shortening—I mean shortly.

First, let's talk about three basic ingredients that lay the foundation for pretty much every story plot: a character, a goal, and an obstacle.

The combination of these three elements result in conflict. Such conflicts can be as simple as a girl who wants a new dress for her birthday but her parents don't have the money to afford it, or as complex as a soldier in an intergalactic war who desires to end the war and bring peace to all intelligent beings, and hey, maybe that soldier also needs to find a birthday dress for his little girl.

This conflict equation is so prevalent, you'll often find it in each individual scene of a story.

A story without conflict is no story at all.

As much as we hate conflict in our own lives, we absolutely love it in tales. Think of your favorite book or movie: What was the conflict?

Would it have been nearly as good without that conflict? You are correct (assuming your answer was no).

Now back to the bread (I've always wanted to say that). The heat makes the bread rise. Turn it up, and that yeast gets a-workin'. Turn it off (or put it on chill), and the yeast slows down. In the same way,

a hero must endure the heat of conflict in order to rise.

It is the heat that activates their inner drive, that sets them ablaze with purpose to reach a goal. It is absolutely necessary.

Returning to story structure: after the first plot point of a story, when we've crossed the threshold into the second act, then comes the first pinch point. The pinch point serves two purposes: it provides a reminder of the antagonist's threat and also a time where the protagonist learns more of the central conflict. It is here things really get tough for the hero. It's a place where the stakes are raised, where the tension increases.

Ahh, tension! Remember, creative tension is the space between what you want and where you are now, the struggle for creativity. The conflict in story plot and creative tension are virtually the same, and tension brings heat. None of this is bad—quite the opposite.

The discomfort of tension leads to a changed life.

Without obstacles, tension, and conflict, we don't change—we remain flat and doughy, practically useless. Have you known a child who always got what they wanted? Were they better for it?

True, the struggle of not always getting what you want may be hard, but without it, there is no appreciation. When you don't have to work for something, you take it for granted—you do not esteem its value properly.

If you always get what you want, you won't learn how to live in the tension. Living in tension teaches you to work hard for what you want and how to get by without the things you don't really need.

This is just as true for creativity as it is with anything else. I've known many a talented artist who did nothing with their God-given skill and instead lived a meandering life while their abilities went to waste. It's a real tragedy.

Learn to embrace the tension, dive head-first into conflict, push your boundaries.

I get it. That's a big ask, so let's start small.

Begin with a willingness to be uncomfortable, to sit in the hot seat, even for a short stint.

Where there is comfort, there is no conflict, and thus no plot and no movement on the journey. No movement means stagnation.

Speaking of which, let's keep moving on our own creative journey.

We've covered the creative approach, which ends with response, but a response is not the end (as you probably guessed, since this book isn't even half over).

To respond or react is to change. It requires a move from inaction to action. But we only move when we see the need to.

During a conference I attended, Rick Rusaw stated, "We don't change when we see the light. We change when we feel the heat." (I later discovered this is from Rick Bezet's book *Be Real*). Much like the storybook hero, we may know the truth, but we don't live it until the lie becomes unbearable.

As long as we find inaction comfortable, we will remain there.

Who doesn't enjoy being the biggest fish in the pond, or at least feeling safe because there are no threats in the pond? The pond is a great place to be a young fish, but there's a problem: you can't stay in the pond. The fisherman is coming and the pond is drying up.

Comfort is a temporary state—it can't last. To live for it is to live for a lie.

Goldfish, and many other types of fish, are indeterminate growers, which means they don't stop growing. If a goldfish gets too big for its home this can lead to problems such as a lack of oxygen, poor water quality, and not enough swimming room. If these problems aren't addressed, it will result in the death of the fish.

While us humans stop growing physically, our potential for personal growth is unlimited. But the wrong sort of environment and lifestyle can impede that growth.

Twenty years down the road, no one will care if you were the valedictorian, football star, chess champion, class president, teacher's pet, honors student, or prom queen. You can't build a life on who you used to be. Eventually, if you want to survive and grow, you're going to have to move to the big lake where the rules are different.

Life is full of stages, such as childhood, adolescence, adulthood, parenthood, and retirement. Every time we enter a new, unfamiliar stage, we undergo changes, uncomfortable ones. Unless we're willing to make those changes, we will flounder through life instead of flourish—we will attempt to live at ease in a tiny pond.

The desire for comfort can be a good thing—healthy even. A baby wants comfort from its parents—nothing wrong there. Comfort is an essential for those dealing with grief. It eases the pain of injury or loss. All good, normal things.

Make no mistake, being uncomfortable does not mean living an unhealthy or unsustainable lifestyle. It's still just as important to develop personal boundaries and practice regular self-care, whether or not you find such habits comfortable.

The problem comes when we get too comfortable with comfort—when we rely on it so much that we don't think we can live without it. We don't grow up, our wounds never heal.

We're in a dangerous place when we fear anything that looks uncomfortable. It leaves us trapped—unable to move forward in life, unwilling to try new things. This mindset stunts our growth and leads to unhealthy patterns such as obsession, addiction, hoarding, immaturity, codependency, perfectionism, and complacency.

When we refuse to leave behind the feel-good familiar stuff, when we instead cling to it with the tenacity of a child with their favorite blankey, we become slaves to comfort.

Creativity is not comfortable.

Trying new things means leaving your safety zone and treading into unpredictable territory. It means taking risks. To be creative—to practice doing and making new things—you have to stretch yourself.

If you've done much in the way of exercise, you've had some

experience with this. Stretching your body helps your muscles warm up or relax. The act requires you to remain in uncomfortable positions, often reaching as close as you can to your limits. It doesn't exactly feel good while you're doing it, but it prevents injury, increases flexibility, and aids muscle growth.

Working out can be equally challenging, but knowing it will be over soon and how good you'll feel afterward can drive you on. It's the same way with any creative task you take on: you push through the setbacks, the failures, and the challenges because you know how great it's going to feel when you're done.

If you want to grow stronger creatively, you'll have to stretch yourself, often to your very limits. Much like a hard workout, it may mean giving it all you have, knowing it will lead to having more the next time. This may require you to go to unsafe places, try unfamiliar things, reach out to people who could hurt you, or even put yourself in a situation that could break you. That's scary. But, much like a muscle,

only by being broken can you be made stronger.

My friend Willie has scoliosis—a sideways curvature of the spine. Remarkably, for much of his life, he ignored it. As you might expect, it didn't make things better. Then he met Beatriz, a no-nonsense physical therapist who changed his life. She taught him how to appreciate and adapt to his condition with every lifestyle choice, down to what shoes he wore and how he folded his dollar bills.

Until his first meeting with Beatriz, Willie had never before stood with correct posture. As he recounted to me, the very first time he got into "correction" everything felt different. He felt like another person.

In the past, his body had compensated for his crooked spine and bad posture. When he finally stood up straight, it felt to him like leaning, even when could see himself doing it in the mirror. It was a strange sensation.

Previously, he'd simply done what was comfortable, what came easily to him. This meant crawling through buildings during inspections, riding his bicycle around town, going to yoga classes. From the outset, these all appeared to be normal, even healthy activities, that required a good amount of effort on his part. Only after meeting Beatriz did he realize that his lifestyle choices were a serious detriment to his health—they were actually killing him.

After that first meeting with his therapist, Willie felt broken down, defeated—everything he'd gotten used to had been suddenly stripped away—but it was a major turning point in his life. It was his first big step toward accepting his condition and adapting to it in a healthy way.

If you want to make the most of your life, you'll have to set aside things that look perfectly fine for "normal" people.

What is your posture toward creativity? What is keeping you from standing tall? You may need to put yourself into some unnatural positions in order to get back into correction, but it'll be the best thing for you.

How can you tell if you've got a comfort conundrum, and what can you do about it? Consider a few questions:

- What is the one thing I do most often because it makes me feel good?
- How much of my time is spent enjoying this thing?
- Is it helping or hindering my own development?
- What is the most recent uncomfortable thing I've done?
- Do I spend more of my time doing comfortable or uncomfortable things?
- Am I challenged, growing, and changing, or am I stagnating?
- What is one small creative practice I can start that will stretch me to try new things?

Why should you choose creativity over comfort most of the time? It's not because comfort is bad, but because creativity is more important.

Comfort is fleeting but creativity lasts.

The interesting thing about comfort is that it is subject to change. What you consider uncomfortable and unpleasant today may become a source of comfort and enjoyment tomorrow. Foods you dislike today may be your new favorite tomorrow. People you didn't think you could stand can become close friends. You might even look forward to a job you once dreaded.

When you practice creativity, you allow a change of expectations.

A comfort-based mindset puts you and your own needs at the center of everything, even at the risk of your own growth.

While comfort, in itself, can be a wonderful, life-giving thing, if our only goal is personal comfort, we start to insulate and starve ourselves. The inner well is deep and holds many treasures, but if it's our only source of inspiration, it will eventually become depleted and can only be refilled by other waters. This is why, ultimately, comfort alone cannot satisfy. It's a dead end. A creative mindset looks both inward and outward.

As Erwin McManus said in an interview,

Because if you live your life for yourself, you can create a pretty comfortable experience and you don't really have to risk a great deal...the moment you start to live your life for others, it moves you into risk mode and moves you out of safety and security mode.

Choosing creativity isn't always easy, but you're better on the other side of it. Sometimes, when the going gets tough, creativity can be the thing to help you get by.

It was a hard year when my mother-in-law discovered she had a soft-ball-sized tumor in her kidney—cancer. Even worse, it had metastasized and spread throughout her lungs. Constant, intense coughing fits had plagued her even before the diagnosis, making her essentially bedridden.

Blessedly, she was able to get on a chemo pill that significantly improved her quality of life, but not without introducing its own set of challenges. If you've had cancer or known someone with it, you likely know about the many complications that arise from the treatment. In spite of her discomforts, my mother-in-law has continued to invite creativity into her life.

While transitioning to the chemo pill, she filled many coloring books. The simple act of applying crayon to paper brought her a sense of peace and calm.

As long as I've known her, she's loved cooking. Not feeling well enough to make food was difficult for her. When she tried cooking again, it wasn't easy. I could tell that the act of standing over a hot stove was exhausting, but she persisted and made something wonderful. I saw a little of her old self come back that day.

Lately, she's taken up tatting, a way of making lace, during her restful days at home. From this craft, she's created bookmarks for her grandchildren and a chew toy for her nephew's son.

One evening, she came with us to an outdoor concert downtown and even danced for one of the songs, taking turns holding my young children in her arms. It brought a smile to my face and my heart, especially knowing how taxing it must have been for her.

Although she's faced some hard changes and had to completely rearrange her lifestyle, she presses on. She still dreams of reliving a fond childhood memory and riding horses again. I believe one day she will.

Everyone, in every circumstance has the opportunity to be creative in some way. At times it can be a challenge, at other times a relief. It may be the healthiest thing you can do and the one thing you need when everything else in your life feels painful.

Creativity is often uncomfortable, but it is necessary. If you need help with the transition from comfortable to creative, find personal examples you can model. Talk to the people you look up to and learn from them, discover how they live with risk and adapt to uncomfortable changes in their own lives.

As Bill Murray's character learns in the movie *What About Bob?*, it begins with "baby steps." On the other hand, extreme measures like "death therapy" are neither recommended nor required. Allow yourself to be just a little less comfortable today and see where it takes you tomorrow.

The more you go places you've never gone, do things you've never done, meet people you've never met, and think things you've never thought, the more you'll welcome growth into your life, and the bigger a life you'll lead. Which means you won't miss out on some great things, like fresh bread.

CHAPTER 15

Process

"Why a process?" I hear you ask (it was you I heard, wasn't it?) "Isn't the creative approach good enough?" (Yes, it is you speaking, I'm certain).

Well, a process is a method or series of steps toward an end. Ultimately, this is what we want—to use creativity with a goal, for a purpose.

On one hand (let's say the left one) a creative *approach* is a way of viewing matters through a creative lens. On the other hand (I mean your other left, of course), the creative *process* utilizes creativity to accomplish something. Both lead to an increase in creative living, but the latter is more focused.

The creative process shares some similarities with the creative approach, but has some important differences.

As a reminder, the creative approach is:
1. Observe
2. Question
3. Respond

And here are the three steps of the creative process:
1. Inspiration
2. Imagination
3. Innovation

Read those again if you'd like—I'm in no rush.

Do you see how they mirror one another? In both, step one begins with an outside influence, step two is an internal work, and step three again is outward action. Such is the rhythm of creativity: out, in, and then back out again.

The difference between steps one and three is that step one involves something on the outside changing you, and step three is you changing something outside yourself. The direction of impact is reversed.

Having looked at how they mirror one another, let's see what is different between the approach and the process.

First, the approach is less purposeful or directed. It's a catch-all for creativity, a treatment that can be applied at any time to anything.

The process, however, is guided. It requires more thought and intent. It arrives at something usable: an idea or invention (you notice I'm using a lot of "I" words, but don't blame me; it just worked out that way).

We talked about goals and how every story is, in one way or another, about a character trying to reach a goal. Tension, as we said, is the space between. The goal—the desired end result—of the creative approach is creativity: to have done or thought about something in a new, creative way.

The creative process looks similar, but the outcome is different. In the creative process, creativity is the means to reach a more specific goal.

Think of it this way: You may give a child a ball of Play-Doh with the instruction to make something. Given such simple instruction, they can do no wrong. As long as they interact with the Play-Doh in some way, they will have succeeded. If they smash it up, they've made a mess. If they throw it, they've made a projectile, or if they eat it, they've made food (that's probably the last thing you want, but I hear it's safe—not like I know from experience).

Though in this case it might not look like much, the child has used a basic creative approach: observe the dough, question what to do with the dough, and respond in some manner.

On the other hand, if you attend a pottery class with the intention of making a mug, you may begin with the same basic approach as the child with the dough (to mold something into a shape), but you will have much more specific guidelines. You have tools to use and methods to follow if you want to make a mug that looks nice, holds liquid, and is without cracks or major flaws.

You might think of other mugs you've seen. You could imagine how you want yours to look and what it will take to get there. At last, you make the mug, working it until you are satisfied with the result. And as long as you make a real attempt, you can say you've given it your best mug shot (sorry, I had to).

The last example has a more defined result and so requires you to use a process to reach the desired end. Just as a person would use a potter's wheel, sculpting tools, and a kiln to make pottery, so you can use the three parts of the creative process as tools to reach an intended outcome.

"But wait," the voice argues. "Doesn't a process kill creativity?"

Not at all! As I'm sure Sherlock Holmes must have said at one point, "Quite the contrary, my good fellow!"

A process allows for more creativity by removing confusion.

I've mentioned the need for creativity to solve problems. Behind every process there is a problem that needs solving. A process is a predictable way toward a solution.

Predictable? How is that creative?

A process creates clarity and direction. It gives focus to creativity. In the first chapter we talked about balance. There is a balance to be found between following the process (performing repeatable tasks in a set order for an expected outcome) and being creative (making something new or unique).

Bill Willson, the founder of Metro World Child, spends his time caring for disadvantaged children both in New York and around the world. There's a particular phrase I've heard him repeat that has stuck with me: "Do what you know and you'll know what to do." This fits in perfectly with the creative process.

In one part, you are doing something you already know—you are repeating. This repetition leads to the discovery of something new, the next thing you should do, the creative bit.

**A process takes away the question of what to do
and gives you the freedom to explore ways it can be done.**

Our life is full of processes that make doing things much easier. They give us time to focus on being creative in other ways. But it took creativity to discover the process to begin with. What's more, the creative approach can lead to the development of a process. See, it's all tied together like shoes over a telephone wire.

A process takes time.

It's not instantaneous. Bread doesn't rise the moment you toss it in the oven. Guess what? Creativity takes time as well. Our greatest creative works are more than a flash in the pan—they are the result of effort, of a thought-out process.

A process requires patience.

Not every process is perfect, and sometimes they need to be reexamined. A process may help us develop good habits as well as bad ones. We need processes, like brushing our teeth, washing dishes, going to work, and feeding the parrot. But throughout time, people have applied a creative approach to such processes in order to make them more effective.

We find processes in stories as well. Take the try-fail cycle. You see it all over the place, from children's cartoons to epic fantasy novels. The protagonist makes an attempt, either succeeds or fails, and then the plot moves on from there. It's a simple process, but an important one.

Mary Robinette Kowal explains this as the "yes, but/no, and" rule. If the protagonist succeeds in their attempt, the answer is "yes, but ... something else happens." If they fail, it's "no, and ... something else happens." This sounds programmatic at first, but it allows for creativity— it keeps the story moving and holds our interest.

Are you still with me here? Very good. I just hate turning back from the chalkboard only to find an empty classroom. Let's examine something a bit more exciting, the first step of the creative process: inspiration.

Apologies, what I mean to say is, let's get inspired, people!

I love the creative process. That's always been the closest thing to my heart, creating something.

~Amy Lee

SECTION 5 REVIEW

What were all those words you just read?

- Comfort can kill creativity and being creative often is uncomfortable.
- We endure discomfort to overcome obstacles and reach our goals, because to do so requires change, and change is uncomfortable.
- While the creative approach leads to a more creative outlook, the creative process leads to creative outcomes.
- Processes are important—they save time and allow us the focus on guidelines we need for our creativity.
- Rather than killing creativity, a process allows us to be more creative by giving clarity.
- Bread is really good. If you can't eat it for dietary reasons (or because it is an entity you worship) I can respect that, yet I pity you all the same.

Interview with a Creative

THE CROSBYS

INTRODUCING THE DYNAMIC DUO–
COLLEEN CROSBY
SHAWN "OBI-SHAWN" CROSBY

Tell us about yourself.

Colleen:

'Who am I?' seems like a complicated question! I am a producer at a motion capture studio (for a living), a producer of independent stage variety shows, a maker of historical and science-fiction costumes, a host of an online radio talk show, and I like to bake when I have any time left over. I'm also a wife, the caretaker of a turtle named Gamera, a reader, and I'm trying to learn to play the ukulele.

Shawn:

I do a little of everything! Artist, actor, costumer, lecturer, puppeteer, radio host, DJ, prop builder and model maker, working for Griffith Observatory, *Star Trek* television and film, Mattel and Playmates toys, Disney theme parks, and Blizzard, Sierra Online, and Vivendi/Universal games. Always ready to do something new and different.

I'm also a semi-professional "Jedi Knight," *Star Wars* geek, and designer/builder of the "H-Wing" and "Z-Wing" Carfighter *Star Wars* art car projects, going to famous places like the Super Bowl, Skywalker

Ranch, Johnson Space Center, and more grounded locations like schools, hospitals, and libraries, teaching science, the path of the Jedi, and lightsaber techniques to kids and kids at heart. I've done up to 160 charity and community events a year in costume portraying characters from *Star Wars*, *Harry Potter*, Steampunk, and other creative realms to further humanitarian concerns and also prove by example that you don't have to be boring when you "grow up."

When do you find it easiest to be creative?
Colleen:
When I'm calm. If my house is cluttered, the dishes are in the sink, there's email to answer, or I have other chores looming over me, it's easy for me to put off figuring out a tough design element to take care of responsibilities. I like working in the afternoons, because I make mistakes when I'm tired.

Shawn:
I need to have my energy level and available time in alignment. I'm fairly nocturnal, so usually that's from 9:00 p.m. to 2 a.m. or later. But sometimes I have to run when inspiration strikes, and I can get fixated on a project until it is completed, regardless of the time.

Where do you look for inspiration?
Colleen:
The internet, movies, books, work done by friends, people at conventions, TV shows, history, and museums.

Shawn:
Everywhere! I can find inspiration in nearly anything, even things I don't like. But a single tangible item, images on the internet, film/TV, and the world at large. I value my friends' input greatly on projects for an objective eye, in case I've become too close. Sometimes I'll wake up with an inspiration in mind, and sometimes I have to fight to find the right path for the project.

What forms of creativity do you most appreciate or enjoy?

Colleen:

My favorite is making general historical clothing. When you make a rec-reation from media (be it *Star Wars* or a painting), you sometimes have to get so exact that it's hard not to be a perfectionist. In women's historical clothing, as long as you understand the shape and materials of a given time period, getting close to your inspiration is usually fine. My favorite event to enjoy is usually picnicking in historical clothing. I get to wear something I've sewn, *and* I get to share a meal that I've created. I find producing variety shows to have been rewarding when the "curtain" falls, but the amount of time it takes to put on a good show will take over every little bit of your life when you're creating it.

Shawn:

I love and practice the art of "modification"—where common objects or materials are transformed into something that better fits my aesthetic, vision, or purpose. I can apply it to anything—props, gadgets, computers, toys, fine art, vehicles, clothing… It requires a variety of skills and exper-imentation, knowledge of available media and technology, and the will to use it in unintended and unexpected ways. It's a fresh approach on every project, often fosters learning new techniques, and because nothing is off limits, the project is only as expensive as you want to make it to achieve your planned result.

When has a creative approach helped you accomplish something impactful?

Colleen:

In an emergency, you find that your creative approach goes into overdrive. We were doing a dress rehearsal for a show two days before it opened, and one of our actors had a costume failure. Her bodice had four darts on the front, and all four of them tore when she was dancing. Keeping her calm was the most important thing, so I had to pretend that it was no big deal, just an easy little fix for me. I ended up taking a day off work, which I spent creatively reworking the front of her costume to make it look like the replacement fabric was a design element.

Shawn:

Being creative beyond what society deems as "normal" has helped me further my goals in working for the "service" of charity and community. With my twenty-years-running *Star Wars* art car project, I had to fight many years through naysayers and haters to create what I knew would be a useful and interesting mobile art exhibit. But now that the cars have had an impact worldwide through enthusiastic online image sharing, public acceptance is a minimal restriction and I find I'm welcome wherever I need to go to be useful. Plus, it's an amazing feeling to travel within your own creative work and to always have it with you as a natural part of life, as long as you're thick skinned to accept the criticism as well as the enthusiasm from the random people you meet.

What is one practice you would recommend to help someone be more creative?

Colleen:

One of the things that I bring to most of my creative endeavors, many of which involve a lot of teamwork, is organizational skills. I have found that if I have to-do lists and calendars that tell me what needs to be done, by whom, and by when, that I can relax and create! This comes with a warning though. It's easy to get pulled into the lure of a journal and spend more time creating it than creating your project. I usually spend a set amount of time setting mine up, and time each day to see where we are. And then I have to let it go, so I can get the actual work done.

Shawn:

Take risks and be fearless! Art is subjective, and only you know what your vision is, and it won't be everyone's cup of tea. But you have to take a chance and do it anyway! Don't be dissuaded because some people might be harsh on you; the people who like it and are inspired by your work will find you, and nothing feels better than having them tell you so—which inspires you back.

Where can people find you or your work?

Colleen:

Docking Bay 94, the pop culture radio show that I co-host, is at http://kryptonradio.com/docking-bay-94/.

For my costumes, I'm on Facebook.

Shawn:

The Star Wars cars can be seen online at https://www.facebook.com/StarWarsCar/

You can hear me live on Internet radio, weekdays at www.kryptonradio.com

Section 6 - Inspired

River

The strong current pushes you head over hindquarters, leaving you disoriented and confused. At last you manage to find your footing on a rock and push up for air.

As your head breaks the water's surface, you hear frantic screaming. It sure is quieter under the water. You surface again to more shouts, close and familiar.

"Ahh! The big fish is gonna get me for sure this time! Help!" You spot me nearby, arms flailing.

You're doing your darndest to swim against the river's force, and I take heart. After a tense battle, we manage to each grab ahold of a driftwood plank.

The ride seems without end, and we fight to avoid drowning or smashing against a boulder, until a tall, pointed rock breaks our board in two and we are again floundering in the rapids.

"Try something, anything!" I sputter. "Be creative!"

A thought comes to your mind, but it seems so ridiculous that you dismiss it.

The water has become too strong to fight, and I've all but given up hope, when we feel something large and solid come up from below—something moving down the river with us.

We rise up out of the water on a smooth turquoise surface covered in a hexagonal pattern—it appears to be the shell of a turtle.

After a collective sigh of relief, we collapse; it seems we're safe and alive, for now.

And so we float gracefully down the river on the back of an enormous turtle. As you consider this, you realize such circumstances, which once seemed strange to you, now feel almost normal.

Much has changed. Even this river, which first brought dread and uncertainty, has now calmed to a place of tranquility. You've taken off your shoes to dip your tired feet in the cool water.

We watch the great reptile's head bob up and down as it carries us onward.

"Sorry," I say. "I may have gotten a little carried away back there."

You offer reassurance.

I pull the little map from my pocket and wring it out. Since it's made of animal skin and not paper, it hasn't been ruined. I unfold it carefully to study it.

There is something strange about the map—it has more lines on it than last time I took it out, even though you never saw me draw on it.

I tuck the map away. "Looks like we should be near the mountain path, the one heading to the peak. I should warn you. Before we reach the top, there's a fortress we must pass through. No way around it. I do not know who resides there—if foe, our passage will not be easy."

Our ride comes to a gradual stop. The river has widened to a pool that, at the far end, drops off into a series of falls. To our left is the mountain. You spot the trailhead. It follows a steep incline but ends abruptly in a pile of boulders.

In front of the boulders, you recognize what used to be a stone gateway, but it has been smashed now, with only the two crumbled protrusions of its base remaining.

"Snakespit! Whatever or whoever caused that explosion back there has blocked up our path!"

You produce the createamobile and blow on it, but to no end—the little disk inside does not even move.

"It's no use. The thing is waterlogged, you'll have to wait until it dries." I grunt, "Nothing for it. We'll need to find another way."

You point out a mossy cave in the wall to our right. Inside, water trickles over round, wet stones on its floor. The tunnel is at a decline but does not look dangerous, as long as we take our time. It is not completely dark—little beams of green sunlight passing through foliage mark the way down.

"I'm not sure. Seems to be leading us the wrong direction." I scratch my chin in thought.

You walk to the mouth of the cave and touch its wet, smooth surface. Light spreads from the place you've touched. It crawls over the stone like little glowing worms and at last forms into one solid shape—an arch.

"Incredible," I marvel. "You found a hidden gateway. That's sign enough for me. I'll take that cave over riding down these falls any day. 'Sides, I think our turtle-friend is ready to head back." I rub my shoulder and suck in a short breath of air through my teeth. I nod toward the tunnel. "You first, partner."

We pat the smooth shell of our animal ferry in thanks, and it sinks beneath the water with a happy *glurp* as we enter the cave.

The cool tunnel has a dank smell of fungus and the constant drip of water. The path takes an occasional bend and follows beside the falls, even passing under at times. A ways down, we spy a circle of light—wide green fronds that hang like curtains over the exit.

The sound of hands and feet slapping against wet rock echoes up to us from below and eventually we see a creature—the same one we spied before—climb between the fronds and make its way into the forest beyond.

"Very strange," I whisper. "Are we following it, or is it following us? Either way, we must keep sharp as a cactus. Who knows what awaits us up ahead."

After some careful footwork and an occasional slip, we reach the tunnel's base. I hold up a hand and point to my ear. You ask if I have an earache, and I whisper, "No, listen. I think I heard someone."

We wait and wait but hear nothing besides sounds of water trickling down stone and gusts of wind through the tunnel. You push aside the wide leaves and step into a sunlit clearing beside the river, now shallow and calm.

I follow close behind and take a long look around the clearing.

A nearby fern rustles, and I jump, but it turns out to be only a little rodent dashing across the clearing. I relax. "It appears we're safe for now."

Ten guards step out from behind the trees, dressed in burnished black-plate armor. The soldiers (a group of both men and women) carry large, polished metal shields with a black dragon painted on them and long black spears, all pointed at us.

We lift our hands in surrender.

"Dark Shields," I explain. "We're not out of the woods yet, so to speak. But it sure is good to feel wanted, right?"

Following our surrender, the Dark Shields take our belongings, bind our hands, and lead us deep into the forest.

Another creature has also joined our party—the same one we saw from afar before the rock-fall. It's tied and being led on a rope by a guard. It stands just above knee height and has dark-green skin with white blotches, a bald head, pointy yellow teeth, little rounded horns under its cheeks, and a gold ring in its nose.

"A merkling." I shake my head. "Nasty things. Looks like this one is enslaved."

The guard holding the merkling's leash walks near—a burly bearded man the others call Buldorf. "The little beast led you straight to us. A fine pet it is." Buldorf lets out a laugh that sounds more like a squelchy croak.

Despite the trouble it's given us, the creature looks pitiful now that we can see it up close.

I bend over and ask it, "How did you do that thing with the rocks back there? Was it magic?"

But the merkling just shakes its head and points in your direction.

Buldorf yanks hard on the merkling's rope, and it topples backward. Other guards laugh and kick at it.

The merkling hisses and scampers back to its feet.

"You best leave it alone if you know what's good for you," Buldorf warns. He gives me a hard poke to the gut with the blunt end of his spear.

From time to time, you catch the merkling staring at you intently, but it says nothing. Though you wonder what it's thinking, you'd rather not risk angering Buldorf right now.

As we walk, other woodland creatures poke their heads out from holes in the ground, behind trees, or through overhead branches. It's difficult to tell whether they're watching the Dark Shields with trepidation or if they're looking at you in curiosity. Did you just catch a deer winking?

"This is a strange place," I mutter as a family of squirrels follows us with beady, unblinking eyes, "stranger and stranger."

I dream my painting and I paint my dream.

~Vincent Van Gogh

CHAPTER 16

Inspiration

Have you ever wondered where creativity comes from? Why do some people seem to be more creative than others? Is it an innate ability only a select few are gifted with, or do we all possess the same creative potential?

All the really creative folks I know hold a genuine and ongoing interest in many things. They possess an increased receptivity to inspiration.

Is this something they're born with or something experience has developed in them? I couldn't say, but I do know this is a posture everyone can develop—it's a wellspring available to all.

What exactly is inspiration?

Interestingly, one definition for inspiration is the drawing of air into the lungs; inhalation. https://www.dictionary.com/browse/inspiration

An inward breath is as accurate a depiction as any, methinks. Here's my definition:

Inspiration is any outside influence that fuels creative thought.

Inspired people are receptive to the things that ignite their inner creativity. They have their antennas up and ready. They breathe in the creative sources around them. But it's just as easy to go the other way, even for creatives.

There are times in my own life when I have kept myself closed off and closed in. As a result, my inspiration waned. But when I've focused on discovering and appreciating more of the world around me, BAM, inspiration hits like a load of bricks (though not as painful).

Some people make the mistake of thinking creativity begins with imagination. But even before we set our thoughts free to roam the playground of our minds, we first discover the motivation to do so from outside influence.

Inspiration fuels your imagination.

Show me a creative, and I'll show you someone inspired (it's the same person, mind you). Though it isn't always easy to trace the source of a particular idea we've come upon, they all had their beginnings somewhere else, beyond our own individual mindscapes.

When we're inspired, it excites our subconscious, fueling it to work in ways we aren't aware of until rational thoughts are produced. Inspiration is an essential step in the creative process. For many, the struggle to be creative comes from a lack of inspiration.

Inspiration can't be forced, but when you open yourself to it, it sneaks up and pounces on you.

So where, then, do we find inspiration? Or where do we let it find us? As I've mentioned, it has similarities to the first step of the creative approach—observation. But instead of merely looking around, you are now on a hunt. You're hunting in order to be caught, so to speak. This step requires active engagement, and so the whole of the creative approach is needed—the practice of question and response will also guide you on the quest for inspiration.

Inspiration takes many forms. It may come to you naturally, but often you must sniff out its scent, follow its tracks, find where it makes its bed, and stake out its den for a night or two, hoping to catch a glimpse of it. Yes, it may take that sort of commitment, but no, we aren't talking about people here, so don't be a creepy stalker for goodness' sake!

And how do you know when you're inspired— when the beast has finally caught you? Oh, you'll know. You'll notice an excitement, a sudden drive, an inward desire to do something with your newly acquired inspiration. It will be undeniable.

This is probably a good time to ask: what's the point of being inspired? What is the end goal? Put simply: the purpose of inspiration is creative action.

I equated being inspired to inhalation. Well, if being inspired is breathing in, then being creative is breathing out. Since you've made it this far in the book, I think it's safe to assume you desire to be more creative, to do more creative things. Being inspired is a perfect place to start.

In the context of story structure, the second plot point or midpoint marks a major change for the protagonist—a turning point. As the name suggests, it comes around halfway through the story. It's a moment of truth for the protag, where they finally get a grip on the central conflict and how to solve it, where they recognize and understand the battle between the truth and the lie (be it an internal or external one).

The midpoint is the mark of a change in the hero, from reaction to action.

As you begin the search for inspiration, you are no longer just responding to what is around you. Instead, you're taking hold of the wheel and choosing where to drive. You choose a direction and make a move. When you follow the creative process, you take creative control over your life.

Inspiration is the bridge from reaction to action.

And just where should you start the inspirational hunt? What sort of bait should you use? And do you need to wear cut-off camouflage cargo shorts? The answer to the last one is no, never ever. However, while I do recommend a pith helmet while out exploring, I'll leave the headwear to your discretion.

This task may seem daunting to some, but it shouldn't. If you feel uninspired, you aren't looking very hard.

Inspiration is all around you, just waiting to be found.

Chances are you already have a good idea of what you find inspiring. Consider what excites you, what piques your interest. What do you find fascinating? Dig deeper until you gain an understanding of why you find inspiration from such sources. This will help you look for it in other places.

When it comes to the inter-webs, Pinterest is a popular source of inspiration. I hardly find a baked good, craft, or room design that didn't have a little help from Pinterest these days. In fact, my wife recently used it to get some ideas for our son's dino-themed birthday.

She discovered a clever way to cut watermelon so it looked like a monster's head. However, we didn't just straight-up copy the design. We added some flavor of our own, including little cantaloupe wedges for teeth and head spikes.

Heed my warning, oh hunter of inspiration: once you find it, never take it as-is. When using it for your own creations, you've got to change it in some significant way—make it your own. This might not seem like a big deal for cake pops and bookshelves, but the more serious you are about growing as a creative, the more important it is that you don't just steal another person's work.

If you've heard Gustav Holst's *The Planets* and John Williams's *The Imperial March*, you'll know what I mean. There are some unmistakable similarities between the two. Apparently, Hans Zimmer's score for *Gladiator* even garnered a lawsuit because of how similar it was to Holst's music.

I'm not one to make a call on legal rights, but if the project matters to you and may be seen or experienced by people who are older than five, don't just duplicate. Besides, wouldn't you rather be known as a source of inspiration than a copycat?

Enough on that. Back to the hunt!

To find inspiration, look for examples from another creative person whom you appreciate. Consider why they made it that particular way. What could you make that is similar but different enough to be your own?

Even if you don't think you know many creative people, that shouldn't stop you.

Unless you live in the middle of Antarctica, you are surrounded by products of creative people. Everything manufactured was designed by a person—even stop signs, fire hydrants, and parking meters—to look a certain way and fulfill a specific purpose.

Sure, those everyday objects might not stand out as much as a three-story art installation that also makes music controlled by the wind, but at one point, they were just as new and interesting. Even graffiti, whether you find it obnoxious or interesting, was someone's attempt at creative expression.

If you really want to be an inspired hunter, spend time in nature. The natural world is full of creative critters and amazing sculptures shaped by the artful hands of wind, water, and time. Whether you're observing how the trapdoor spider captures its prey, marveling at the survival abilities of the wood frog, or taking in the wonders of a national park like Yosemite, there is virtually no end to the inspiration nature has to offer. Even the critters, plants, or rocks in your own neighborhood can hold more inspirational value than you expected at first bush—I mean blush.

If nothing else, explore something you know little to nothing about. Delve into a historical documentary. Find someone with an unusual career and ask them about it. Watch a movie or read a book you wouldn't normally entertain yourself with. Go somewhere new, like another country.

Find people who live and think differently from you. They might be just down the block. Try a new restaurant and feast upon a dish you've never before tried, maybe one you can't even pronounce. Go to a concert with a style of music you haven't listened to.

Heck, just try a different flavor soda at the fountain or combine a few. I don't know if I'd call Sprite-lemonade-black tea inspirational, but it might just open your mind to a whole new world. Point is, you need to get out of your routine and do something different.

You could even take a trip to the museum. It's the most obvious place to start, which is why I saved it for last. Keep in mind: being in the presence of art does not guarantee inspiration. That's the amazing thing about it—it's unpredictable.

As I hope you've realized while practicing observation, when you focus on what's happening around you, you see things you never saw before. So it is with drawing inspiration from the arts. Start asking questions about the artwork itself:

- How does it make you feel?
- What draws you to it, or what is lacking in it?
- Does it tell a story? If so, what kind?
- Is it entirely original, or does it remind you of something else?

- What do you think the artist was trying to express through it?
- Does its message seem clear or confusing?
- Do you think the artist succeeded in expressing their message?
- How might you use a similar medium to express a message you feel is worth sharing?

Don't feel like you have to break the bank on this. You can make it as challenging and expensive or as easy and cheap as you want. Creative works such as inventions and art are all around you—you just have to train yourself to stop and notice.

Inspiration hits different people at different times and in different ways. Over time, you will discover the sorts of things that inspire you the most, but always be open to discovering new sources.

One of my favorite things to do in the grocery store is to stop at the wine section and look at the bottles. I find both the names and the artwork on the labels interesting. While looking them over, I consider what the artist's choices say about the contents and company behind that brand of wine. I think about what sort of expectations they generate. I read the write-up on the back of the bottle to see what kind of story they are telling. Each is unique, and some of them are quite amusing.

Think about Georgia O'Keeffe for a moment. She took a common subject matter, the stuff that was around her, and made it stand out, made it unique. One of the most iconic subjects was cattle skulls. Sounds pretty strange, but she portrayed them in such a striking manner, you can't help but look at them. She uses that same style with flowers and landscapes, a subject other artists had covered for a good long while, yet hers are distinctly different. And just why did she pick flowers? I'll let her explain:

> Nobody sees a flower really; it is so small. We haven't time, and to see takes time—like to have a friend takes time.

And also,

> I decided that if I could paint that flower in a huge scale, you could not ignore its beauty.

As you search for inspiration, think about how the common things around you could be transformed into something more than meets the eye. Who would have thought cow skulls could look so amazing and paintings of flowers could be so surprising?

There are endless places and methods to find inspiration. Once you begin the search, you'll be surprised what may turn out to be an inspirational source.

I invite you to let your mind stray down roads it has never before taken. Open yourself to new ideas and experiences (not too dangerous ones, mind you), and then take time to reflect upon them.

When your mind is presented with the unfamiliar, it is forced to take notice, to think in new ways.

As an article from Trello points out, just doing your usual day-to-day work in a new location can cause a mental shift.

> Essentially, when confronted with new stimuli your brain responds by creating new pathways and mechanisms to accomplish tasks. By doing this, you are climbing out of the stale rut you were in before, activating your brain's ability to think about things in a new way.

People who make the grave mistake of living comfortable lives by doing the same thing day in, day out will have a hard time being inspired because everything is old and familiar to them.

Instead, be adventurous. Don that pith helmet and get pithy: you are the intrepid explorer in search of the new and interesting.

One parting word of advice: If you have a particular creative work you are about to begin, don't wait to start until you feel inspired. If you do, you'll never actually begin. "Feeling inspired" is a subjective term. The need for inspiration can easily become an excuse you tell yourself to avoid the challenge of the creative process or the struggle of creative tension.

Instead, begin the work and allow the inspiration to present itself as you go. If, after you've spent some time at it, you run into a roadblock, then take some time to go out on the hunt. A short stroll outdoors may be all you need to get the blood pumping and the gears turning (especially if you're a cyborg).

Inspiration is a funny thing, sometimes unpredictable, but when it strikes, be ready to catch it. It's powerful, like lightning in a bottle. On the other hand, it's not so mystical as to be unobtainable. From the artsiest of artists to the simplest of simpletons, anyone can find inspiration with a little effort. If you search for it—if you put up your lightning rod—it will hit you one way or another. Just be ready for the aftershock of ideas to follow.

Fiction is art and art is the triumph over chaos...to celebrate a world that lies spread out around us like a bewildering and stupendous dream.

~John Cheever

SECTION 6 REVIEW

Let's recap:

- In the midpoint of a story, the protagonist begins to understand the truth and shifts from reaction to action.
- Creativity begins with inspiration, it is fuel for the imagination.
- Don't wait for inspiration to fall into your lap—hunt it down.
- Inspiration is all around you, look for it in unexpected places.
- Look, just because Georgia O'Keeffe used animal skulls, doesn't mean you have to. All I'm saying is, be careful about digging up a bunch of bones—it's not just gross, you may actually be disturbing some ancient Native American burial ground, and if so, you're in for trouble!

Interview with a Creative

JENNIFER GARRETT

Tell us about yourself.

I'm a visual artist, writer and a storyteller. Or, to put it more creatively, I make various marks on paper that allow me to transform my imagination into reality. Sometimes other people pay me to transform their imaginations into reality as well.

When do you find it easiest to be creative?

It's not so much about a specific time of day; it's about being able to minimize distractions and having the freedom to let my mind run around in a world of possibilities, about having times of quiet. There are times when quietness seems to come more naturally—before and after others are in bed, when I'm doing something repetitive that doesn't require a lot of mental focus, or on those rare days when I have the house to myself. But as nice as it is when those times just waltz up and invite me to be creative, I've been thinking lately about the importance of being aware of how I am cultivating times of quietness rather than just snatching the moments that happen to come my way. If I wait for ideal times to come along, the reality is that I'm not going to be very productive—certainly not consistently productive—in my creative life. But if I'm deliberate about making and guarding my time to create, and I employ simple but effective tools such as shutting the door, turning on music that helps me focus, turning off device notifications, and communicating that I'm going to need uninterrupted time to focus, then I don't have to rely on chancing upon ideal moments—I can create my own times when it becomes easier and more effective to be creative.

Where do you look for inspiration?

Everywhere. And that's not a copout answer. We live in a gloriously beautiful world, and I'm convinced many of us don't take nearly enough of it in on a day-to-day basis. I think we sometimes get dulled to it by the idea that "we've seen it before." The thing is, no, we haven't. Not really. Not today. Not the way it all looks right now. Not from the point of view you have today that maybe you didn't yesterday or five or ten years ago. There's so much creative inspiration to be gained just from actively observing and engaging with people and the world as a whole—from nature, architecture, science, history, visual arts, books, music—and even engaging with our own thoughts, taking the time to ponder and imagine and allowing ideas to germinate and grow over time. It's like an open playground of discovery out there. So, go see how many types of green you can find in just that one tree, marvel at the moon, read a book, research that question, give the person in front of you your undivided attention, daydream. The more we engage in life, the more we begin to uncover the extraordinary in all the "ordinary" things around us, and if that's not inspiring, I don't know what is.

What forms of creativity do you most appreciate or enjoy?

This could become an extensive list very quickly, but if I really boil it down, it always seems to end up coming back to story as one of the big "constants" I enjoy, whether in the form of books, movies, dance, or painting. I'd venture to say I've learned as much about truth through fiction over the years as I have from any study of facts, and in many ways, a story can take my understanding of something far deeper than it might go if someone just told me "Here's how this aspect of life works." Like so many seeming "opposites" in life, I believe reality and fiction need each other, and that each makes the existence of the other better and more complete.

Music is another lifelong love. There's something so pure and direct in the way beautiful sounds go through our ears and straight to our souls. I think the need for beauty is something ingrained deeply into our psyches, and it's something really wondrous—that music can be such an intense experience of beauty without any visual element to it. I think that really validates the whole idea that the kind of beauty our souls truly yearn for is something far deeper than what we see on the surface, despite what culture tells us. Of course, there are many things in the visual world that radiate this deeper beauty as well, but music has a special ability to demonstrate this in an especially clear way simply because we can't mistakenly attribute its beauty to anything we can see.

When has a creative approach helped you accomplish something impactful?

Something I took away from my time as an art student was observing how the teacher would sometimes come at the same things from a variety of angles to help us understand what we needed to do, especially when we were having trouble or stuck on a concept. As an art teacher now, I feel the need to apply creativity to not only my own artwork, but also to figuring out ways to convey the process to different people, not to reinvent the wheel, but to sometimes put a new spin on the information so that it hopefully makes as much sense as possible to each individual student. The ability to apply creativity to exploring different ways of approaching things and of looking at the processes of art making has been a hugely valuable tool in being able to help others further their own artistic journeys.

What is one practice you would recommend to help someone be more creative?

This kind of ties back in to the inspiration question. Choose to be an explorer of the world around you, both literally and conceptually. If something interests you, go research it, google it, put books on hold at the library. Be a curious observer of art and people and nature. Study everything. The more you know and experience in a range of subjects, not just the ones that come naturally easy to you, the more you'll ultimately have to pull from when you need fresh perspectives and ideas. I remember how much I bucked having to take algebra in high school, because I was already dead set on an art career, and I thought anything past the basics in math would be useless as an illustrator and were therefore largely a waste of time. What I realized later when we were asked to apply a geometry-style logic to drawing in art school was that even my math experiences could contribute to making me a better artist. When the world ceases to be broken up only into separate little compartments in our minds and instead we see the bigger picture of how our experiences can feed into each other, the creative possibilities only become greater. So yes, always, always, always explore because what's out there to discover is limitless.

Where can people find you or your work?

My art site and links to social media can be found here: www.jngarrettart.com

Section 7 - Imaginative

Forest

Bound and led at spearpoint by the Dark Shields, we trudge deep into a pine forest. We follow a rugged dirt path, winding between clusters of brightly colored ferns, some taller than a bear standing on its back legs. In some places, the foliage is so thick, the path is entirely covered in shade. You've got to admit, the shelter from the hot sun is not unwelcome.

After a few hours, the smell of smoke reaches us. We are led to a wall nearly two stories high and made of spiked wooden poles. A gateway in the wall reveals a second, smaller wall a little ways beyond.

After Buldorf whispers a password to a gatekeeper, we pass through, walk between the walls for a time, and then pass through a second gate. We then enter a large encampment with cook fires, tents, and wooden buildings. Red flags with a black dragon symbol decorate the camp.

Although some trees have been cleared for walking paths, most remain, which make it difficult to measure the size of the Dark Shield camp and the army within.

"I think we're in Forest Town," I say, "or what's left of it. Never been this far around the mountain before."

While marching through the encampment, you note that many of the

202 | THE ENDLESS CREATIVE

residents have…animal parts. Some of them have patches of fur. Others have tails, snouts, hooves, or claws. Is it a curse similar to the one that plagues Plateau Town?

I nod to you as we pass an elderly man with lizard eyes and slits for a nose. "You see it too? But where does it come from? And notice, none of the Dark Shields have it. What's protecting them?"

The sun has begun to set, giving the forest canopy an orange hue, as if the overhead leaves were wreathed in flame.

We at last arrive at our destination: an open space between a long row of tents. A crude wooden platform rises in front of us, carrying a high-backed chair, which is also made of roughly carved wood. The chair is empty.

It appears to be some form of theater but without any seating. Buldorf makes us sit on the ground and wait in silence.

The light dims as long shadows play over the branches, giving them the appearance of unnatural movement. Soon, torches are lit, their unsteady shadows making nearby roots seem to twist and writhe underfoot.

At last, a man walks out from behind the platform. He wears a long, black cape as well as brown leather garments that cover all but his head, upon which a golden circlet rests. His movements are stiff as he climbs up the steps and takes a seat upon the wooden chair. You hear it creak under his weight.

The man is impressive in stature, almost bearlike, were it not that he is hunched over with age. He sports bushy white eyebrows and a matching white mustache, which stand out from his dark complexion.

The man upon the throne motions for us to stand, and we obey. "So, it seems we found you at last." There is a ragged softness to his voice, like a worn blanket.

"Greetings, Lord Obvious." I make an exaggerated bow. "Are you the king of this army?"

"Show some respect to our leader." Buldorf thwaps me on the back of the head.

The leader holds out a steady hand toward Buldorf. "Easy, my over-eager captain. We don't often get visitors." Is that a tired smile on his face or a trick of the lighting? "Alas, I am no king." He laughs uncomfortably. "I'm just the person put in charge."

"What do you want from us? We are no threat to you," I say, keeping a wary eye on Buldorf.

The leader turns to me, a look of sadness in his eyes. "No more questions from you now. After all, you are not the one we are after. Your time is near an end. It is the other we want."

The leader points to you and squints one eye. "It is you we consider our highest threat. I know your plans to reach the mountain peak, to defeat us with a great weapon. There are many who have attempted the same journey and failed."

The leader tugs at his thick white mustache and looks up to the treetops, as if something were hovering over him just beyond the branches. "I myself once resided up there upon the mountain. Then the curse came and everything changed. You believe we're the cause, don't you? You are wrong, of course. We fight against this curse. Can't you see that we who serve the Great Master are protected? Here we are safe."

"Lies!" I shout. "Don't believe him."

Buldorf shoves me hard to the ground, and a rotund female guard sits on my chest so that I can barely breathe.

Through all this, the leader, his brows furrowed, has not broken eye contact with you. "I'm afraid, in a sense, your friend is right. This place is not safe for you—nowhere is. Tomorrow you shall be our great offering, and then at last these lands will be pure once more." The leader motions to a high wooden pole nearby; it appears they intend some form of sacrifice. "Now, to the pit with them both. Let no one converse with them until the morrow."

We are taken to an area on the edge of camp. On the way, we pass the merkling, who has been tied to a wide stump. It appears to be asleep, exhausted from the rough journey.

A little farther on, we are tossed without care down a deep hole in the earth. We land on our hands and knees in a soupy patch of mud. Night has fallen.

"I owe you an explanation," I say after I've taken some time to wipe mud from my face. "You're troubled by this turn of events, and I haven't been entirely honest about my mission. Don't be angry. I meant no harm. I…I just wasn't sure. But it's true. I'm not the one they're after. They're looking for the Endless Creative. The one spoken of long ago who will again restore these lands, who will bring great change. They want to blame someone for the curse, to make people afraid so they will join their ranks and serve the Great Master, whoever that is. But the Endless Creative is the only one who knows how to end the curse. Is it you? You don't have some secret solution you've been hiding, right?"

You shake your head.

"I was afraid not. I don't know who the right person is, but I've been searching for a while, and you're the closest I've found. You saw something back at the Pool of Dreaming—a sign. And the things you've done, well, it harkens back to the time of legends. I'm still not sure I believe any of it myself, but—"

"Psst," a voice says.

A lantern hovers over the pit. Its light shines on the face of a woman bordered by long red hair—a guard.

She speaks again. "I don't have much time, so listen well. You have a friend or two among us. We're just…scared. And outnumbered. But we can help. This pit is surrounded by some of their best guards, but I'll make sure they're all sound asleep come midnight. Until then, this should help."

The woman tosses down some food: a sack with a loaf of bread, a slab of meat, and some cheese. "And I believe this is yours. Not sure if it's much use now." The createamobile lands in the mud beside you. It has a big crack down the middle, and the disk inside is bent. The woman glances over her shoulder for a moment, then turns back. "I know you'll find a way out somehow. We believe in you." She disappears into the night.

"That could have been worse," I say while tearing off a piece from the bread loaf. "Look." I pull out the map. "This is the edge here, but from what I can tell, we're in the Forest of Defeat. It's just a matter of who will be defeated, us or them. Between your smarts and my charm, we're sure to find a way out of this mess."

You study the map, but something is different about it. The names on the map shift, the letters and landmarks rippling as if they're sitting on the surface of a pool, but you can't quite understand them. Then you catch it, just for a moment. The name of the forest is Hope, not Defeat. As you consider this, the map returns to its former solid form. You pause, glance around the pit, and then turn to me with a fixed expression, resolute.

"So," I ask between mouthfuls of bread, "you got a plan?"

The power of imagination makes us infinite.

~John Muir

CHAPTER 17

Imagine

The heat is on and the water has begun a slow boil. If inspiration is the fire, then ideas are those little bubbles rising to the surface, popping into your mind.

In our trip through story structure, we've reached the second pinch point. Things are heating up for our hero.

Like the first pinch point, there is again a sign of the troubles ahead—the road becomes even rougher for the protagonist. This part of the story lies in the shadow of the protagonist's darkest hour and foretells of what is to come. However, it is also the time when the protag is in full swing, doing their best to solve the conflict (both outer and inner) and overcome the antagonist.

**This new trial presents an opportunity for the
hero to show us what they're made of.**

Once you have been out on the hunt for inspiration, you will return with a head full of ideas—your hunting trophies, so to speak. Whether good ideas or bad ones (there may be a skunk hiding in there), it's not important at this point, only that you have them.

You probably already had a few already hiding in there, but inspiration will help raise them to the surface and make them stand out.

However, just having ideas isn't enough. Like koi fish in a full pond, they are slippery things, and you must draw the best ones out if you want them to be of any use to you. Inspiration is throwing bread on the water, causing the koi to gather in front of you, but then you need a net to catch them. You must learn how to imagine.

When you imagine, you summon to mind something not present.

As Ken Wytsma puts it in *Create vs. Copy,*

"All of us breathe things into existence every day that didn't beforehand exist in this world. We are all creators. Creativity is a mindset of imagination and potential. It takes the building blocks of today and uses them to make space and expand horizons for tomorrow."

But how do we learn to imagine if we've gotten out of practice? Think back upon your sources of inspiration—use your memory. In this way, inspiration becomes a reliable link, a sure path to imagination.

To remember is to imagine—to willfully bring to mind something that does not exist at present.

When it comes to the creative journey, making a conscious leap from inspiration to imagination is not always easy. One of the inherent challenges when using the imagination is to take the emotional response of inspiration—your enjoyment or interest in a thing—and transfer that energy into a useful idea of your own, something of substance you can show the world.

To be imaginative, you must be willing to overcome your own inner doubts and distractions and use your mind with purpose. There is a natural balance here between allowing your mind to roam free while also giving it a focused direction. This can be a challenge.

Just as the protagonist must strive forward into the conflict with a confidence of victory, so you must learn to embrace your ability to be imaginative in the midst of trying, and often distracting, circumstances.

But do not despair.

The wonderful thing about imagination is how accessible it is—anyone can do it anytime and anywhere.

Sadly, not everyone does. It is a rare and valuable skill, often neglected.

Our capacity to imagine is a spectacular thing. I heard this from copywriter and coach Joshua Boswell in a video course: "As humans, we have the unique ability to imagine and turn those imaginations into reality through a process called creation. If you don't imagine something, you can never create it."

If you're like me, you're hearing the voice of dear departed Gene Wilder sing "Pure Imagination." It sounds so lovely, so magical. But let's be honest. We don't all have a bunch of money and a crazy chocolate factory in which to live out our wildest (or wilder) imaginations.

If we want to put our imaginations to use, we've got to take the magical and make it practical, even practice-able. Yes, imagining is an important practice. This is why it's part of the creative process—it's something repeatable, something leading to a result.

Utilizing our imaginations isn't always our go-to habit. These days, we can be so task oriented, so goal focused, we forget to take time to daydream, to "waste time."

Okay, critics, I hear you. If our heads are always in the clouds, we'll never get anything done. We're in danger of being called a good-for-nothing layabout by some old-timey person—heaven forbid.

Sure, it's good to be a hard worker, but sometimes you need to look up from the task at hand and see the sky above you. Sometimes you have to step back and ask why you're doing what you're doing and, ultimately, where you're going. You have to take a break, remember the past, and envision the future.

To imagine is to let your mind free, to allow it to think whatever it wishes without hindrance. Some folks will tell you imagination is a waste of time—a pointless, idle practice. And yet those people rely on methods and tools that were imagined by someone else.

Take the ballpoint pen, or biro, for example. John J. Loud was the first to patent a ballpoint pen design in 1888 in an attempt to create a pen that could write on rough surfaces like wood and leather—something fountain pens couldn't do well. But John's pen was not adequate for letter writing. Only later did the brothers László and György Bíró work on perfecting the ink as well as the ball-socket mechanism to allow for more control of ink flow. This pen, patented in 1938, was at last fit for writing and commercial use.

The telephone is another great example. What began with two cans and a wire is now something we can carry with us everywhere to talk with people almost anywhere, and so much more. For better or worse, phones have become a major part of our livelihood. There are many notable jumps along the way: from needing an operator to connect the parties to being able to dial a contact, from using a rotary dial to push button, from wired to wireless, from landline to cellular. Both the pens and the phones we have today are the result of many people stopping to imagine how an already existing device could be improved.

Every useful tool and practice we now have
is the result of another's imagination.

Our imaginations may take us to far-off worlds, but it is in those far-off worlds where we discover the keys we need for this one.

An essential part of the hero's journey is the step from the ordinary world into the special world. This is what it means to imagine—to depart from the regular day-to-day trappings of the mind and visit the unexplored realm—a place only your imagination can take you to.

But the hero does not remain in the special world. They must return home again to the ordinary world where they began. Though they return, they come back changed—they have a new attitude and a treasure—something to help them in their normal world, such as a tool or a new realization.

While in the special world, your imagination is what will guide you to said treasure, and the bigger imagination you have, the more treasure will be available. Don't be mistaken—this treasure is much better than money. There are many good things our imaginations may lead us to, things like peace, joy, and contentment—the things that last.

The ability to walk between worlds takes skill. Naturally, we stay to one side or the other.

Some want only reality and sniff at any mention of the fantastic—the world of pure imagination. They miss out on the inward journey. They cannot look beyond the surface of life and see the deeper meaning hidden under each little stone of reality. As David Farland has said, "It is not until we begin playing in the woods of our subconscious that we can find ourselves lost in them."

Others desire endless escape to their fantasies and dread any return to ordinary life. What they don't realize is that their ordinary world holds adventures of its own. The real world, when seen in the right light, is just as amazing as any world with dragons, aliens, or magic.

Our fantasy will always, in some way, be predictable. Reality, like it or not, is surprising. As terrifying as it may be at times, it is equally exciting not knowing what will happen next.

As Dean Koontz puts it, "Truth is always stranger than fiction. We craft fiction to match our sense of how things ought to be, but truth cannot be crafted. Truth is, and truth has a way of astonishing us to our knees. Reminding us, that the universe does not exist to fulfill our expectations."

Creatives must learn to enjoy both worlds and to accept the merits and dangers of each.

To be a creative is to be a person of two worlds.

The finest of imaginers can be in both worlds at once. They see the fantastic interlaced with the ordinary. A flower by the side of the road, a weathered ship abandoned at port, a glisten of sunlight on wet stones—each may be a container, a portal to wonders untold.

The ability to see the world with new eyes is a powerful one. Indeed, it touches the very heart and center of creativity.

To see the fantastic in the ordinary, the beauty within the broken requires hope. It is looking at a pile of shattered glass at a dump and seeing an intricate mosaic. To hope is to be in a state of expectancy, to believe a situation can be made better. When you see with eyes of hope, you discover the path to change—to lasting improvement.

CHAPTER 18

Contemplate

Now, before you float too far up into the heavens, we return again to the grounded and practical. There are steps to this process, habits of the imaginative.

You can imagine anything you want any time you want, but not everything will be helpful. If you want your imaginings to take you somewhere useful, you'll need to learn focus. You'll need intentionality.

There are no bad ideas at first. However, you can't stay there. Those meager first ideas are not enough. They must lead you on to better ones or else grow stale and useless like old bread.

If you're out on a fishing trip, you don't leave after the first thing you reel in—you stick around for a while. You wait for that big, juicy fish. An old boot simply will not do.

It's perfectly fine to start by exploring the untamed wonderings of the mind and even return there often—just don't stay there.

If you set your mind to ponder something in particular, you will accomplish more. Just as there are tools and tricks to successful fishing, so there are ways to better direct your thoughts.

Think of a landscaper. They take the natural form of the earth around them—the slopes of the ground, the rocks, the trees—and fashion it into something beautiful, something more useful.

**When you direct your thoughts, you become
a landscaper of your own mind.**

The following practices will aid you in the mindscaping process.

Where, then, do we begin? First is contemplation—this is how you set aside the time to feed your imagination.

Quiet contemplation is a simple, often forgotten practice, but a crucial one.

Start with just five minutes of being by yourself in a place where you will not be distracted by anything else. Turn off or hide all electronic devices. If you need music playing (perhaps to drown out other sounds or if you find it helps you think), turn on something calming that has a slower tempo and no vocals. If you still have trouble thinking, write down a few questions beforehand to ponder.

As you begin this practice, it will be difficult to put aside your regular worries and concerns. The giant list of to-dos you have will fight for your attention. This is expected. It's normal. There are many ways to deal with such thoughts and clear your mind.

If something is bothering you, write it down and set it aside. If you can't stop thinking about a task you need to do, plan another time when you will do it, then let it go for now. If a disruptive thought continues to invade your mind, then it's likely something you'll need to address before you can move on.

A friend of mine suggested this practice to me when I felt under the control of troubling thoughts: imagine you are in a room in a house. Now recognize the disruptive thought that is in you. Breathe it out. The thought is now in the room with you, filling the air around you. Examine it. Then look around the house and walk from room to room. Now leave the house and the thought within it. Close the door behind you. Look at the house from the outside and take some time to explore the surroundings. That practice alone may be a good segue into quiet contemplation.

Maybe you need more time. Try ten or twenty minutes to allow your mind to settle. If the questions aren't helping, simply think about the things that bring you joy and consider why you love them—go back to your sources of inspiration.

Contemplation can look different for different people and it may take some time to find what works best for you. Perhaps you think more clearly in a busy coffee shop or spending an afternoon on a bench at the park. My editor, Dori, has found that brainstorming, either alone or with other authors or editors, has been a form of contemplation that produces amazing results.

The important thing is that you take a break from anxiety and stress-inducing thoughts and instead allow calmness to set in. Your goal is to create an environment where you feel unrestrained, to let your mind venture down unexplored avenues. To do this, you must be at ease.

A preoccupied mind is not an imaginative one.

Try quiet contemplation for a week or two and see where it leads you. You may even find it helpful to do a little journaling or praying during this time, just as long as you are giving your thoughts the space they need.

It may be hard to find the time at first, especially if you live with other people who require your attention. Let them know this is important to you. After all, everyone needs a little time to themselves.

As you give yourself time to think—as you let creativity blossom in your brain—you'll be surprised when a good idea sprouts. It may be in the car on the drive home or during a morning shower.

The idea may show up completely out of the blue. It's true—some of our most creative thoughts come when we least expect them, often when we're doing something mundane.

I once came up with an idea for a board game while I was getting a haircut. Such ideas seem random and unexplained, but they are the natural result of planting those seeds of inspiration and giving them time and space to grow—they are the product of subconscious thoughts, which are constantly at work in the background.

Though I hadn't been thinking about anything related to board games moments before, I had been giving attention to certain games and thinking over which mechanics I found most enjoyable.

At last I presented my mind with a problem and a goal: how to make a game that relied on some of the mechanics I enjoyed—ones that made sense for a game about thieves and guards. Suddenly, all those inspirational ideas that had been tumbling around in my noggin rose to the surface. They were there all along, but only showed up when the need arose, when I gave them the space they needed.

While I didn't come up with the entire game on the spot, the general idea hasn't changed. I've since developed a working prototype and plan to get it published someday. I've come up with and built two other games in similar fashion. For one, the idea came to me of making a game where the goal rather than getting ahead is to simply not fall behind. This one came while staying at a hotel the night before a friend's wedding.

Another game (this one about creating customizable characters to fight with other players) came the night of my brother-in-law's engagement party. I find it interesting that both were triggered by major life events. You could say I find relationship celebrations to be inspiring.

If you'll bear with me, I've got one more example. As a child, around ten years old, I had a vivid dream about how to create a Darth Vader out of various Lego sets. Keep in mind this was back before Lego had sets based on another company's intellectual property, like Harry Potter or Star Wars. Like many boys my age, I often played with Legos and loved Star Wars. For whatever reason, my brain worked out the perfect way to join the two and, by doing so, rule the galaxy (or at least my bedroom). When I woke up, I built the infamous Sith Lord and was pleased to find the results perfectly matched the vision from my dream.

On a basic level, this is how your imagination works. It combines the things you know and the things you like in new and interesting ways. Remember, it takes time and patience. Even the best of fishermen (and women) come up short some days. Much like fishing—if you do it for the experience, you won't be disappointed.

In case you haven't gotten it yet, the goal here is to have fun. Let your mind climb up the slide, hang upside down from the monkey bars, and take a reckless leap off the highest point of the swings.

Until you take some time to just be and think, you'll never know what you're missing. You'll never be able to release the creative inside you. And believe me, it wants out badly.

CHAPTER 19

Mind-Map

All right, so you've given quiet contemplation a go? Spectacular.

I've got another suggestion for you—a real dandy.

It turns out you have a secret weapon at your disposal: the magical solution. It will activate the amazing abilities of your subconscious and turn you into a powerhouse of ideas. Sounds too good to be true, doesn't it? Which is why you may be surprised at how basic and obvious it is.

That weapon is mind-mapping.

Go ahead—laugh if you want. It's fine. You won't hurt my feelings.

Mind-mapping, also called brainstorming, or, even less appealing, brain-dumping, may sound simple enough, elementary even, but if you practice it and do it right, there's really no end to where it can lead you.

The mind-map is an all-important first step to gather the many ideas you have for one particular subject and get them down somewhere concrete. You record them for future analysis.

When you mind-map, you become the
uber-scientist of your own ideas.

I can't overstate the importance of this practice. It isn't difficult, and that's part of the beauty. You may develop your own special methods, but this is how I recommend getting started.

First, you must come up with a topic. It can be as specific or vague as you want. You might have ideas for a book, what you're looking for in a spouse, types of food you love, ways to develop a better watering system for your garden, or…well… anything really. As long as you've been thinking about this problem or subject for a little while (if it is something you care about, you won't be able to help but think about it), you can mind-map it.

Next, get a big piece of paper—the bigger the better (you don't want to run out of space or feel cramped). Set a timer for half an hour (you can go longer, but I'd recommend this as a minimum). Write down the subject or problem in the center of the paper and put a big circle around it.

Now, begin! Just start writing everything that comes to mind. It doesn't have to be good. It doesn't have to make any kind of sense at all. Heck, the messier it is, the better.

You can draw lines connecting different ideas and circles around each one, but it's not required. Do what feels comfortable and natural.

The main goal is that you just keep writing things down for the whole length of time and fill up as much of the paper as you can.

When the timer goes off, take a deep breath. Give yourself a pat on the back, a rub on the belly, and a little treat: you've done good work, champ.

When you're finished, it should look like the work of some deranged conspiracy theorist. If a friend of yours walks in and sees it and they aren't at least a little bit concerned about your mad scribblings, you haven't done your job.

Did you realize you had that much stuff stored up in your head? Probably not, because for most people, the conscious mind can only think of about four things at once, but the subconscious has been working away on it while you do other things like work, eat, sleep, poop, and veg out.

While your conscious mind has mostly forgotten about the topic, your subconscious is working like gangbusters to come up with whatever it can. You have a whole factory of thinkers inside you working away nonstop. You've just gotta stop and ask them what they've come up with from time to time.

Maybe it's more like you have a pen of yipping dogs and you turned the volume down on them. As author Ray Bradbury puts it, "My stories have led me through my life. They shout, I follow. They run up and bite me on the leg—I respond by writing down everything that goes on during the bite. When I finish, the idea lets go, and runs off."

Hopefully, your experience isn't quite so painful for you.

Now that you have all those related thoughts in one place, set them aside for a day or two. They'll still look like a crazy jumble when you return to them, and that's totally fine.

The next step is to separate each individual thought from your mind-map. You could do this on sticky-notes or in a writing application.

Then, group each thought under a category or subcategory. Some thoughts you might need to duplicate if they belong in multiple categories.

What you do next is entirely up to you and will depend on what sort of creative project you hope to accomplish. If you're writing a book, each category might be a chapter. If you're teaching a class, each one could be a lesson for the day. If you're remodeling a home, each might become a different task that you can then organize by priority.

I used mind-mapping to write this book. Even though I had a vague idea at the outset, until I mind-mapped it, I really didn't know what exactly I was going to write. Creativity is a pretty broad subject after all. In fact, after the first (chaotic and incoherent) draft, I mind-mapped again to come up with the idea of organizing it around story structure. Though the final product looks quite different from those two mind-maps, they helped me organize my thoughts and figure out where to go next with them. And much of their content has ended up in the book, in one way or another.

Our studio has also used mind-mapping meetings to come up with some of our in-house projects such as an animation about a motion captured character acting in the real world. We've also used it when figuring out how to tackle particularly challenging jobs from other clients.

Mind-mapping is great for turning that tangled mess of ideas you have about one subject into something manageable—useful even. But what about your other stray thoughts, the ones that, like little lost puppies, don't have a home to call their own? Don't worry. There's a place for them too.

CHAPTER 20

Write

Besides quiet contemplation and mind-mapping, there's one more practice I highly recommend.

It's even easier, but requires more diligence on your part. It's a little something I like to call "write it down as it comes to you."

I know. Highly original, right? Really, this is something you should start doing *all the time*. I mean it. Here's why: If something matters to you, you're going to think about it. If you're thinking about it, ideas will pop into your head.

If you don't write your ideas down, you may lose them…forever.

Like me, you may find yourself trying to recall that great (or even halfway decent) idea you had, and you just can't do it. Count every idea as a little treasure sent down to you from above, and you won't be sorry.

I'd even suggest writing down ideas you don't think are all that great. What could it hurt? You can just toss them later if you're that embarrassed by them. It's not like they're your kids. I've had plenty of ideas I wrote down that I rediscovered years later and thought, "Hey, that was pretty good," then ended up using them. There's no way I would have remembered them otherwise.

Here's the other benefit of writing it all down: it frees your mind, giving you more time to spend in imagination land.

Writing stuff down isn't just helpful when you have a great idea. It's useful every time you think of something to add to that ever-growing to-do list.

What happens when you don't write it down? Those tasks circle around in your head again and again, like a brick in a clothes dryer, just banging and bumping away, setting everything else off balance. Your mind gets stuck reprocessing the same stinking thing. This state of mind is known by some as "monkey brain." It's an inability to focus due to constant mental interruptions.

Even the most mundane thoughts can become constant irritants, ones like, "I should send Joey a card;" or, "That song would be perfect for the party playlist I'm making;" or even, "I should do the laundry soon and maybe take that brick out of the dryer."

Hey, why are you storing bricks in your dryer, anyway? Well, if you don't write them down, all those distracting thoughts and ideas will keep returning to you until you do something about them. Since you can only hold a few thoughts in your mind at a time (four to six), your capacity for thought gets all jammed up, like a backed-up, overflowing soft-serve machine. You thought I was going to say toilet, didn't you? You're so gross.

**When you write your thoughts down,
it allows your mind to release them.**

Your head clears, and you can again focus your attention on matters at hand. When your mind is cleared of the incessant rambling, then the really good ideas come.

Think of panning for gold. If your mind is all backed up with the big dirt clods of daily distractions, the shiny gold nuggets never make their way out. No good. Instead, write down every idea (good or bad) and every thought of something you should address in the future. Then choose a time (such as the end of the day) to revisit them and reflect on what you've written.

I suggest you keep a journal, notebook, or notecards on hand at all times. You techies may want to use an app, but I recommend trying it with the paper version first. The minute you pull out your mobile device, you're faced with a whole host of distractions in the form of text messages, emails, social media posts, etc. Instead of writing down your idea you'll be loading up the ol' noggin with more dirt clods. Until you've built up enough self-discipline to ignore all those things, write it down by hand.

Whether or not you get into the habit of writing down your thoughts and ideas as they come to you, I also highly recommend taking up regular journaling. If you can't do it daily, at least commit to a couple times a week (that's what I'm currently doing).

The wonderful thing about journaling is it allows you to take that heavy cloud of fears, worries, hopes, and expectations looming over you and instead dump them onto the pages of your journal. They won't necessarily go away, but now at least they've been recorded somewhere else—giving them less control over your thought patterns. You gain distance from such thoughts, freeing up the mental energy you once used while holding on to them.

Journaling is especially useful right before going to sleep. It allows your mind to unload the heavy weights it's been carrying and finally take a break, letting you rest at ease.

You can journal about anything and everything, whether it's a record of recent events, things that have been giving you the emotional run-around, or ideas you have about something you want to do in the future. It's all good and it's all right.

Your journal is a safe place where even your wildest, most uncivilized thoughts can be at home. No one else needs to read it. That said, you might want to store it somewhere away from prying eyes, or at least make sure that only people whom you absolutely trust have access to it.

And while you certainly don't have to do it for this reason, there is something sentimental about a journal. After we were married, my wife made a scrapbook for me filled with photos and little souvenirs of our adventures and experiences while dating. In the book, she included many pages from her journal during that time. I'll tell ya, it was pretty darn special.

Life is valuable. Your experiences and how you felt about them matter. Why not record them? If nothing else, you can look back one day and realize how much you've changed.

All right, you have your assignment. Go write. Right now!

Write "Write It Down!" on a piece of paper, any paper you have on hand (well, not toilet paper—that's kinda hard to write on).

Once you've given time for your imagination to sprout, directed your thoughts, and written down everything that comes to you, you'll have heaps of creative ideas on your hands.

If you want to read more about coming up with good ideas and how to take them all the way to a finished project (and in a timely manner), check out my free e-book *Done!* You can find it at my website: *creative-andbeyond.com/done*

There's no end to where your imagination can take you, but as the great LeVar Burton said when recommending books in pretty much every episode of *Reading Rainbow*, "You don't have to take my word for it."

Try these methods out yourself. If they don't quite work for you, adapt them into something that does. If you want an active imagination, you must nourish it.

Treat your thoughts like children, ones you love dearly. Children need playtime just as much as they need instruction.

When you give your mind the room it needs to stretch out and have fun, it will soon learn to spread its wings and fly. When you take ownership and direction over your thoughts, they will soar to new and undiscovered lands.

Alright, so you've explored the extraordinary world of the mind, gathered your treasures, and brought back some shiny new imaginings. What now?

The next step is figuring out what to do with them all. It's time, my thought-filled, finely feathered friends, to innovate!

Logic will get you from A to B.
Imagination will take you everywhere.

~Albert Einstein

SECTION 7 REVIEW

How about we retrace our steps:

- Imagination is accessible to anyone at any time.
- Imagination may not seem immediately useful, but only by using it can we discover the ideas we'll need and use tomorrow.
- Begin with unfocused thought, but later direct it toward a goal.
- Three practices that can help you beef up your imaginative skills: quiet contemplation, brainstorming, writing everything down.
- Put away your usual distractions and give space for your imagination. Go ahead—be bored out of your mind…you have my permission.

Interview with a Creative

DAVID WOLVERTON, a.k.a. DAVID FARLAND

Tell us about yourself.
I'm a novelist, the lead judge for one of the world's largest writing contests (Writers of the Future), and I'm a writing coach.

When do you find it easiest to be creative?
In the morning, definitely, just after I wake up.

Where do you look for inspiration?
Most inspiration comes from looking outside yourself. You find it in books, movies, talks with friends, or while traveling or studying. Going to a library or visiting strange places on the internet can help too.

What forms of creativity do you most appreciate or enjoy?
I like a lot of them. I'm a writer, obviously, but I've also been an amateur photographer, painter, and sculptor. I've helped design video games and movies too, and I love music.

When has a creative approach helped you accomplish something impactful?
Gosh, that's what I do. For example, years ago, I was co-leader on the design team for Starcraft's Brood War video game, which became the most popular in the world. I've written novels that have been bestsellers,

and helped a publisher push the book *Harry Potter*, which became the bestselling book of all time. Then I helped one of my writing students do a little brainstorming for what became the novel *Twilight*, and so on. I've even had a hand in creating a couple of big films.

What is one practice you would recommend to help someone be more creative?

Don't look at what has been done—look for what might be done. I like to think about what the audience wants, not what they've seen before.

Where can people find you or your work?

You can learn a lot more about me at www.mystorydoctor.com, and from there you can get links to my classes, my books, and so on.

Section 8 - Innovative

Hilltop

After several hours of effort, we're able to carve a few steps into the side of the pit, with a little help from the broken createamobile.

"It's past midnight," I whisper as I glance at a nonexistent watch on my wrist. "Let's hope that guard wasn't setting us up."

We climb up to the edge of the pit and peek out. Sure enough, all the nearby guards are sound asleep. In the distance, lights hover between the trees: patrols carrying lanterns.

"She's good to her word, but we'll still need to be careful. If one of them sees us, the gig is up."

You lead the way as we crouch from the cover of one large tree to another. You pause when we reach the merkling, still tied to the stump and asleep.

"I know what you're thinking," I say, "but I wouldn't recommend it."

At the sound of my voice, the merkling awakes and stares at us for a moment. You'd never noticed before, but it has large, glistening yellow cat-like eyes. It speaks in a scratchy whisper, "Rescue. Please." The creature pauses in contemplation. "She help you, know secret way up mountain."

She? We look at one another in surprise.

I scratch my chin. "That sure would be useful, but I don't trust it—ah, her—for a moment. But you're the one with the plan here. You make the call."

Without further hesitation, you move to where the ropes are tied behind the stump and loosen them.

I sigh, and I kneel down beside you. In a short while, the knot is undone and the merkling is free.

She doesn't run away, but instead climbs upon the stump and looks down on us. "Wretch they called her, but that not her name. Free now, need new name." She rests her hand on her hips and stares at you with a wide-eyed expectation.

You look to me, and I shrug. "I think…maybe she wants you to give her a name?"

After some thought, you suggest Timble.

She considers it, rocking her head side to side, then nods in satisfaction. Something about her looks a little different—she seems less hunched, or slimy, for that matter. She jumps down from the stump and, before you can do a thing about it, snatches the createamobile from your pocket.

"Hey!" I say loudly before catching myself. I continue in an angry whisper, "That's not yours."

"Timble fix it," she says as she examines the broken contraption.

You nod to her, though I remain skeptical.

"Who goes there?" One of the patrolling guards calls out.

I duck down. "High time to make like a pest and flea!"

Someone calls out—they must have discovered the empty pit. Soon, the camp is buzzing with activity.

The three of us make a run for it, but before we get far, a group of five Dark Shields block our path, swords at the ready, glinting in the torchlight. From among them, out steps Buldorf, a menacing smile flashing from within his thick beard. "You know," he says, "I was hoping you'd try to run. Gives me an excuse to beat you to a pulp."

He no longer has a spear but instead sports two spiked metal gauntlets, gleaming in the torchlight. Buldorf laughs, more of a growl really, and the other Dark Shields advance at a steady pace.

We turn to run in the other direction, but come face to face with the white mustachioed leader. He stands as still as one of the trees with his arms crossed. He looks even bigger up close, and his old age seems more formidable than a sign of frailty. He raises one bushy eyebrow. "Going somewhere?" he asks, as if he'd just happened upon us during a walk in the park.

"No," I say, "but you are." Then I turn to you. "Well, do something, quick!"

Buldorf is only a stride away when a flurry of movement stirs up the leaves around us. A family of skunks dash out from the forest. The animals stop, lift their tails at Buldorf and his men, then release a foul spray.

The guards fall back, coughing and holding their noses. Another group of guards begins to approach from our side, but then trip and fall head over hindquarters. We see their legs are wrapped up in a tangle of roots.

An enormous grizzly bear crashes through the brush and charges at the leader, but he dives out of the way just in time and slides down an embankment.

You look around to see the whole camp is in chaos: creatures of the forest run wild, trees wave their branches about, knocking over the Dark Shields like bowling pins, and even the campfires have come alive and roam freely, setting tents ablaze.

"It appears we've got friends here," I observe, "but we'd better get going while the going is good."

We both race toward the edge of camp, gripping Timble by the arms. As we run, her legs barely touch the ground, but she doesn't complain.

Our pace slows as we head up a treeless incline. We stop to catch our breath at the top. You see an odd pile of rocks surrounding a large boulder. The camp below is still in confusion, but the Dark Shields have begun to fight back and retake control of the situation—they'll soon be on our trail.

From behind the rocks, a group of twenty guards emerges, carrying an assortment of weapons.

"We're in for it now," I say.

However, you recognize among them the woman who spoke to us in the pit.

236 | THE ENDLESS CREATIVE

"So it was all a trap?" I ask.

The woman shakes her head. She walks up, kneels before you, then removes her helmet. A pair of tiny antlers sprout out from beneath her red hair.

"My name is Saren," she says, "and we are glad you've come. Your actions give us boldness, but as we forsake our fears, we also fall prey to the curse. You are our hope of rescue now."

Without knowing exactly why, you reach out and touch Saren's antlers. They shrink into little nubs.

Some of the other guards gasp, and even I am taken aback. To her credit, Saren appears unfazed.

"Thank you," she looks up and smiles, "but I believe any healing you bring here will only be temporary—until you destroy the source of this curse. You must leave us. I have gathered supplies for you." She hands us our packs, now filled. "There is one problem. To escape, you must pass through the wooden barriers, but they are too tall to climb, and their gates are well guarded."

Saren stands, and her soldiers gather behind her. "What would you have us do?"

You glance at Timble, the merkling, but she hasn't had any time to work on the createamobile yet. You take in your surroundings. The double walls made of wooden posts lie just below us. You hear Dark Shields shouting in the distance and see the army has spotted us and begun to charge toward our hill. It's time for action.

You direct Saren and her troop to the boulder, and she understands. The stone is taller than it is wide—oval in shape. After removing the surrounding rocks and expending considerable effort, the soldiers manage to push the boulder sideways, and it lies like a beached whale upon the hilltop.

Buldorf shouts up from the base of the hill, but you can't make out what he's saying. A large army has assembled behind him, surrounding the half of the hill facing away from the wall. They advance upon us in a clatter of stomps and steel.

Saren's group gathers to the side of the tipped boulder and begins to roll it, slowly at first but then faster and faster. It crests the hill and tumbles down like a giant, bouncing watermelon, then obliterates both walls as if they were made of toothpicks.

We all cheer, but the celebration is short—Buldorf's army below will soon be upon us.

You feel something wet against your neck and turn to see two large stags with antlers nearly tall enough to touch the branches above. One is a dark gray and the other a light beige color, almost white. They stand at attention.

I shrug. "They aren't horses, but I'll take any ride as long as it gets us out of here."

"Go," Saren urges. "We will hold off the Dark Shields. We have an advantage here, and I don't believe they will kill their own—not yet. Besides,"she winks,"I've got some beef with Buldorf."

Saren's guards roll the smaller stones down at the approaching army, thwarting their progress.

We leap upon the stags—you take the lighter one, and I, the darker. Timble climbs up behind you and holds fast your belt. With a "Hya!" the stags take off at lightning pace.

Wind rushes by, wet with morning mist, as we speed down the hill, past the broken fences, out of the camp, and into the forest beyond.

"I'll be!" I shout as branches whip past us in a blur. "You sure know how to show someone a good time!"

Timble chuckles in her raspy voice, then pumps a fist in the air.

We rush on, beams of light streaming out around us from behind the trees, straight into the dawn of a new day.

Innovation simply is the application of new ideas or methods to an established way of doing something. It's the result of purposeful application of creativity to our challenges, opportunities, and systems.

~Ken Wytsma, *Create vs. Copy*

CHAPTER 21

Innovation

Do you know why I love creativity so much? You don't? Oh. I was really hoping someone here knew. Well, here's one reason:

Being creative is just plain fun.

Creativity has its challenges, sure. Sometimes it takes considerable effort, but at the end of the day when you step back and look at what you've come up with, it's pretty dang exciting.

I can't recall a single time I've looked back on my creative efforts and felt like it wasn't worth it, even when they didn't turn out how I hoped or garnered the attention I'd expected. I still feel satisfied knowing I took a chance, made a change, and stepped outside the safe, normal, ordinary world.

We've come to one of the most fun and rewarding parts of the creative process: innovation.

There comes a point in the protagonist's story when they reach what seems to be a victory—when everything is going right.

They may believe the conflict has ended, and it's likely they've even gotten what they wanted (or at least had a good taste of it), but the story isn't finished yet.

The real conflict is just on the horizon, and the hero will soon discover what they wanted isn't quite what they needed—they remain unfulfilled. At this point, they've begun to understand the truth but have not yet fully abandoned the lie.

They may think they've reached the end, but they're actually at a crossroads between the two paths. Their greatest decision lies just a few steps ahead.

Although the hero enjoys a moment of triumph before the main conflict, the audience knows their darkest hour looms further down the road. Even so, this temporary triumph is important—it is proof of the hero's accomplishment, evidence of their progress, a sure sign their journey is close to the end—there's just one final hurdle.

We've reached the part where I'm supposed to tell you all about innovation, where I say how great it is, how it gives feet to your creative efforts and allows it to run free in the world, how it mirrors the response of the creative approach, how it is the completion—the end result of the creative process, how we all must be innovators if we want to survive in a changing world.

I could tell you all those things, but I won't.

In fact, I'm hardly going to talk about innovation at all. This may strike you as unusual, uncouth, unacceptable even.

Fine. I'll say something, briefly mind you, just to appease your perplexed mind.

To innovate is to bring your imagination to life.

Innovation ushers your thoughts from their metaphysical existence into the solid domain of reality. It turns your ideas into practice.

There, done. Easy, right?

Not so much.

Just like the hero's partial victory before the climax, innovation is an end to itself, but it's also a start—an important marker in the race, but not the finish line.

What I will talk about are two aspects of innovation you have no doubt already encountered: failure and success.

Failure and success are so closely linked, they're almost inseparable.

They are two splashes of paint on the same page—bleeding into one another so that parts of them can become difficult to tell apart.

You might be wondering why we're talking about failure in a chapter that should have a more triumphant tone. After all, a victorious hero knows no failure, right? Not hardly.

CHAPTER 22

Failure

As you adapt the creative process into your life, there is one thing I guarantee you will encounter: failure. I'm sure you'd rather I tell you how to circumnavigate failure entirely and just skip to the success part, but regardless of what anyone might promise you, failure is inevitable. More importantly, failure is necessary.

But don't close the book just yet—there is hope.

The good thing about failure is it always comes before success.

We've got to learn to think differently about failure, because when it comes to innovation, it's a key ingredient. Instead of seeing it as a setback or even a necessary evil, we must see it as an opportunity, a sign—dare I say it—a friend.

Until you fail, you won't know the right way to do something. As Thomas Edison famously said, "I have not failed. I've just found ten thousand ways that won't work."

There is a difference between failing and *being* a failure. When you've failed at something, it simply means the thing did not go the way you expected—you experienced a failure. But that doesn't make *you* a failure—someone who has, after failing, given up. Do you see the difference?

You have a choice. You can keep trying.

**You can choose to let failure define you, or you can
let it lead you on the road to accomplishment.**

According to Denis Waitley, "Failure should be our teacher, not our undertaker. Failure is delay, not defeat. It is a temporary detour, not a dead end. Failure is something we can avoid only by saying nothing, doing nothing, and being nothing."

If you've never failed, you've never really tried.

There is nothing wrong with failure, no matter how great, as long as you learn from it. Every implementation of a creative idea you have will not turn out the way you planned. Why is that? Well, for starters, you can't know the future, so you have no way of telling how something will go until you try it.

After you have tried and failed, you've now got a recorded history. You can take what went wrong, tweak your approach, and try again.

There's a way to be smart about it. Don't start out by putting all your gold in one ship. If what you're attempting simply "can't fail," you need to find another approach. The exception to this is if you're in a life and death situation with limited options (which, I hope, is rarely the case). If that happens to you often, might I recommend a lifestyle change?

Try something you can afford to fail at because, chances are, you're bound to fail (partly, if not completely) the first time you do something.

How many people do you know who landed a strike the first time they bowled or sunk a nothing-but-net three-pointer from downtown the first time they threw a basketball at a hoop?

Listen to the king of B-ball himself, Michael Jordan: "I've missed more than nine thousand shots in my career. I've lost almost three hundred games. Twenty-six times, I've been trusted to take the game winning shot and missed. I've failed over and over and over again in my life. And that is why I succeed."

No one questions whether or not Jordan is a basketball pro, but when you look at it, his career has been marked by far more failures than successes. That didn't hold him back. He experienced many failures, but failure did not define him.

Here's the secret: in the end your failures don't matter a whit.

Failures aren't strikes against you—they're marks of accomplishment.

Yoda may have said there is no try, there is only do or do not, but I'm here to tell you he's wrong—*GASP!*

Trying *is* doing. Look, we're not talking about some mystical force-power here. As strange and unpredictable as creativity may seem at times, it is just as much practical. Furthermore, it's practice-able.

By trying and failing at something you're practicing—you're doing the thing. By doing the thing, you're getting better—not perfect, but better—and that is what it's all about. Maybe that's what Yoda was trying to say all along. I don't know; he confuses me—out of order his words always are.

A friend of mine, also named Michael, once recounted to me his struggles during his education at MIT. He felt like the least qualified student there, and as such, his one goal was to simply last as long as he could before they kicked him out.

If he were like most people I know, he wouldn't have bothered. After a failure or two, he would have been out that door like a kid on the first day of summer. But not Michael. He put in hard work. Fixed his mistakes. Talked directly to teachers about how he could improve. He stuck through to the end and graduated.

When he told me the mindset that drove him on, I couldn't help but feel inspired: "You can make me fail, but you can't make me quit." That's one atom bomb of truth. It's the attitude every creative needs.

You will fail on many accounts and for many reasons (sometimes because others have caused you to), but no one on earth can make you give up. That choice alone is yours to make.

A failure gives up when the road gets rough, a hero walks it to the end, no matter how many setbacks there are on the way.

When it comes to failure, I think Thomas J. Watson Jr. said it best:

Would you like me to give you a formula for success? It's quite simple really. Double your rate of failure. You are thinking of failure as the enemy of success. But it isn't at all. You can be discouraged by failure, or you can learn from it. So go ahead and make mistakes. Make all you can. Because remember, that's where you'll find success.

As the hero, it is not your goal to avoid failure like a Star Warsian Sarlacc pit. Your goal is to try and keep trying, come what may. Only through failure can you learn and grow.

It's time to get used to failing. A lot. That means learning how to accept your mistakes.

CHAPTER 23

Mistakes

Let's look at a near-and-dear-sister of failure: the mistake.

Mistakes, like failures, are a normal part of innovation. If a failure happens when something doesn't go the way you expected (or even the opposite of what you expected), then a mistake is when you do something you didn't intend to.

Mistakes can lead to failures and vice versa. Be it a wayward stroke on the canvas, accidentally hitting Reply All to an email intended for one person, or throwing a green sock in with the white laundry, mistakes happen all the time (at least you've got plenty of clothing options for St. Paddy's Day now).

While they can be pretty dang frustrating, mistakes shouldn't bring us down. They are, after all, unintentional.

Feeling bad about a mistake isn't just unhelpful, it's nonsensical.

Why should you beat yourself up about something you did accidentally? It's illogical, yet we do it all the time. We hold our mistakes so closely they become attached to us—part of our identity. It need not be this way.

We don't need to enjoy mistakes, but we shouldn't hate them, and we certainly ought not fear them. If we live in fear of mistakes, we'll never create anything worthwhile.

You simply can't control whether or not you will make mistakes. You can, however, reduce the number of mistakes you make while doing a particular task. Guess how it's done: by making mistakes!

Backward (and wackbard) as it sounds, mistakes are the best way to learn how not to make them. Mistakes are the difference between a novice and a pro. As a creative, the more mistakes you have under your belt, the more experienced and better equipped you are.

The only other way to limit your mistakes is to learn from someone else's. Even so, mistakes are made.

At the end (or even the start) of the day, mistakes are unavoidable. It's impossible to prepare for every single potentiality and to account for every detail. Things happen you didn't anticipate, you get distracted, you have a mental malfunction (happens to the best of us), and then, voilà, a mistake.

Like weeds after a good rain, mistakes sprout in abundance when we try something we've never tried before—that is, when we're engaged in the creative process. They're a sign you're doing something right, just in a kind of wrong way. They give flavor to life. They make things interesting.

As unwanted as they are, mistakes lead to a better outcome.

I can't tell you how many times I've made a mistake in a painting or drawing only to find it came out better because of it. I've played a wrong note on a guitar or piano only to discover I liked it better, and then I take the song in a new direction.

As John Cleese recounted in a lecture, he once lost an entire script he had written and had to rewrite the whole thing. Afterward, he found the old script and was surprised to see how much better the new one was.

Mistakes are unexpected discoveries.

Every mistake can be used not just as a learning opportunity but as a creative exercise—a path to new possibilities. The next time you call someone by the wrong name or miss the exit on the freeway, don't get angry at yourself or grumble about it. Think of how you can use that mistake.

Maybe your accidental misnomer could be a new joke you share with the person, or you could tell them a story about someone you do know with that name and the similarities they share.

If you end up on the wrong road, look around. Is there something interesting on this unintended route, perhaps a restaurant you should try, some unusual architecture, or even a person you wouldn't have seen who needs help?

Failures and mistakes can seem like bricks at times: weighty and upsetting if they come flying through your window. But they also are great if you want to build a solid wall, a set of stairs, or a fine road on the way to success. So let's paint those babies yellow and head that-a-way. Which-a-way? To the Emerald City of success, where things aren't all they're cracked up to be.

CHAPTER 24

Success

We've talked about failure and mistakes—now let's move on over to their BFF, success.

We all want success, right? Why would we innovate if we have no hope of our efforts eventually leading to some form of success? But success, as great as it is, can be a shifty, unreliable thing. One thing's for certain: real, lasting success is not free.

Success always comes at a cost.

I previously mentioned wants versus needs as they relate to a protagonist. We all want success, but it may not always be the thing we need in a particular moment. It could be the success you have in mind isn't realistic, or when you obtain it, you aren't satisfied in the way you thought you'd be. In another instance, you might have to give up something more valuable in your life to obtain it.

Even "instant" success (I'm not convinced there is such a thing) can prove detrimental—it may land you in a place you're not yet ready to be, it could make you a target for those who do not bask in the warm glow of your triumph, or it might just turn out to be a huge disappointment.

Most people recognize this at some level. As much as we fear failure, we can develop an even greater fear of success. I'll admit I have, and it's kept me from finishing many a project—or even trying in the first place.

Success can be just as intimidating as it is enticing. We don't know where it will lead, how it might change us, or whether we're really ready for it. But it doesn't have to be that way. Success can be small, approachable, friendly even—but no less powerful.

Here's the thing to remember, the phrase to write down in your sequined trapper-keeper, one which you will likely find printed in bold font later in this book: success is a mindset, not an event.

Success is a mindset, not an event.

Okay, by *later* I meant *immediately after*. Hey, repetition is great for memory, right?

In Derek Doepker's book *Why Authors Fail*, he points out how both success and failure can work for or against us based on how we define them. His argument is that we should view success as a *process*, not an *event*.

The same goes with failure. This sort of outlook can change everything for you.

If you only see success as achieving some milestone, then you'll run into problems.

First, if you don't reach your goal in the time you hoped to (or at all), you will feel the weight of discouragement and failure. This could dissuade you from ever trying again. You might begin to question whether you'll ever succeed at anything. You lose hope.

If you do reach your goal, despite failures and setbacks along the way, the glorious feeling of achievement only lasts a little while. When it passes, you're on to the next thing or stuck trying to repeat what you just did in order to keep the blissful feeling of success. In this case, you're constantly searching for success but never truly reaching it because there will always be something more, something bigger you can do.

However, if success is a process, then you can be continually successful, not just when you reach a goal. As long as you are continuing to take the necessary steps toward your goal (even itty bitty ones), you are living in success—you are a success story.

Doesn't that sound more rewarding than basing your success on some far-off goal, whether or not you ever reach it?

Success is right in front of your nose, or rather, between your ears.

You get to decide your measure of success and what it looks like on a daily basis. How? Take the creative approach: look at where you want to go, ask how you could get there, and then come up with your own unique, specialized answer.

Your goals can sometimes feel like a weather balloon—so far off and out of reach. But every balloon comes down eventually.

Weather balloons are important, they collect useful meteorological information. Your goals carry within them the necessary steps toward completion, they may hold the key toward progress on your creative journey.

Let your goals be exciting and inspiring. Let your dreams be so big they sound impossible. But make sure each and every step you take toward them is one within reach.

With the mindset of success as an event, you can remain reasonable and grounded until your goals finally land home. Whether the weather seems to pull them closer to or farther from you on any given day, you'll know it's only a matter of time before they're realized.

Find the balance, or you'll get lost in the clouds and eventually brought down by the harsh storms of reality.

Make it about the attempt, not the results. Forget the words of Yoda. Try and try again. As long as you put forth a real, honest effort toward your goal, you are succeeding, even if things don't turn out the way you expected—in other words, even if you fail hard.

Consider the following questions when it comes to your own process of success:

- Are my standards of success helping or hurting me?
- What are my long-term goals?
- What is the smallest, simplest thing I can do today to progress toward one of those goals?
- What would need to happen for me to consider today a success?
- Are those requirements within my control?
- Are my expectations reasonable?
- Can I still consider the day a success even if things don't go according to plan?
- In what past attempts have I failed to reach a goal, and what could I do differently now?

Remember, creativity is its own reward.

As long as you've used a creative approach and followed the creative process, you have reached an important goal—you are living creatively.

As author Steven Pressfield shares in the "about" section on his website, "The work is everything."

He's right.

Love the work. The work is all you have.

When you're grabbing those scant few minutes to spend a little time working on the thing you love, when no one understands why you're doing it or even cares, when you're exhausted and terrified—you're at your best.

Success is not someday when you're rich and famous, when the world loves you and thinks everything you poop out is gold, or when you're on your own private jet on an extended trip to paradise. You're a success, sweating it out and being your true creative self, right here and now.

Enjoy the here and now, but don't ignore the future. As the carriage of creativity leads you down the path to future success, think about what the ultimate result of your creativity will be. Where will it lead you, what will it make you, and how will it affect others?

The beauty of creativity is, like the striking of a gong, it rings on and on long after the initial impact. Relish the reward of creative success, but don't hold it in. Let it sound out to everyone around. Keep banging that gong until it echoes across the planet and your neighbors start complaining because you're hitting a gong at 3:00 a.m.

I've given you a little time to celebrate. And if you haven't yet, take some time to do just that.

If you've followed a creative approach to anything, then bravo, you're on the right track. You are just where you need to be.

If you've adopted the creative process (even in the smallest way) and you've wound up with a result you didn't expect, it's all good. You're going somewhere. Take a little time to rest, give a war whoop, eat a cookie, or do whatever it is you enjoy doing. You've earned it!

But don't pause for too long—the hardest part is still ahead. The winds have picked up, and those clouds are getting dark.

The creative journey leads through many bright and beautiful places, but to get there we must also be willing to face the dark and dangerous. As we pick up our pace, we see a great mountain ahead. The third act awaits, and with it, the dreaded climax

So I tell people, look, you don't know how it's gonna play out, you don't know what the future holds, you don't know if you're gonna succeed or fail. So what becomes important is giving yourself to something that matters whether you succeed or fail.

~Erwin McManus

SECTION 8 REVIEW

What were we talking about again? Oh, that's right:

- To innovate is to put your imagination to use—to take what is imagined and make it real.
- Failure, mistakes, and success are all necessary ingredients when it comes to innovation.
- Just because you fail doesn't make you a failure, as long as you learn from it and don't give up.
- Mistakes are opportunities to learn and become better. They are the marks of experience.
- Success isn't all it's cracked up to be: it's better to celebrate the little daily successes—to have a mindset of success—than to have it all ride on one major event. Therein lies disappointment.
- Give yourself a little reward from time to time. Enjoy your victories, small or great, but don't forget to keep a move on. One cookie is fine, maybe two, but don't overdo it and eat the whole tray, like I just did. *Groan.*

Interview with a Creative

BEN HALL

Tell us about yourself.
I am a believer in Christ, a constant cutup, and a filmmaker. I love creating motion pictures that emit wonder, excitement, and thought-provoking narratives!

When do you find it easiest to be creative?
The moment a small spark of an idea hits me. My mind then takes it down several avenues of thought, and I can't stop thinking about it until I find an avenue that, at least for the time being, fits. That spark though, usually comes from something mundane. I don't think I have even once thought up an idea for a script by sitting down and "trying" to be creative. You find the idea in the sometimes mundaneness of life. Or, if I'm watching a film, I might say I want to do a picture like that, but I usually won't figure out a concept until later down the road. I think that's the basis of creativity. Allowing normality to spark ingenuity!

Where do you look for inspiration?
FILMS...novels, news articles as of late, and like I said above, normality. What happens when we bend normality?

What forms of creativity do you most appreciate or enjoy?
Hmm...I really enjoy the personal selfish form. Ha-ha. What I mean by that is, allowing an idea to bounce around in your head. It's yours. It's special, even if it's only good to you. Once you open it up for collaboration

264 | THE ENDLESS CREATIVE

or start to put it on paper (which obviously is the best thing to do and most constructive next step), in a way, for me, it loses the excitement a bit. The work of it sets in. The deliberation of what plays and what doesn't in a screenplay of film. It takes time, patience, writer's block, etc., to accomplish. While it's still in your head, for me, is almost pure enjoyment. I really love that spark, the brainstorming-with-myself form of creativity.

When has a creative approach helped you accomplish something impactful?

With my latest feature film, *The Man From Outer Space*, I knew I would have immense budgetary constraints. I had two ideas in my head. One was a straightforward, one-location story of a writer creating a story in his apartment with his dysfunctional family. The other was about an astronaut from the future that crash lands on a desolate Earth. I thought, *Why don't I put them together?* The writer is writing about this astronaut, and we'll see both stories and how they blend together in the same narrative. This allowed me to do something wondrous, but at the same time ground over half the movie in an inexpensive apartment set. Synthesizing those ideas made a huge impact on the story and on the themes.

What is one practice you would recommend to help someone be more creative?

Don't stress out trying to find the "idea." Let it come to you. And when it does, jump on it, explore it. Even if it goes nowhere, it can be great fun and can help in the future.

Where can people find you or your work?

You can find my latest feature film on Amazon. Search:
The Man From Outer Space
My reel is on YouTube. Search for:
Ben Hall Director's Reel

ACT III

The Pursuit

Section 9 - Marsh

Marsh

As we ride on, the morning mist settles into a fog, the trees thin, and the ground becomes wet—we've entered a marsh.

Our rides, the two great stags, have grown tired. They slow their pace, then stop to kneel in the wet mud, and we dismount. With a pat, you thank them for their help. Each bows its head to you, then turns back to their forest home. In a single, graceful bound, they are swallowed by the mist.

"We're now officially lost," I announce as I stare at the map. The markings on it have been covered by a big, gray blob. I sigh and tuck the map back into my pocket.

"No, Timble knows way," the merkling says.

Is it your imagination, or did something large just slither through the mud between your feet and disappear?

"Do you trust her?" I ask. I wince and rub my shoulder.

You look back at the merkling in consideration. Again, something seems different about her: Have the horns under her cheeks gotten shorter or the bright blotches on her skin grown larger? Even her voice sounds smoother.

"Look." She holds up the createamobile to you. "Fixed."

You examine the contraption, and it does indeed appear to be mended: the disk is no longer bent, and the crack down the middle of the case has been sealed with a sturdy substance. Hardened spit, perhaps?

You give it a try, blowing gently on the disk. It begins to spin and shimmer, and you detect a hint of nutmeg. It shoots out wispy blue arrows in all directions. We wait for more, but the arrows simply fade and dissipate into swirling mist as the wheel slows to a stop.

"Not the way," Timble says, a tinny sound to her voice. "Close eyes and look." She adds emphasis to the last word.

Though confused, you close your eyes. At first you see nothing. But then, even with your eyes closed, you envision the swirling motion of the fog. It parts in areas, and you make out dim shapes in the distance. You recognize them: great constructions like those you saw in the valley.

You open your eyes, and they are gone, but you remember seeing one up ahead to our left, and you point in its direction.

"Yes," Timble says, "you see."

I shrug, but we follow your lead. Before long we approach something like a giant metal stagecoach, but with only two wheels as tall as the rest of the vehicle. It has partly sunk into the wet ground and is half covered with vines. You hand the createamobile to me and ask if I can do something about the vines.

When I use it, the vines begin to writhe, then loose their grasp on the coach, marked with a smell of steamed spinach.

We climb a ladder into the vehicle's one large room and approach the waist-high plate of dark glass at its helm. It has a round panel in the middle, surrounded by buttons and switches. Timble studies it for a time, then pumps a pedal below the dashboard and flips a green switch.

Nothing happens.

She opens a hatch beneath the dashboard and jumps in. There is a sound of banging and yelling before she emerges with dark smudges on her hands and clothes. She again attempts the pedal, and soon we hear the sound of gears turning as the vehicle shudders to life. The engine begins to make a low *puff-puff*, and the round screen blinks on.

At first, the screen displays a thin line of light. The line warps and waves, then the whole screen lights up. We're presented with what looks like an ancient map. It bears similarity to my own map, but some of the landscapes have changed, and the locations are unnamed.

"I know where we are." I point at the map. "This is the Marsh of Despair, if I remember right." I tap the screen, but to no effect. "How do we move this thing?"

Timble looks at you, then points to the screen. "Direct it. Close eyes. See where to go."

Following Timble's instruction, you place your hand on the screen. As you'd done previously, you shut your eyes, but this time you imagine the peak high atop Mount Dread. The vehicle lifts up, then lurches forward. We grab hold of the dashboard to keep from falling over.

"Incredible," I say. "Hey, I've got an idea." I blow on the createamobile again, and a single blue directional line shoots out. "Looks like we're headed toward another gateway." I place the createamobile into a recess on the dash, which fits it perfectly.

The giant wheels of the coach slosh on through the muck, carrying it on the same path as the blue line. We rumble past other broken-down structures, dilapidated cabins, ancient ruins, forgotten places of worship, and abandoned towns.

"Doesn't look like this place has seen activity in a long while," I say, staring off in the distance.

While passing a large ghost town, you have a flash of vision: the town bustles with activity, just as alive as your own Plateau Town had been—maybe more so. Some people operate tall devices with hooks and ropes in the construction of new buildings. Some ride moving platforms from place to place—marvels you have never before seen. In the center of the town is a great square where many are gathered, a place where ideas are shared openly and freely.

In an instant, the vision is gone. You turn and notice Timble staring at you.

"You see," she says, "not what was, what can be."

You look back at the dashboard screen and notice new words on the map. The places you once tread are different: the Worrisome Valley is now Inspiration Valley; the Canyon of Indecision is one of Determination; the River of Doubt is Progress; the forest, as you saw before, is one of Hope and not Defeat. Even the marsh, instead of Despair, is a place of

Confidence. You look ahead to the mountain and the fortress atop it, but the words blur, and you can't quite make them out.

Timble tugs on your shirt. "Friend," she says, "not well."

At first you think she might be motion-sick from the coach, but then you realize she's pointing at me. I'm huddled in the back corner, head lowered. When you approach, you notice something around my collar and the edge of my sleeve: my skin has turned a deep purple, and my veins pop out dramatically.

You reach out to touch my shoulder, and I whip my head around to look at you, eyes wide with a crazed expression, "It's coming for us!"

You jump back in surprise, then the coach lurches to a halt. The gears grind as the vehicle struggles against whatever is holding it. Thick black tentacles wrap themselves over the windows.

From a hidden compartment on the coach, Timble pulls out two round metal devices, each with red buttons on top. She presses them and drops the metal balls down a chute in the back of the coach. "Front, front!" she shouts, and we move up by the dashboard.

Two explosions follow, and the back of the coach is blown wide open. The damaged coach groans and moves again. You look out the back and spy something like a slimy black hill rising out of the marsh. Then the hill opens. It's a massive, globular head with a mouth full of jagged teeth. Its muddy skin appears to be made from the marsh itself. From the mouth you hear what could be described as a croark—something between the sounds of a bullfrog and an earthquake.

More tentacles smash through the windows and slither inside the vehicle. The coach again slows, but continues to drag on, throwing a spray of mud in its wake. The marsh monster pulls itself closer and croarks again.

"We're doomed!" I bend over, clutching my head in my hands.

You feel something tight on your ankle—one of the tentacles coils around you. It pulls you down toward the gaping maw of the beast.

"No!" I straighten and shake myself, then run over and kick the tentacle away. "Not you, not today." I pause and lean over with my hands rested on my knees, panting. Then I look up. "There, the gateway!"

You see it, just a few paces ahead of us.

"Go, both of you. Now!" I rush to the dashboard and grab the createamobile. "I'll handle this."

You hesitate, unsure about leaving me.

"Go!" I say again. "Don't worry. I'll be fine."

You aren't convinced, but there's no time to think, so you snatch Timble and leap out of the coach, barely clearing a waving tentacle. You both land with a *sploosh* in knee-high sludge. Heart racing, you hoist the merkling onto your shoulders and rush to the stone arch as fast as the muck will allow.

Just as you are about to cross the threshold, you stop to look back. You hear the mingled sounds of shouts, twisting metal, and low gurgles. Flashes of light shoot out of the stagecoach, and tentacles fly off in all directions.

The light fades and the coach sinks into the mud with slurping sounds, and soon the vehicle is completely swallowed. All is quiet, save the buzz of insects and an occasional pop of a bubble that rises to the surface where the coach and monster had been.

Timble grabs your arm. "Timble sorry. Must go now."

You see tears in her big yellow eyes and know she is right. The fog of the marsh disappears as you step though the tall stone arch, collapsing on rocky ground at the base of Mount Dread.

Once you've had time to catch your breath, you look ahead and find a narrow stairway crawling up and around the mountain. It's going to be a long climb.

We are all either building our own dreams or building somebody else's. To put a sharper point on it, we're either building our own dreams—or building our nightmares.

~Jeff Olson, *The Slight Edge*

CHAPTER 25

Pursue

At the opening of the third act, our protagonist faces the third plot point. This is a dark time for the hero, when it seems all is lost and the hero may be on the verge of giving up hope. The third plot point brings what is likely a complete reversal from the victory the protag experienced at the end of the second act.

All right, you say. That's nice and all, but what does it have to do with me or creativity?

Just hold on a sec, will you? I'm telling a story here.

At this point, the protag either believes the thing they want is impossible to obtain or they found it and discovered it wasn't all it was cracked up to be. Though it's a low point for them—a time of reevaluation—it's also when they are closest to embracing the truth and realizing the thing they need. Or, it's when they are just on the edge of fully and irreversibly embracing the lie.

In the film adaptation of Neil Gaiman's *Stardust*, the protagonist Tristan has acquired a piece of the fallen star (actually the hair of a woman, Yvaine) and brings it to the lady he thought he loved, Victoria.

Tristan soon realizes his true love, Yvaine, is not only at risk of being destroyed in the barrier between his world and hers, but has also been captured by an evil witch desiring to kill Yvaine in order to restore her own beauty and vitality. Though Tristan is about to lose everything he truly values, he has also realized he no longer must prove himself to a person like Victoria. He has yet to discover his true identity as a rightful heir to the throne, but he is well on the way to learning this truth as he returns and fights to save Yvaine.

It is such dark moments as these, such trials of the soul where the things we love seem lost or out of reach, where we step back and see what really matters to us.

Change is a challenge. As I've heard a motivational speaker say, "If you want to be who you've never been before, you've got to do what you've never done before."

It's time to leave the well-traveled road in the dust.

It means going so far from home—from the ordinary world—that you've lost sight of the way back. You're out of cell service. Your map no longer makes sense. You wonder if you need to figure out how to build a proper campfire and if that cluster of berries over there is edible.

Until you reach such a place, the life of the creative will always be optional, something you try from time to time but never fully adopt as your own.

In the same way, until the storybook hero goes through a crucible where they are refined, where they reach an end of themselves and everything they thought they wanted is stripped from them, they will always be tempted to return to their lie.

It is the third plot point that forces the hero to look straight at the truth and decide, once and for all, if they will pick up their sword (or pen, paintbrush, potholder, banjo, sewing needle, or whatever your creative tool is) and become the hero their journey has called them to be.

Such is the path to true and lasting creativity.

In the dark moments when it is the most difficult to be creative, this is when we need it most. When everything inside you wants to turn back, give up, and go home empty handed, this is the time to stand up, shake off the dust, and press on. This is the time when you must no longer dabble in creativity, but pursue it with all you have—you must decide to make it a lifelong aim.

CHAPTER 26

Momentum

I'm borrowing this little anecdote from my eBook *Done! Finish Your Creative Project in One Month*, but I think it's worth the retelling.

As the story goes, back in the day an old man sat next to a friend at a railway station, looking at a steam engine for the first time. He peered far down the tracks at the many box cars in tow and shook his head. Steam began to shoot up in the air, and the old man muttered to his friend, "They'll never get it started."

But the whistle blew, and the powerful engine started to slowly turn its wheels and pull the heavy load behind it. Before long, the train was gone; all that remained was a lingering cloud of smoke.

"Well?" his friend asked, nudging the old man.

The man shrugged. "They'll never get it stopped."

We're all headed somewhere,
as certain as that train leaving the station.

Even the most sedentary lifestyle will land you somewhere—possibly an early grave. With that in mind, there are two questions I'd like you to ask yourself: Is the destination I'm heading toward the one I actually want? And how fast will I get there?

Our journey, which began with the creative approach and led to the creative process, at last takes us to the creative pursuit. This is the final part of the creative journey, at least as far as this book is concerned.

Though each step leads to the next, you never fully abandon the

280 | THE ENDLESS CREATIVE

previous one. You've made your way through the creative process, but you don't stop taking a creative approach. Each step is important, and we should return to each one often, but there is a natural order to them: there is a momentum, an increase in speed.

In an approach, the change is from a standstill to movement. The creative process is where the pace begins to pick up; it's a jog instead of a casual stroll. At last, the creative pursuit is a marathon—you're in it for the long haul.

The three parts of the creative pursuit are: courage, confidence, consistency.

I could break down the creative pursuit into dozens of aspects (maybe all beginning with the letter "c"), but this book can't go on forever, and those three are some of the strongest and most crucial.

Unlike the other parts of the creative journey, there isn't necessarily an order to these three. They work in tandem with one another.

Let's take a big leap back and look at the creative journey again as a whole. Here are the three steps with each of their three parts.

The creative approach:
1. Observe
2. Question
3. Respond

The creative process:
1. Inspiration
2. Imagination
3. Innovation

The creative pursuit:
1. Courage
2. Confidence
3. Consistency

Every journey requires movement: going from one place to another, though not necessarily physically. After all, you can read this whole book while sitting in the same spot, though your mind has been going places the entire time.

A pursuit is part of that movement—it's a reason behind the movement. It means following after something definite. You pursue something you can envision, whether with your eyes or in your mind. To pursue is not to catch the thing, only to follow it, to chase it.

As the title of this book suggests (nay, loudly proclaims), the creative journey is an endless pursuit. Endless? But why would you run a race with no end? It sounds exhausting, not to mention impossible. Yes, it is endless, but that's not to say there are no rest points or resolutions. There are many stops on the road, but never an end.

Just as every story resolves, so does every creative undertaking. Yes, nearly all things end, but every end leads to a beginning, a new story, a new task or opportunity. The creative pursuit itself goes on and on and on (like the Energizer bunny, but more).

In a creative pursuit, and indeed the creative journey itself, the point is not the end—it's how you run. How, then, do you keep running without exhausting yourself? In order to run well, to not abandon the pursuit, you need to build momentum, a force that carries you on.

Think of an object in space: once it has built up speed, if there is nothing in its path, it will continue to move at the same speed without any further thrust necessary. If you can burn enough fuel to launch a rocket out of the atmosphere and then give it a boost from more fuel or sling-shotting it around a planet with the help of gravity, that thing is going to fly far and fast without any extra effort needed. This is the beauty of momentum.

From the approach to the process to the pursuit, each transition is a gradual increase. It's impossible to go from motionless to a hundred miles (or 160 kilometers) an hour without hitting all the speeds in between, if only briefly. You also can't stay at a sprint forever. Eventually, you will have to slow down, rest, and recoup.

The creative journey is a lifelong marathon. If you treat it like a sprint, you'll get exhausted, probably throw up, and find yourself flat on the side of the road, soon to wake up in urgent care. Or you'll just quit right away.

If you want to be a creative, you've got to be in it for the long haul. You've got to learn the rhythms of creativity, to find your own personal stride. You must learn how to manage your momentum.

Momentum is a wondrous thing, but it's difficult to begin.

This may be obvious, but the hardest part about momentum is getting it going in the first place, like trying to escape the pull of gravity from your own planet. When you start out with nothing, progress will be slow.

As Newton observed: objects at rest tend to stay at rest. It's difficult to get out of bed or off the couch while you're still lying there with your eyes closed, snuggled up with your good pet, Mr. Fluffynippers. However, once you get off that thang and start the ball rolling, it becomes easier and easier to keep pushing on.

When you begin something new, it can feel like pushing a boulder uphill. You might even slip backward a time or two. But when you reach the top, it's an easy ride down.

Life is full of such up-and-down patterns—times when we must push with a great deal of focused effort and times when the wind is at our backs and everything falls into place.

It takes effort to build momentum, but much less to maintain it.

Just how do you build the momentum you need to reach your goals? Simple, repeated, continual effort over regular intervals of time.

In Jeff Olson's book *The Slight Edge*, he makes a strong argument for doing the small and simple things daily and how they result in incredible results down the road. This practice is just as true with creativity as it is with any aspect of life.

The key is to start now and stay consistent. Don't stop, no matter how slow you may feel you're going. When you stop, you lose momentum, and you have to exert more energy to get the machine cranking once more.

You start with a little creative exercise, you pause to consider an important question or begin mind-mapping a new project, and before you know it, you step back to find you've completed something you're proud of, something of great creative prowess.

What seemed impossible at first gets done with the aid of momentum.

One of the best things about momentum is the exponential growth curve. While progress seems slow—nearly imperceptible at first—and the work and arduous, it builds quickly.

As I've heard it said, the days go slow, but the years go fast. What started with a snowflake, given time, becomes an avalanche.

When you use momentum to your advantage,
time becomes your friend instead of your enemy.

When you take daily creative steps, your momentum builds. Over time, it becomes easier and easier to repeat the process, to come up with ideas, to create something new.

As creative habits become a permanent part of your schedule, you'll find your own internal resistance breaking down. It becomes easier to get out of bed, to make that call, to pick up that pen, paintbrush, needle, ruler, measuring cup, or chainsaw. Be careful about picking up that kiln, you might hurt your back.

The more you work at it, the more external resistance becomes less of a problem. Not that it goes away—it just doesn't stop you in your tracks like it once did, all thanks to momentum.

If a boulder gets moving fast enough, there is little to stand in its way. Even a pebble flying fast enough can smash through a cement wall.

The start of a creative endeavor is often difficult because you have little progress to back you up and a lot of work ahead of you—your momentum is at an all-time low. However, this is also when you have a lot of excitement and expectation to carry you onward. As you continue, momentum builds and tasks become easier. But a new challenge arises: the initial excitement dwindles in the presence of challenges and setbacks.

When the hard times come, momentum can get you through them. Think of a roller coaster: they nearly always start with a long, slow trip up to the top, but once there, the downward slope gives the coaster enough momentum for the rest of the ride.

Like the coaster, you will face many uphill battles after the initial rush, and they will slow you down, but with enough momentum behind you, you'll be carried to the next peak and regain the speed you've lost on the next drop, without ever coming to a complete stop.

When it comes to creative momentum, consider these leading questions:

- Do I consistently practice creativity?
- What most often prevents me from staying creative?
- How often do I end up starting something over or abandoning it altogether?
- What is the simplest task in my current creative project that I know I can do consistently until it is complete?
- What would motivate me to "keep on keeping on" with my creative habits?

We all could use more momentum working in our favor, but what is the best way to build it—the most surefire, tried-and-true, foolproof, fire-resistant, weatherproof method? Practice!

Wait, practice? Whoa, that sounds like work. I know, I know. Hang with me.

CHAPTER 27

Practice

Doing the same thing over and over again may sound like the furthest thing from being creative. I get that. But creativity is more than just coming up with a bunch of cool, new ideas. There's also this important bit about turning those ideas into something real—something with substance and value. To do that takes practice, and maybe a little bit of magic, but mostly practice.

The importance of practice cannot be overstated. But, it can always be restated. Practice!

They say practice makes perfect. That's debatable. However,

it is impossible to become better without practice.

Even the term "better" indicates an improvement on previous results. The better we become in any particular area, the more momentum we gain from it.

We practice by making an attempt—many, many attempts. Notice I didn't say we talk about an attempt or plan on an attempt. You must make an actual, honest-to-God-and-your-neighbor-and-everyone-else attempt.

Here's some often-repeated advice from the writing world: show, don't tell. If you've spent any amount of time studying creative writing, you're probably rolling your eyes right now. It's textbook advice, and you've heard it one thousand and two times before. But "show, don't tell" is an important lesson—when done right, it draws the reader in rather than bore them with needless explanation.

When it comes to the creative pursuit, *show, don't tell* is equally important. It means *doing* rather than just *talking* about your plan. Most people have some creative project lurking in the back of their minds, something they'll get around to one day: build furniture, paint a mural, write a book, start a YouTube channel, make an army of gopher statues from sawed up logs, that sort of stuff.

Talking about doing those things is easy, but until you put your mind and your hands to practice, all you have are a bunch of empty words. As Henry Ford said, "You can't build a reputation on what you are going to do."

Oddly enough, just talking about what we're going to do gives us a sense of having done something, even though no progress has been made on the task itself. It's a weird chemical reward our brains give us.

Here's my advice:

Save the talk until you've got something to show.

Instead of *you* jabbering on, how about you give *them* something to talk about? This gives you a clear sense of progress, and it's much more impressive.

We all know a bragger or two—the person who can talk a big game—but like the boy who cried wolf, eventually people stop taking them seriously. Eventually, even the bragger knows their words are nothing but hot air.

Don't cry novel, painting, or Adirondack rocking chair. Go make. Get doing. Start practicing.

I admit, practice isn't always a peachy process—it can be problematic (geez, that is a *lot* of *P*'s). We've developed some highly unrealistic expectations when it comes to practice.

These pesky untruths can get in our way:

- You can excel at anything after only a few attempts.
- If something requires a large amount of time and effort, it isn't worth doing.
- If you aren't instantly great at it, you should move on to something else.

After reading those, you might say, "Pah! I don't believe such untoward rubbish." But why do so many of us live according to those lies of practicion?

We want the fast track to perfection. We're bombarded with advertisements promising we can have all and be all with little to no practice. Someone always has a guaranteed honest-to-goodness shortcut to help you circumnavigate practice and get to the good part.

Whether it's the promise of developing the perfect golf swing in a week or amazing abs and bulging biceps with just one little pill, we're being fed a pack of lies. The pros laugh at such things. They know this all too well:

there are no shortcuts around practice.

There are times to experiment before committing and there is a need to abandon certain pursuits in order to focus on more important ones, but many of us are in danger of becoming a generation of drifters—only willing to take on what is easy, what requires little to no effort, and what has a minimal risk (if any at all) attached. It's not even a path to mediocrity, because at least mediocre means you've met the base standard. This indecisive, noncommittal route is a path to nowhere.

Improvement requires commitment.

It's a misconception to think creativity is nothing more than moments of spontaneity.

Creativity takes determined effort and hard work in the form of practice—trying something over and over again until you improve and then pushing onward and upward. Little successes every day.

If you want your creative work to be excellent, you must be willing to put in the time and energy required. Find something you enjoy and make a serious commitment to improving at it. Some things are harder than others: becoming a concert pianist takes more work than being an awesome scrapbooker, but both require commitment of some form to reach a place of skill.

If you want to do fine, put in the time. Sounds cheesy, but it's true.

Before you begin any task, great or small, take time to weigh how much effort it will require. In other words, count the cost.

Eugene Cho puts it more elegantly than I have: "Take the time, and make a commitment to be an expert in the areas of your passion."

Practice makes better. That's the process. But what is the end goal, the final result?

The whole point of practice is to create something of value.

If you value something enough, be it a skill or project, you will be willing to pay the cost to reach completion—you will persist in practice. However, if you keep abandoning projects because the cost is too great, I'd urge you to reexamine your expectations. Do they line up with reality?

Anything worth doing is worth an honest attempt—doing it over and over until you've improved. If nothing else, this is a commitment of time.

When I was nineteen, I decided I wanted to learn how to play guitar. Maybe because the people I knew who could play were cool cats. Maybe because it seemed like an easy enough instrument to learn for a person with no inherent musical talent. Though I asked for a pointer from time to time, I mainly taught myself. Looking back now, I'd recommend getting a teacher—it goes much faster that way.

Anyhow, I picked up my dad's old, mediocre guitar, found a book of chords and just went to town. I didn't do anything special and most of the time it felt like I wasn't getting anywhere. Most of the time, the fingerings seemed just as hard as they had the day before and I didn't notice any improvement in sound quality.

I don't recall when it happened, but at some point I realized I could play well enough and other people didn't mind listening, even if I still messed up now and then. I ended up playing for our church's youth group for a few years. It was a good experience and it was nice to have something to offer.

Truthfully, I still can't do anything impressive with a guitar, but I'm glad I took the time to practice until I learned how to play one. Though the going was slow and progress difficult to notice, I genuinely enjoyed the time spent alone, plucking away at those strings. The music I made wasn't always beautiful, but it still carried with it as much meaning and emotion for me as anything Eric Clapton or Bob Dylan created.

Though practice takes time and effort, it doesn't always need to be painful or even all that difficult. Yes, you need to work hard, but you can also be efficient and even have fun while doing it.

Everything takes time, but that time can be spread out and sliced up into small chunks. Develop simple, daily tasks that lead you on the gradual road to improvement. The other option—trying to do everything at once—will leave you drained and disappointed (like pretty much every science fair project I've tried to finish two days before the big show).

How do you know when your practice was worth it? When you've made a masterpiece.

Contrary to popular belief, a masterpiece is not your final crowning work. It's the first work that proves your mastery over a subject. A masterpiece is the proof that you're no longer an apprentice, but now a master.

A master still has room for improvement, but they've reached a standard of accomplishment. It's the difference between saying "I'm writing" and "I'm a writer," or "I'm sewing" and "I'm a seamstress."

It's one part accomplishment, one part mindset.

You don't need to be a paid professional to create a masterpiece, but you must have creative ownership. There are many people who have mastery of a subject who haven't received a dime for their efforts. Then again, if you have become a master, there's no shame in making a living (or even a few bucks) from it.

Making money from your creative work does not lessen its value. When you get paid for your creation, it doesn't make you a sellout. It's simply an exchange of value. You have created something of value to another person or persons, and they give you something they value in return.

Also, when you get paid for your craft, it gives you the time and resources to put in more practice, resulting in repeated, improved performance on your end. Don't be ashamed to get paid, but also don't believe the money is what validates your work. Money, after all, isn't the only form of currency.

My buddy Shawn and his wife, Colleen, (whom I interviewed in this book) are into costuming—they create and sometimes design their own costumes. Shawn likes to dress up as Obi-Wan from Star Wars (plus some other popular characters) and volunteer his time visiting children in hospitals. It makes a kid's day when not only do they have a visitor, but a Jedi Knight comes to see them. There's no price you can put on that experience.

Admittedly, there are varying levels of mastery, and just about every possible skill has a group who sets the standards for it. You have to decide what mastery looks like on a personal level.

Let the level of mastery you desire be a reachable goal, something measurable. If your standard is absolute perfection, you'll face continual disappointment and discouragement. Practice makes better and better is a more rewarding goal than perfection.

Not everyone can be Yo-Yo Ma, and some incredibly famous and successful artists have little more than an average level of technical skill in their craft. I'm sure you've seen a work of art on display and thought, "Hey, I could have done that." I could likely teach you how to play Cash's *Ring Of Fire* in less than a week. It's how you use your acquired skill that makes the difference. It's the creativity in your craft. But without the skill, you won't get too far.

Practice builds momentum. Momentum, once begun, soon becomes a force to be reckoned with. However, it is just as easily lost when we get sidetracked. It takes a force of will and determination to continue a thing once begun.

CHAPTER 28

Determination and Motivation

In 2007, the young Professor Randy Pausch gave his final talk to a packed auditorium at Carnegie Mellon University. In his talk, appropriately titled *Last Lecture*, Randy shared some of his life experiences and what he'd learned from achieving (and not achieving) his childhood dreams.

As he recounts some of the challenges he overcame, there is one observation in particular that Randy repeatedly makes: brick walls are there for a reason. They aren't there to keep you out. They give us a chance to show how badly we want something.

Without determination, those brick walls will look like dead ends.

Determination is the drive to stick with something no matter what comes against you. It begins with motivation but goes beyond that.

**Determination is not only an indicator of how badly
you want something, but also the key to achieving it.**

Some folks seem to have it in ample supply, while others come up short. If you don't feel the drive of determination, it could be that your end goal isn't big enough or you don't want it badly enough.

It could be you've fallen into complacency—a satisfaction with less than your best. Maybe you don't yet believe that facing the resistance is worth the outcome. You'd rather stay mediocre, stagnant, stunted, and immature.

I've sure been there. Sometimes I even fall back on the easy old ways. I might "give myself a break" far too long and digress, letting my creativity and personal growth wane. But the cost of giving in has never compared to the cost of staying determined.

It's hard to stay the course now,
but it's easier than facing your regrets tomorrow.

As Levi Lusko says, "Now yells louder, but later lasts longer."

With the proper motivation, you can live a life of determination now. This is why a creative approach and a creative process must come first; they build your creative momentum.

When you observe, question, and respond, you discover your end goal—your motivation for being creative.

When you're inspired, imaginative, and innovative, you develop determination, which will lead you to a desired end. The creative approach develops your motivation, and the creative process transforms it into determination.

When you find you've slipped into a complacent lifestyle, go back to your goals. Examine them with questions such as these:

- Where is it you were headed before you lost your way?
- What were your plans? Can you pick up again where you left off?
- Are the goals you set realistic?
- What will your life look like once you reach them?
- Who else is missing out because of your actions?
- In a few years, will you look back with regret at the things you could have done, or will you have satisfaction that you did the best and most you could with the time you had?

It might feel like we're getting extreme, but if you're stuck in a rut, extreme thinking is what you need to get out of it.

Remember, the third plot point is an extreme—the lowest point the protagonist reaches. It takes serious determination to get out of a pit once you've fallen in.

Determined people are extreme. They're obnoxious to everyone else around them. When others resist change, the determined person demands it.

Resistance from others is the fuel of the determined creative.

If determination is about reaching goals, motivation is about focus.

When you're looking through a camera lens and there are many objects in your view, you must decide what you want the camera to focus on. When one thing becomes clear, everything else gets blurry.

If you focus on how you're feeling at the moment, you often lose heart. If you focus on the obstacles in front of you, they're all you will see and you'll get tripped up.

However, when you focus on what it takes to reach the end and how you'll be when you get there, you'll have the motivation to continue.

Of course, it's easy to tell someone to stay motivated and determined—it takes almost no effort. It's much harder to live it yourself. As C. H. Spurgeon pointed out, "It is easy to use words, but it is difficult to feel their meaning."

It's difficult to be creative when you are in pain, sad, stressed, overwhelmed, depressed, defeated, or without hope—but it is in these times you most need a creative mindset, one that makes and does new things, one that accepts and moves toward change. Without it, everything will remain the same—you won't escape the pit.

When the hero faces their darkest moment, the easy path leads to surrender, defeat. But that doesn't make for a good story.

In the most powerful tales, the protagonist not only faces outside opposition from some antagonistic force but also must overcome an internal battle—by far the hardest struggle of the two.

There is one thing that will kill your creative drive faster than anything else, and it comes from within: fear.

To quote a tagline from the sci-fi movie *Moon*: "The hardest thing to face is yourself."

What do you do when face to face with your greatest antagonist—your inner fear? Join us next time when the story continues. Or just read on.

Never, never, in nothing great or small, large or petty, never give in except to convictions of honour and good sense. Never yield to force; never yield to the apparently overwhelming might of the enemy.

~Winston S. Churchill

SECTION 9 REVIEW

One more time, with feeling:

- It is during our times of crisis, when all seems lost, that we finally see what matters most, when we truly evaluate our lifestyle and are closest to understanding the truth.
- When it is most difficult to be creative is also the most important time to do so.
- Creativity is a lifelong pursuit.
- Though difficult to begin, momentum gives us energy to push on, especially through hard times.
- Practice is a requirement for creative mastery.
- Like the hero who fights on in the face of defeat, determined people pursue their creative goals in spite of resistance.
- The most difficult battle for the creative is the internal one.
- If you plan to name your pet Mr. Fluffynippers, might I suggest a Great Dane or some form of mastiff?

Interview with a Creative

AMERICA YOUNG

Tell us about yourself.
I am a filmmaker and stunt person in the film, TV, and video game industries. Professional storyteller.

When do you find it easiest to be creative?
When I'm under deadline, consistency, limitation, and surrounded by creative, supportive people.

Deadline: So much of being creative has to be self-motivated. If you have a full-time job as a lawyer but have always wanted to be a novelist, that's all on you. Staring at the blank page/canvas can be daunting. Whether it's a script or a short list, having a deadline looming over me forces me to start, to sit down and just face whatever it is I have been avoiding. Once I do, I am able to really create!

Consistency: Also for this reason, having dedicated time to spend on it—for me, every morning for thirty minutes—means I will work on it consistently. Like anything else, consistently doing it can only make you better. The more you practice throwing baskets, the better you get. So the more you practice being creative, the better you will get it.

Restrictions: To have limitations put on you can be so frustrating, whether it be time or budget or physical. But my favorite moments in the films I've either made or I've watched have all come from someone having to think outside the box to fix the problem or limitation. When you are backed into a corner, your mind's creativity reaches outside the usual and typical ways of thinking because it has to.

Surrounded by other creative people: Surround yourself by people who are excited to create, who build on each other's ideas instead of knocking them down. This is my favorite environment in which to create.

Where do you look for inspiration?
Books and conversations with people. I love hearing what is important to people, what moves them. The best creations we make are ones that speak to and move others. The only way to do that is to create from truth, which you learn from examining yourself but also listening to those around you.

What forms of creativity do you most appreciate or enjoy?
Novels and music move me the most and I admire the most because I don't think I could do either.

When has a creative approach helped you accomplish something impactful?
I recently directed a short for National Domestic Violence Awareness Month. The creative approach gave me the ability to use creativity to tell a heartbreaking story but leave people with hope and inspiration.

What is one practice you would recommend to help someone be more creative?
Just do it. Sit down and make yourself write for fifteen minutes every day if you want to write. Make yourself draw every day if you want to draw. Make yourself play an instrument. The doing helps with the creating. That, and commit to a deadline that you will have to stick to. And stick to it no matter what. Just like anything else, with each attempt at creativity, you learn and grow and develop confidence for the next one. So do it and keep doing it.

Where can people find you or your work?
www.americayoung.com

Section 10 - Courage

Fortress

The hike up Mount Dread is tiresome and treacherous.

The winding stairway to the top has seen better days—many of the steps are uneven, and some shift or crumble when you put weight on them.

Your body aches and you desire rest, but Timble urges you on.

All you can manage is to simply keep moving by placing one aching foot in front of the other.

There is little to see beyond the barren rocks of the mountainside. Even the view you might have enjoyed is hidden in clouds.

As you ascend, it becomes more difficult to draw breath in the thin atmosphere, as if your chest were locked in a steel cage. A cold, relentless wind penetrates the very marrow of your bones. Despite all this, you have to remain focused—one slip on the jagged stairway could be your downfall.

The higher you go, the more Timble grows silent. Your attempts at conversation are rewarded with short answers, even for her.

At last, you arrive at a flat outcrop, where you stop to rest. A weathered stone plaque rests in the center and you walk closer to examine it. At the top are the words "Welcome to," but the rest of the original writing has either faded or been removed. Underneath, the word "Failure" has been roughly carved by someone who could use a typography lesson or two.

Timble gasps and points up ahead at a towering stone fortress. You had been so focused on where you stepped, you missed its approach. It is more grand (and imposing) than you'd imagined.

Timble shivers. For a moment she looks more like her old self, but after you pat her on the head and offer a word of encouragement, she regains her composure.

You can make out a few glimpses between the cloud cover. The sun has begun to set, casting a dark-red hue over the valley below.

As far as you can tell, there is no path around the fortress. Each of its side walls sits atop sheer cliffs. The only way up is through.

The towering outer gate to the fortress is open and unguarded. Strangely, Timble doesn't look relieved by this.

You both enter with caution, eyes darting about for signs of hidden attackers, but you see nothing of alarm. In the great circular courtyard, you find a dried-up fountain with a statue of children dancing. Their heads have eroded away or been smashed off.

From the courtyard, there are many other paths leading back down the mountain. As far as you can tell, the only way onward is up a wide flight of steps to the fortress's main entrance, which is so high most trees could fit underneath. You look again at the steps and realize they are occupied, but not by the living.

On the steps are many statues, made of rusted metal, all frozen in mid flight, running away from the castle. Worried by what you may find inside, you press on. Timble hesitates, but at last follows.

The main hall is deserted except for more of the unusual statues—all facing in the opposite direction of where you are headed. Not having been out in the elements, there is less rust on these, some still maintaining a dull sheen. They depict not only adults and children but also an occasional creature similar to Timble. The expression on every one of their faces is the same—terror.

The hall is dead silent. As you walk, your footsteps echo off the tiled floor to the buttresses in the arched ceiling above. Deeper in, windows become scarcer, and darkness fills the empty rooms. Timble pulls something from her pocket and holds it up: a thin steel rod. Light shines from one end, a mere pinprick in the towering dark halls, but it is enough to see the way forward.

Everything about the place looks abandoned. While the building itself is in good condition, nearly all the furnishings and personal items have vanished. The occasional paintings and tapestries are in bad condition: many have fallen off their walls or been torn to shreds. Despite your unease, the empty fortress at least offers protection from the frigid wind outside.

Eventually you arrive in the throne room. It is vast and, more than anywhere else in the fortress, holds a deep feeling of emptiness. There are no statues or decorations here.

The ceiling and back walls of the room are hidden in darkness. Thick marble pillars border the path to some stairs. A high-backed chair sits at the far end, which you can barely make out in the dark.

Timble is no longer beside you. When you look behind, she stands far away at the entrance to the room. Is she cowering?

"C...can't. Can't. Can't help it." Her voice is raspy again. "Must obey master." She shakes about as if something invisible were crawling over her. She pauses—mid crouch—and the light of her little torch reflects off her yellow cat eyes, now wide with fear. "If you are truly the one, you will make it. Timble knows!" She raises the steel rod in her hand and throws it to the ground, then turns and runs.

You begin to run after her, but when you hear the rod beep quickly, you duck behind a pillar. A blast shakes the room, and when the dust clears, all that is left of the entrance is a pile of rubble.

With no other option, you walk toward the throne. Something is still lighting the room, and you soon find the source of light: in front of the steps leading up to the throne is a shallow, circular pool with a soft green glow. In the center of the pool is the stone carving of a dragon, just above the surface of the water. The design matches the shields and flags you saw in the forest. Though the air is still, the surface of the pool ripples.

"You've come at last," says a weary voice.

You start when you realize someone is sitting on the throne, very still. The dim, shifting light casts an eerie glow on the figure. It takes you a moment to recognize him as the old leader from the forest.

"Master was disappointed when he heard you'd escaped," the man says, leaning forward in his chair. The leader does not look angry with you. Instead, he seems sad and tired. He stands, with some effort. "This was my castle once. King Goodvin I was called back then. It was a happy time and my subjects loved me, until the Master arrived."

Slowly and with a few grunts, Goodvin descends the stairs, the light of the pool further illuminating his face from below. "I resisted the Master's call at first, though others gave in. But then this—" with some difficulty, Goodvin removes one of his gloves and holds up a hand made entirely of solid metal with fingers frozen in a clawlike pose.

"I fled, but alas, my daughter was lost to the curse. Many of my loyal servants followed me to the forest. Eventually, even I gave in to the Master's call. As will you." At that, Goodvin reaches into the pool and stirs the surface of the water with his metal hand. It shimmers and glows, undulating images drifting in and out of view.

The water's movement entrances you, and you discover you are staring at a reflection of yourself—but changed. Your image looks older, haggard, like King Goodvin has become.

Horrified, you try to pull away but can't. Your reflection speaks to you: "Foolish to come all this way for nothing," it snickers. "There is no escape from here. You will never reach the top."

You try to run, to close your eyes, to scream, but the words of the reflection leave you paralyzed.

"What did you hope for? Did you think you were special? No, you are lost and alone, like everyone else."

You shake your head to dismiss the lies—the reflection is playing off your fears.

"I don't know your fears," it says as a forked tongue flicks from its mouth. "I *am* your fears!" Its mouth opens, and you lean forward into the water.

Just before your nose touches the glowing blue pool, a hand grabs your shoulder and yanks you back.

You whip around, ready to face whatever foe is behind you, but stop when you recognize me. A sigh of relief escapes your lips, followed by a laugh. Then you catch your breath—something is not right. I have two short tentacles sprouting from my back and dark-purple splotches over my arms and face.

I bow my head low. "Yes, it got me too, but not totally. I finished off that marsh horror but was weakened by the fight and my wound. Then something flew down and carried me here, probably to stop you."

I collapse into a seated position. "Listen, I don't have much time, before I...turn. But you can still make it. This may be the Fortress of Failure, but it's also the Fortress of Success. It's both, but you have to decide which one it is to you.

"You have to pass through the Cavern of Fear. You have to face the Shadow Dragon. He's the one who cursed this place, who convinced people the only way to not be transformed was to serve him.

"But the real curse is becoming his slave, believing his words. It changes people on the inside, makes them forget who they really are until there is nothing left. It happens even to the best of them."

I point behind you, and you look back to see King Goodvin has also become a metal statue, still bent over the glowing pool of water. "It's not too late," I say. "The dragon's in charge now, but you can stop him. You are the Endless Creative. I believe it now—I know it for truth."

With resolve, you stand, then ask for the createamobile.

"That thing?" I shrug, "It went down with the coach in the marsh." I stop to wince and grab my chest, then continue on with effort, "It's just a toy, a neat trick. You don't need it. Besides"—I cough—"you were awful at it. It was you, not the contraption, doing all that amazing stuff." I cough again, and thick dark liquid drips from my mouth. "You and only you can do this. Now go." I pass out.

You turn to leave, but stop when I convulse on the floor. You bend over and search my pockets. I make wet gurgling sounds, and my hands become fists.

At last you find it: the vial of water from the valley spring. You open it and pour the cool liquid into my mouth. The convulsions cease, and my eyes again close as a faint smile plays at my lips. I release a sigh of relief, and my tensed muscles relax. "Thanks, friend," I breathe, and then fall into a peaceful slumber.

You hoist me on your shoulders and carry me up the steps to the tall throne at the top. Part of its back has been broken off and one of the arms is missing, but you are still able to leave me with some dignity in a seated position. I begin a series of loud snores.

Behind the throne, a giant hole has been smashed in the wall—the entrance to the dragon's cave. You can smell smoke and see the flicker of fire deep within.

There's no turning back.

Good stories are driven by conflict, tension, and high stakes.
~William Landay

CHAPTER 29

Fear

I'll give you fair warning: this is a hard chapter. It has a lot of things you won't want to think about. You should probably skip it.

I didn't even want to write it. And yet, here it is for the world to read. Then again, if you don't read it, you won't know what you've missed—and there's some important stuff here. I'm not even sure if it's possible to be a creative without doing the following things. I'll let you decide.

As a reminder, there are three parts of the creative pursuit: courage, confidence, and consistency. We'll start with courage, and as you might have guessed, this means we must also talk about fear.

If you've seen *The Wizard of Oz*, you'll remember the Cowardly Lion and his emphatic song and speech about courage. The fearful feline makes some bold proclamations, but at last ends it off with, "Whatta they got that I ain't got?" Everyone answers, "Courage!" And the lovable lion responds, "You can say that again."

In many ways, creatives also proclaim bravery they have not yet attained; they dream about the day when they too will be the fearless king of the forest. But even kings are afraid of something.

Every single person on this planet has some fear they've yet to confront. As creatives, we cannot afford to hide from our fears—to turn tail and take off in a sprint at the first sign of trouble. Instead, we must face our fears head on.

We've reached the beginning of the climax—the confrontation between the protagonist and the antagonist. It's the point every story builds to, where everything comes to a head.

In the climax, the hero faces not only their outer antagonist, but also their inner conflict. A duel must take place, to the death. Be it literal or metaphorical, the story cannot progress until either the hero or the antagonist have been neutralized—until the hero has conquered their inner demon or died trying.

This is where things get spicy, when the audience hangs on the edge of their seat. Who will win? Will our hero walk away unmaimed, or at all?

There are many outer forces that impede our own creative goals, things such as a lack of resources, people who oppose our efforts, or even painful life situations. These present incredible challenges to us. But the greatest struggle is and always will be the internal one.

According to Plato, "It is the first and best of all victories for a man to conquer himself."

What holds us back? What internal force must we defeat in order to march forth in creative victory? The answer is our great opponent: fear.

Fear is the great enemy of creativity.

If you subject yourself to it, you will become its captive. As a captive of fear, you will be restrained every time you attempt to be creative, too frightened to go on.

Fear is at the root of why we choose safety and comfort over the risk and discomfort creativity requires. Fear is what makes us avoid change. It keeps us from growing, from trying something new. Fear is even the source of creative's block (a.k.a. writer's block)—the dread of the blank page, the formless lump of clay, the white canvas, the struggle of starting something from scratch. The voice of fear tells you that you can't do it, you aren't good enough, you're just a fake, and you're all alone.

There are many causes for fear, and it leads to different reactions, few of them good. Have you taken time to consider your own fears? Take a glance over the list below. Do any of these strike home?

Rejection
Insignificance
Being unloved or unlovable
Incompetence

Helplessness
Being an outcast
Failure
Success
Pain
Lostness
Disconnection
Weakness
Unworthiness
Shame
Mockery
Missing out
Being alone
Unimportance
Getting trapped
Confusion
Being broken or defective
Purposelessness
Loss
The unknown

I've been held back by more than a few of those. And if you're honest, you have as well.

But wait. Isn't it normal to be afraid? Yes, but remember that normalcy doesn't make something right. Even so, fear can serve a useful purpose.

Fear is a natural response—a recognition of potential harm.

It is right to fear burning yourself on a hot stove or hurting someone's feelings by saying inconsiderate words. Those are regular, normal fears.

Some fears, however, are not reasonable, such as the fear that frogs will fall from the sky into your mouth and suffocate you, or the belief your pajamas will come to life at night and attack, or even a concern your house will one day turn into pudding (actually, that would be kinda cool, for like a day).

All those are ridiculous, of course, but even reasonable fears cause us to do irrational things. Because you fear burning your hands, you might refuse to cook or even walk near a stove. An extreme level of fear goes beyond logic. After having been betrayed by someone close, you could harbor a sense of mistrust until, eventually, you believe the whole world is out to get you.

We can allow fears to grow so large, they dominate our entire lives. If you dread the disapproval of those around you, you may stop taking risks. If you fear damaging your reputation, you may be driven to make yourself always look good in front of others, never willing to be honest, hiding your real self from those around you.

While a dose of fear is healthy, it can quickly become a toxic brew—poisoning the way we live and think. Even creative success can lead to fear. Many an author or artist, having completed a work that was widely praised, did not produce any further works, for fear they could never surpass their initial accomplishment.

Fear leads to unhealthy comparisons and unreasonable expectations.

You may have heard of imposter syndrome: a belief that you are really just faking it—nothing more than a hack—and not a true creative.

The fine folks on the *Writing Excuses* podcast have discussed this topic often, sharing their own personal struggles. By openly admitting their fears, they demonstrate something important for all creatives:

When our fears are exposed, they lose their power.

When we drag them out in the open, we begin to see our fears for what they are: common and weak. There is comfort in realizing that almost every creative struggles with imposter syndrome, even (especially) the most famous and accomplished.

Through camaraderie and encouragement, we learn not to let unrealistic expectations stop us from trying our best. Everyone is still figuring it out, even the pros—they've just been doing it longer and have learned some useful tools to get through the hard times.

Fear is self-generated and invisible, yet as we feed it, we transform our fear from something imagined to something real.

Imagination is a powerful thing. It can help you create something from nothing, but it also can be your undoing. A life consumed by fear, one in which we only believe the worst will happen, is a life of enslavement.

Fear is a strange thing. It may begin with something small and common to everyday experience: an unkind word, a mistake, an injury. Given time and attention, it can swell so big that it far surpasses the original source. Fear then becomes the thing we dread, instead of a potential outcome.

I have heard it said the reason we're so enamored with social media platforms is that we are afraid of death. In an attempt to feel significant, we perform thousands of little meaningless exchanges to prove to ourselves and to others that we matter, that our lives are important. Those things are easy, but they give us a false sense of value. The real problem comes when we are afraid to die, so we just pretend at living.

Instead, we should be concerned about a wasted life, reaching the end having left behind nothing of value.

To quote from the game *That Dragon, Cancer*, "I think greater than my fear of death is that of insignificance. Rather, my default assumption is that my thoughts and passions, loves and the stuff of my being are insignificant."

That's not to say there's no value to be found in social media. I've seen many excellent and creative uses as well, but often the way we use it is uncreative, unhealthy, and born out of a fear of change instead of a desire for it.

Instead of using social media to promote ourselves, we should use it to lift others up. Instead of wasting most of our time with meaningless interactions that are soon forgotten, why not instead focus on meaningful, lasting ones? Why not reach out and make a real impact? After all, you can't give a long-distance hug.

There's nothing inherently wrong with sharing a picture of your happy family and saying how thankful you are for the people in your life. But why not send a private message, email, or, better yet, a handwritten letter, to someone in your life explaining in detail how much they mean to you?

Sure, you can blast out a long rant with some data and a lot of opinion on the refugee crisis, gun control, abortion, or suicide. Maybe that'll help somebody. But how much better would it be to reach out to a person who has endured trauma or suffered loss and just talk with them?

And who doesn't love to post pictures of an amazing meal they're about to eat? Why not also share that great recipe you found with your cooking pals? Or, take a meal to the lonely woman down the road, foster parents with twenty kids, or the young family that just moved in right before their sole provider lost their job? Or serve at a local food bank?

So much of what we do on social media is mindless and easy. It's the true and lasting interactions that are difficult and scary.

It's not just social media. There are a multitude of ways we can live in safety, comfort, and utter insignificance—in fear of change. Scientists determine the death of the universe occurs when there is no further change. It's the same with human life.

Every one of us every day is faced with the choice of life or death, to bring change or resist it and, in doing so, die a little more. To grow colder and harder—to surrender to fear.

Yes, fears are real, just as death is real, but it is only when we give up, lose hope, and lose faith, that we give them power over us.

Your own reflections upon fear make it great or small.

We give strength to fears by thinking of them, by believing in them, by giving them credibility. Your fear is really just a trick of the mind, a beast of illusion. Only by feeding it do you give it teeth and claws.

If you entered a dark back room of a circus warehouse, you'd be startled if you noticed a tall figure looming over you, ready to attack. But if you switched on the lights and discovered it was only a cardboard clown holding a banana, you'd be relieved (though, perhaps, still a little uneasy).

Sure, it's a clown, and those can be a little scary, but at least you know it can't harm you (unless you're deathly allergic to cardboard bananas).

If instead of flipping the lights on, you ran as fast as you could from the room, you might go away with the belief that you have a stalker on your trail and nowhere you go will be safe. That could become a very deadly lie by which to live.

Your fear becomes exposed only when you shine the light on it—when you confront it.

Just how should you confront your ever-growing fears? With creativity, of course!

CHAPTER 30

Courage

When fear rather than creativity becomes our motivator, we tend to close ourselves in and shut out the world. We can become narrow-minded—in bondage to a feeling.

Creativity, however, leads us to take steps in a new direction, to see the world from a different perspective, to take risks. As counselor Mike Foster has said, "Courageous response builds confidence." But a person driven by fear refuses to take that first step.

Creativity sets free. Fear enslaves.

What should you do when fear pounds at your door, when it makes you want to curl up in a ball and hide in a corner, when it lifts you up by the collar, demands you give up your snack, and pours milk on your head? Ah, good old elementary school.

As in the case of the *Cardboard Banana Clown* (sure, I'd read that book), you must turn and face your fears in order to see them as they really are. Instead of giving in, fight back with creative boldness.

Remember my friend Michael, whom I mentioned previously? He's the MIT grad who said, "You can make me fail, but you can't make me quit."

Well, he's also the self-proclaimed shyest man on earth (just ask him—he'll tell you the same). But he recognized his shyness was holding him back, so he did something about it: he started attending Toastmasters and developing his skill in public speech. That's a big step, considering a lot of people are more afraid of speaking in public than they are of death.

Michael committed to improving in this area and is now an extraordinary speaker (my humble opinion) who lectures all over the place about fascinating topics like black holes, Bitcoin, and whether the universe is expanding or shrinking (small stuff, really). In fact, he's even done a TEDx Talk on artificial intelligence.

If you struggle with fear—let's be honest, we all do—it's time to call it out and make a change, or at least begin by recognizing that you do struggle with fear, which can be a challenge in itself.

First, identify what it is you're afraid of. Is it a legitimate fear, something likely to happen? As I said before, fear is a natural reaction to danger. The problem is how we respond.

Fear can be helpful and even healthy at times. However, besides the immediate, seen dangers, there is a hidden danger: fear can get in the way of our most important goals or our goals themselves may become fear-based. If we allow it, fear can creep in and dominate every aspect of our lives.

As part of your creative pursuit, it's time to examine the things you want out of life, why you want them, and the steps you'll have to take to get there.

Consider your life goals: What is the main emotion driving them? Do they look more like running to or away from or running toward something?

Fear and creativity are often at odds, pushing against one other like two opposite sides of a magnet.

Fear is inward focused—it's you-centered; it's based on your personal desires. Creativity is outward focused—it is influenced by and influences the outside world. It requires you to look beyond yourself and your own wants.

Fear withdraws while creativity reaches out.

When faced with change, the unknown, or danger, the typical response is fear. That's normal. It's a starting place. From that point, you have a choice: to allow fear to control you—suppressing your creativity—or to do something with that fear, even if it's uncomfortable or downright terrifying.

It takes a purposeful, creative decision to not capitulate to your fear.

It takes the creative approach to instead find reasons for joy, hope, and courage in the face of frightening situations.

Let me be clear: some of us face significant emotional hurdles, some of which we may not ever fully overcome in this life. I myself have struggled with anxiety and panic attacks. It's not fun and it isn't something you can just make up your mind about and move past. I get that.

However, creative courage is always an option, even if it takes a lot of time and effort to get there, even if the fear doesn't go away. And, thankfully, there are more avenues and resources available to help with such struggles than ever before. At the very least, talk with someone, share your story, seek help. That, in itself, is courageous.

Extreme cases aside, the regular old run-of-the-mill fear can sometimes be a good thing. It isn't wrong to want to get out of a dangerous situation or to protect yourself from potential harm. There is a reason they built walls around castles—to keep the attackers out. But if no one is let in or out of a castle, its community dies and survival becomes impossible.

This is why a blockade is such an effective tactic. It's much slower than a direct assault, but it eventually starves out those within the walls. Fear can become our own personal blockade, where we close ourselves off to the trade of ideas and we cease to be nourished by inspiration.

We should be wary of living a life that's always on the run, one that never rests, never builds connections, never takes time to grow and develop in the place it is.

In a conversation with one of the actresses who frequents our studio, she recounted her childhood. Her family moved all the time, so she ended up bouncing from school to school, always playing the role of the new girl.

While she was talking, a few people expressed how hard they imagined such a life to be. But the actress countered that concern. Actually, she told us, it was great. She learned how to make friends quickly wherever she was. She also learned how to let people go. It was a valuable lesson. A situation most consider undesirable taught this woman how to overcome many relational fears, things that take some people a lifetime to learn, if they ever learn it at all.

I've said this before and I'll say it again: no matter where you are, you can be creative. If you want to face down your fears with hope and confidence, you will have to be.

To be creative is to be courageous.

You will have to look beyond the hurt and danger and see the potential for good. You will have to come up with interesting ways to ignore those fears and instead move in the direction you should go.

Here are a few questions to consider:

- Are there any ways fear may be holding me back?
- What is the worst that could happen, and how likely is it to actually happen? Could I go on with life if it did happen?
- What are the things I've been wanting to do, and know I should, but haven't because I'm afraid of the consequences?
- What would my life look like if I had no fear at all?
- Is there a safer place I can go or person I can talk with in order to better deal with my fears?
- If there is a particular goal or project I haven't been able to do because of fear, what is the one smallest, safest step I can take to once again make progress toward reaching it?

So to be courageous creatives, we have to remove all fear, right? Nope.

I have a poster from the game *Portal* that you might call motivational. It depicts a stick figure standing boldly, arms akimbo, while an energy ball hurtles toward his head (maybe the figure is a *she*—I have trouble telling with stick figures). These words are emblazoned across the poster in thick black letters: "Courage is not the absence of fear."

Fear and courage are not always at odds. Neither are fear and creativity. They often go hand in hand, much like failure and success. If you don't have any fears, chances are you aren't challenging yourself, you aren't stretching your limits, you aren't growing—in other words, you aren't being creative.

To have fear is to recognize risk and without risk, there is little gain.

Yes, fear can be your downfall, but it is also necessary. Like everything, there is a tension, a balance between fear and confidence.

While the Pixar movie *The Good Dinosaur* had some major missteps, and could even be considered their first throw-away film, I still appreciated its message: only crazy people have no fear. To be brave, you have to face down your fear, not eliminate it.

Besides that, the film was incredibly beautiful. Seriously, just turn the sound off and enjoy the spectacularly computer-generated landscapes—you don't even need to go outside anymore. (I kid—the real world still looks better, if only by a slim margin.)

To quote Elizabeth Gilbert again from her book *Big Magic*,

> Creativity is a path for the brave, yes, but it is not a path for the fearless, and it's important to recognize the distinction. Bravery means doing something scary. Fearless means not even understanding what the word scary means.
>
> It isn't always comfortable or easy but it's always worth it, because if you can't learn to travel comfortably alongside your fear, then you'll never be able to go anywhere interesting. And that would be a pity, because your life is short and rare and amazing, and you want to do really interesting things while you're still here.

Despite what movies may lead you to believe, overcoming fear is not always a grand showdown between you and the monster you dread. Often, it comes down to little, uncomfortable decisions, like talking with someone, journaling, searching for a new job, sending a letter, or enrolling in a class.

What is the smallest step you can take toward the place fear has kept you from going? Once you make that step, take another. With each step, you grow bolder, and you find the road ahead isn't nearly as dark as you expected.

In Levi Lusko's book *Through the Eyes of a Lion*, he writes about the death of his daughter and how he and his wife found healing after that tragic event. He uses two phrases I appreciate: "run toward the roar" (or face the thing that scares you rather than running away from it), and "lean into the groan" (or accept and embrace the difficulties life throws at you). Having such a creative mindset will give you the courage to move on, not without fear but in spite of it.

While your fears are your own, there is no reason you must face them alone. A creative community, or even just one or two like-minded friends, can be the very strength and support you require to press on through the dark moments. This is one of the great challenges of fear—it tends to isolate. Don't let it. Instead, make the effort to find someone who cares, and share what you're going through with them.

Facing a fear is not a one-time event because no matter how many times we succeed at it, or how many fears we overcome, they always return. In a way, fear is like a cactus: even long after it has died, it's still dangerous. Sometimes you don't see it until you've already been pricked.

As you continue the creative journey, there will be new dangers to face, new obstacles in your way, new risks to take. They will often be unpredictable, and you will feel unequipped to overcome them. Don't be dismayed. This is a sign that you are growing. You will always have the choice of how to respond, whether to cower and hide in fear or to step up to the challenge with creative confidence and walk on.

But know that until we are willing to give something up, we will never gain something better. We will be stuck in the comfortable normal world, not knowing what we're missing. To slay the dragon, get the treasure, and reach our goal, a sacrifice is first required.

CHAPTER 31

Sacrifice

Before you commit to pursuing anything, you should consider the cost. Creativity is no exception.

Even Jesus gave some practical advice on the matter:

> Suppose one of you wants to build a tower. Won't you first sit down and estimate the cost to see if you have enough money to complete it? For if you lay the foundation and are not able to finish it, everyone who sees it will ridicule you, saying, "This person began to build and wasn't able to finish." Or suppose a king is about to go to war against another king. Won't he first sit down and consider whether he is able with ten thousand men to oppose the one coming against him with twenty thousand? If he is not able, he will send a delegation while the other is still a long way off and will ask for terms of peace. (Luke 14:28–32 NIV)

In the verses following the above passage, Jesus tells the crowd in no uncertain terms they must give up everything to be his disciple. Talk about a steep price!

Everything of value has a cost, and someone has to pay it. As they say, there is no free lunch. "They" being the cold-hearted cafeteria ladies from Slovakia who won't cut a hungry guy some slack. But I digress.

How do we determine the value, or worth, of a thing? That becomes a personal question. What I find valuable might differ greatly from your own values.

What may seem like an inconsequential amount of money to a millionaire may be a fortune to someone in poverty. One person might throw away a bottle of water, but that same bottle could mean life to someone stranded in the desert. A birthday present might be no big deal to a child who often receives gifts, but it could mean the world to a kid who has never been given one before.

Value is based on what we determine important. Put another way:

**How much you value something is determined
by what you're willing to pay for it.**

Consider the personal cost of creativity. What are you willing to give up to be creative?

Sacrifice is a word we don't use as often these days, perhaps because it's an uncomfortable word that generates images of some poor sap being offered to the gods atop a great Mayan temple. Indiana Jones sort of stuff.

We're not talking about that kind of sacrifice, mainly because the one being sacrificed is not a willing participant. Personal sacrifices, however, involve willingness, even if a reluctant one. Personal sacrifice is just as necessary today as it has ever been.

You've likely heard the phrase "You have to spend money to get money." That's investment in a nutshell. Oh, you're allergic to nuts? How about an eggshell? You're vegan (and you didn't even tell me)? A bombshell then? Of course, you're a pacifist. Fine then: a candy shell. Most people like candy. You like candy, right?

Where was I? Right, investment. The same is true of creativity—we should invest in it if we want to reap the benefits, to further develop our creative abilities. We have to give something up to get something in return. It's a sacrifice, but not a pointless one.

If you've come this far, my hope is that you have begun to see the incredible value of creativity in your life.

Creativity is worth investing in. It is worth the sacrifice.

Just as with money, if you bury it in the ground, you won't make any more, no matter how much you have. If you don't practice creativity, you will stagnate, and your creative drive will wither away. You will risk nothing and gain nothing.

So what is the sacrifice creativity demands? We've already talked about facing down personal fears. That in itself is a sacrifice because fear bids us to hold on desperately to the things we don't want to lose. To face your fear is to be willing to let go of those things to pursue something better.

With every step we take in pursuit of the creative, we leave something behind. The cost may be valued resources like time, money, and energy. It could be some things we enjoy, such as comfort or entertainment. You may need to surrender a finely crafted image and instead expose your true self. The creative pursuit might even demand we give up our deeply held visions of fortune, fame, and power.

However, as with any good investment, what you sow into creativity, you will later reap, but at an increased return.

What you give up now, you'll get more and better later on.

Why is sacrifice worth it? Because in the end it makes you stronger— not just a stronger creative, but a stronger person. When you willingly give up those things you don't need, you make room for the ones that matter most. By necessity, you become more free.

This will mean something different to every person. Only you, and hopefully those closest to you, know what is holding you back, what must be relinquished before you can take the next step. This may look like something big (a relationship, a reputation, a house, a mindset, a career) or something seemingly small (a chocolate bar, a game, a favorite hangout, a t-shirt, a word you often say). If it has a hold on you, if you fear letting it go, if it keeps you from being and living the way you know you should, if it hinders your creative output, then it's a prime candidate for sacrifice.

The more free you are, the greater your creative capacity.

Even when the benefits are obvious, that doesn't mean sacrifice is easy. It can leave you feeling empty for a time. It may just break you. But brokenness can be the first step to wholeness. Sometimes lives are like a damaged bone that has grown back incorrectly, it must be broken and reset before it can be restored. That's painful.

And this isn't a one-time thing either. I hate to break it to you, but sacrifice is a lifelong process. There will always be something, whether big or little, old or new, that you'll need to say sayonara to. It could be something that was just fine yesterday but has now spoiled, stinks to high heaven, and is fit only for the trash heap.

Surrender hurts, but you don't have to go it alone. There's no shame in getting help and asking for accountability. Doctors and healers come in all shapes and sizes. The difficulty of giving up is made easier when done with a friend. If you've ever fasted, you know it's easier to do when someone else is feeling your pain rather than just you at the table while everyone else partakes of a meal.

Maybe you need a grieving buddy. I have a friend and life coach who gives talks about the importance of grieving what we've lost, even if it wasn't good for us, even if it kept us from the unlived life. Grieving our loss is an important step in letting go, it comes before rebuilding. An old, decrepit house must be cleared to the foundation (sometimes even that must go) before a new one can be built. Grieving is a recognition of transition, of struggle, of a departure from the familiar.

Can you think of someone to assist you with this—a good listener who can help you shoulder the burden of loss? Then you've found a treasure. Can you be that sort of person to someone else? That's twice the reward. Helping others is itself a sacrifice, but as you guide another on the path of creative freedom, you walk the same road.

Yes, sacrifice is necessary, but it should be made within a community. And just because you can give something up doesn't mean you should. Not every creative pursuit is worth the cost. This is why it must be considered before you begin. Don't just think about what you have to lose or gain, but also how your actions will affect others.

Some sacrifices may actually prevent you, or others, from being creative in the future. Cashing in your retirement funds, giving up unhealthy amounts of sleep, and cutting off all friendships so you can build a three-story bird sanctuary in your back yard might not be the wisest decision, but only you can make that call.

The right kind of sacrifices can hurt—very much so—but they're worth it because they yield better results. They lead to more opportunities for yourself and others.

Sacrifices do not need to be senseless.

Beneficial sacrifice happens when you lay aside an immediate pleasure today for a lasting one tomorrow.

When considering the cost, there is a level of necessary risk required. Not everything will work out the way you hope, and some benefits are more difficult to measure than others, and yet, some of the immeasurable ones have the greatest personal value. It's hard to determine the exact results of an improved relationship or a stress-free workplace, but they're clearly a change for the better.

There is nothing wrong with calculated risks. At some point, it becomes unwise to invest any further in something that has not produced any positive results. Pouring water into a pit in hopes something will one day float to the top becomes worse than pointless when you realize how thirsty you've become. Take a drink and then go water a garden.

Develop patterns that allow you to be the most creative you can be, while also living a healthy life. It's all connected: creativity can improve the way you eat, sleep, work, play, think, get along with others, etc. In turn, the attention you give each of those will have a direct impact on your creative levels—they can lead to inspiration and a greater capacity for creativity.

Here are a few questions to consider when you're weighing the cost of a creative undertaking:

- How much (time, money, attention, etc.) am I willing to spend to see this through?
- At what point will I know I've spent as much as I can afford and I need to invest in something else?
- Are the potential benefits greater than what I'm giving up?
- Is this something I actually care about? Am I taking this on for good reasons?
- What personal goal does this fulfill?

- How will I know when I've either reached completion or failed?
- Even if I do not achieve the desired results, is the potential benefit worth the risk?

Willing sacrifice means estimating your wants versus your needs and choosing the latter. It is giving up the things you can do without to gain the things you can't. It is a denial of self. It is dying to self.

Death? Wait. I thought we weren't talking about that kind of sacrifice! Ah, but remember the difference: willing versus unwilling. You must be willing to die—in a manner.

Yes, the final turning point in the hero's journey is death and rebirth. True, in stories it is often a metaphoric one, but it is a drastic change nonetheless.

After all, death is the ultimate sacrifice.

**Only when you reach the end of yourself,
when you've given it all, do you become something else.**

Rebirth requires you to put to death the old ways, the old habits, the old desires, and instead take up the new life of the creative—a life of change, of newness. This is your breakthrough moment, your transformation.

While the initial act of surrender will be the most powerful, it won't be the only time. The hero's journey is completed in a single cycle. The creative journey goes on and on. Endless.

You will have to continually die to yourself in order to live creatively. There's no way around it.

Every creative act is, in one way or another, a rebirth—a bringing forth of something new after the passing of something old. It is a process that can be painful but is ultimately freeing. It is a worthy sacrifice.

To follow the journey of the creative, one must learn the balance of life and death, of putting things to rest so others may spring forth. Even on a cellular level, you are undergoing this process. Your cells are constantly dying as new ones are being made in their place. Every day, you are a new person.

When you are willing to bury the old and make space for the new, you change on the inside. In turn, this gives you the power to change the things on the outside. It is a painful but necessary process. The death of a seed makes way for a forest.

Like marriage, the creative pursuit should be a lifelong commitment. You never get to the point where you're a good enough spouse and you don't have to try anymore. There is always some new thing to learn, some new way to grow, to better yourself and discover more about the person you pledged your life and love to.

There is always room for change. And that's a good thing. It keeps life interesting. It gives you a goal to strive for.

Facing our fears and living sacrificially will lead to the most difficult challenges we'll ever have to take on, but they are part of our change arc—they are what make us the creative heroes we were meant to be. They are what lead us to the climax—the moment of triumph.

Fear is a dead tree riddled with hopelessness, cynicism, and self-doubt. Be a sapling, reaching up with courage and bravery and faith. Fear gets a lot of attention—way more than it deserves. It's not surprising because fear is never content on the fringes; it always demands center stage.

~Maria Goff, *Love Lives Here*

SECTION 10 REVIEW

Here's what we covered, mainly and plainly:

- Fear is both the enemy and counterpart of the creative.
- Fear is a natural response to keep us safe, but becomes dangerous when it holds us back, when it keeps us from change and trying new things.
- Overcoming fear can be done through little steps. It's not always a grand showdown.
- You will face many fears on the creative journey, but they act as signposts, pointing you toward the next step.
- Consider the cost of creativity. What are you willing to give up for it?
- The right kind of sacrifice leads to more freedom.
- The denial of self, or self-death, leads to creative rebirth.
- Slovakian Cafeteria could be a great name for a military operation or a jazz group. Also, if you can sweet-talk those lunch ladies into dishing out some extra schnitzel, it's more than worth it. As "they" say, a little extra schnitzel goes a long way.

Interview with a Creative

CATHERINE COLELLA

Tell us about yourself.

I am a junior high English language arts and yearbook teacher, along with orchestrating the associated student body (ASB). My job is to not only educate middle schoolers in the ways of sentences, grammar, spelling, and reading comprehension, but also in the ways of being an individual who strives to be the best at whatever they want to do or be. All of this imparting of knowledge takes place in the economically challenged high desert of Southern California, where classroom resources are as scarce as the water, the budgets are slim, but the locals always make do with what they've got!

When do you find it easiest to be creative?

There are two types of creativity for me. The first is what I would call *recreational creativity*. I find it easiest to be recreationally creative when all of my "adulting" is done and out of the way. This allows my entire brain and self to focus on a fun project.

The second type is *occupational creativity*. I find it easiest to be occupationally creative when there is a time crunch and limited resources. Working under pressure normally brings out the best in my educational abilities, whether it is limited time or a limit in physical or monetary resources. Once I see what I have to work with, I can mentally form the shape of my completed project before I begin, creating logical steps along the way.

Where do you look for inspiration?

One of the places I go to brainstorm is Pinterest. I use it to help me visualize what exactly I do or don't want to make. If I need a tutorial on how to make or do something specific (i.e., a recipe, a classroom strategy, or how to clean a carburetor), I generally turn to YouTube. As a visual learner, these two online tools are a great help. I will say, though—nothing really beats the old standbys: art galleries, novels, picture books, a favorite music album, nature, and paramount to all: necessity! The mother of invention.

What forms of creativity do you most appreciate or enjoy?

When I was younger, being creative meant that I could draw a picture or paint a painting. As I grew older, this art form was replaced by writing poetry, short stories, or just getting the words out of my head and onto paper. I currently find that I use my words and visual knack for imparting my love for words to junior high school students. When I really need a break from academia, I'll normally saunter into my garage and paw through the wood and metal scrap piles. I'll then jigsaw a side table or another useful object out of the scraps of whatever is lying around. Making something useful and beautiful out of what other people might consider trash is extremely satisfying to me. As an earth-conscious person, I also try to use what I already have at hand, only buying new materials when I must.

When has a creative approach helped you accomplish something impactful?

I revel in the challenge of getting a twelve-year old who thinks that they don't need to know how to write to morph into a kid who is excited to complete their first personal narrative essay. You could call it "lesson planning," but I feel that what I do is more about finding creative ways to get kids to engage in learning something new. One of the most difficult forms of writing for young students is argumentative writing. Don't get me wrong—they love to argue. But it is teaching them to back up their arguments with facts, statistics, and quotes that is the difficult part. I was teaching seventh grade argumentative writing during my first year of teaching. My students were mostly minorities from big cities, who had been transplanted into a hot and barren Barstow. They had a hard time relating to my small-town, white-privileged upbringing. After plenty of researching the internet, reading a few biographies, and digging through audio archives, I eventually found an argumentative topic that my students latched on to wholeheartedly: Who was the better orator—Martin Luther King Jr. or Malcolm X? I had them read and listen to two of their most famous speeches: "I Have a Dream" and "The Ballot or The Bullet." The students had to find figurative language and rhetorical devices in both speeches and then discuss which orator left a greater impact on the civil rights movement. They loved it! And they learned from it! And all because there was a small difference between us.

What is one practice you would recommend to help someone be more creative?

I highly recommend observing people who show determination and grit. Those are the people who will always find the creative edge to cut through a problem. By watching how others have handled problems or obstacles, you'll pick up a trick or two. Hell, if you're lucky, that person might ask for your advice on something, and then the creative juices can really start to flow!

Where can people find you or your work?

Follow me on Instagram @catherinejcolella or check out my classroom blog: www.colellanotes.blogspot.com

Section 11 - Confidence

Cave

Leaving the throne room behind, you take one reluctant step after another deeper into the cave. The soft crunch of your feet in the dirt is barely audible over the sound of your heart pounding; *thump-thud, thump-thud, thump-thud.*

A dim flicker up ahead is your only light. It casts long, twisted shadows along the rocky cavern walls—unfamiliar beasts writhing in some mad dance.

Everything inside you wants to turn back, but you know you must go on. The cavern seems to stretch on and on without end.

At last, you round a corner and come to a great arched stone doorway built into the wall of the cave. The doorway is up on a platform with two lit braziers beside it. The blazing fires are so intense, you begin to sweat as you approach.

There are remnants of what used to be a set of wooden doors, now smashed to pieces on the ground. Perhaps some of that wood is being used to fuel the fires.

Intricate designs decorate the braziers and doorway. Their overall pattern reminds you of tightly woven vines, but their shape and variation also resemble a written language. An image has also been carved into the platform, just in front of the doorway—the menacing head of a dragon. This one does not match the skilled artistry carved on the rest of the doorway, but is crudely rendered, as if it had been hurriedly scratched into the platform with a sharp rock.

You step up onto a smooth stone platform. A deep darkness awaits beyond the arched stone doorway.

After one long, slow breath, you walk beyond the door, glad at least to move away from the fire's heat. You hear nothing except your own breath and footfalls as you step forward, waiting for your eyes to adjust to the dark. Though you strain to look ahead, you can make out little of the vast cavern in front of you. Then you hear a deep rattle: the breath of something large.

You dare another step and a gust of wind blows past you, nearly knocking you over. The fires behind you extinguish. The chilly darkness envelopes you entirely. It awaits your next move.

This is the part where we must break from the story. Remember, this is your story, not mine.

You are the Endless Creative, and you alone can choose whether or not to let fear defeat you. Only you have the intimate knowledge of your inner fears, the ones that keep you up at night and prevent you from moving forward. You alone know what it means to face them, to call them out, to move beyond them, to embrace change and the life of the creative you were born to lead.

I could cover in great detail your battle with the Shadow Dragon—how awful a thing it is, the lies it taunts you with; how you are almost defeated by it and nearly give up entirely; how it offers you an escape and promises to give you everything you've ever wanted if only you will serve it. It is a tempting offer, and you understand why others have accepted it.

I could do this, but no matter how terrible I make the cave of fear and the dragon within sound, it will only be a mockery compared to the real thing you know all too well. In the end, everyone must enter the cave and face their dragon.

Only you know what it means to follow your dreams and what stands in the way.

Remember this: to face your fear, to triumph over it, is not to eliminate it but to move on in spite of it, to continue walking in the dark while fear still whispers in your ears, tempting you to turn back and run to safety.

You've discovered the true path—the one that does not lead around but through your obstacles. Others can help, but only you can choose to take that path. All that's left is to press on.

In this particular story and, I pray, in your own life, you reject the dragon's lies. You walk on through the dark despite everything telling you to run away or bow down in submission.

It is not easy. The darkness presses in around you, so heavy it feels as if you are moving underwater. At times you feel suffocated by it, fighting for every breath.

With each difficult step taken, you realize your journey has prepared you for this confrontation. The lessons you've learned (even the failures) and the people you've met have given you the confidence to keep going when all seems lost and hopeless.

Somehow, in a way that is not entirely clear, you feel the strength to continue. It is a nearly tangible thing that rises up from a power that is both within and around you.

You learn this about the dragon: he cannot touch you. Yes, he may mislead you, may remind you of all your failures and the things you hate about yourself. His fire may be hot, his smoke blinding. The wind from his mighty wings may buffet you on every side. But in the end he is just a shadow.

The dragon cannot stop you from moving. He may make you fail over and over, but he can't make you quit. That is entirely up to you.

You realize the dragon, though awful, has no more power than your imagination allows. That thought weakens him.

You take another step, groping in the dark but still finding nothing.

Another step. Then another. You hear a different voice, not at all like the whispers of fear. At first it's just a sound, but then you understand the words, a single phrase repeated over and over: "Be not afraid."

It is soft and gentle at first. Fear tries to drown it out, but with each step you take, it grows louder and louder until it becomes a shout. Now you are shouting, "I am not afraid."

At last you see something at the far end of the cavern—a thin stream of light piercing through the rock walls. Your hand finds the cave wall, and you follow along it toward the light.

Something inside your pocket bumps against your leg. When you reach inside, you find one of Timble's explosive devices. She must have slipped it in when you were climbing up the mountain. Good thing it didn't go off on its own!

You've reached the crack in the rock where light streams through. Recalling how Timble had used them in the marsh and the throne room, you compress the button on your own device, shove it into the fissure of light, and run like you've just planted a bomb (because, well, you have).

The explosion shakes the whole cavern, and you are nearly blinded, not by the blast but instead by the sunlight that now pours in. The hole is now big enough to walk through.

In the light of the day, you can see the cavern wasn't nearly so large as it felt. You see the Shadow Dragon clearly now. While he is still frightening, he's not as terrible as you had imagined. He hisses and howls as the sunlight vaporizes his dark scales. He is injured, but not defeated. And now he's mad. He flaps his wings, and a gust of wind knocks you on your back.

Those wings, you think, what would he do without their strength? They turn into kites. The dragon continues to flap, but without effect.

The dragon rears back and takes in a deep breath, ready to roast you in flame. You wonder if instead of fire he breathed something more…fun.

The dragon thrusts his head forward and opens his mouth…confetti bursts out. The dragon gasps in confusion. His scales fall away and reveal the skin underneath, made of brightly colored papier-mâché.

You can't help but laugh at him now. As you laugh, the dragon shrinks. Before long, he is small and pathetic, hardly bigger than a cat. Soon, he's a tiny lizard.

The dragon squeaks angrily and scampers off into a little crack. Now seeing it for what it really is, you wonder how you could have been afraid of that thing in the first place.

The dragon is defeated, and you have no reason to stay in his home any longer. You climb out of the darkness of the cave into the blessed light, victorious. But it's not the end—not just yet.

Valor grows by daring, fear by holding back.

~Publilius Syrus

CHAPTER 32

Change Arc

The time has come. Time to celebrate, that is.

This is your climactic moment: you've won the battle, saved the princess or prince, defeated the dragon, nabbed the treasure, and—most importantly—embraced the truth in a big ol' never-let-go bear hug. You've won.

In story terms, the climactic moment is reached when the protagonist's goal is met, when the central conflict is resolved. There may be some smaller conflicts to face, but the main one, the focus of the story, has reached completion.

In terms of the creative journey, this means you have at last overcome the obstacles, both internal and external, that kept you from living a creative life. They cannot stop you any longer.

Your character change arc has been completed. You have transformed from being one sort of person to another. There will be struggles down the road, but you have embraced the truth, accepted the life of creative freedom you were meant to live.

It's time to throw off the old robes—your old ways of thinking. It's time to step into your new skin, to run free, unashamedly showing the world what you're made of. Okay, okay, let's not get out of hand here. There are some regulations—indecent exposure not the least of them. You can't just do anything, can you?

**When you discover the power of creativity,
you become unstoppable.**

At the least, you won't stop you. Those old fetters are gone—whether your situations, the views of others, or your own views. You are a creative, and you can be creative anytime and anywhere. If you believe it, if you practice it, you are on the journey. You are a creative.

Does this mean you'll never face another obstacle again? Do you get to walk off happily ever after into the blissful sunset of unending success? Not quite.

There will always be new challenges, from without and within. Failures will always come before successes. But now you know the truth, your truth.

Creativity is and always will be a valuable tool at your side, ready to lead you to and through the most uncomfortable undertakings.

Yes, it's an ongoing process, but a good one. In one sense, you'll never arrive. In another, you're always arriving—and moving on. You're always progressing, always moving forward one creative step at a time, even when you're failing.

But wait. Are we placing the wagon before the wheels here? Have you truly and finally begun the exciting adventure of the creative life, or is there yet something in your way?

Our own opinion of ourselves is often the most biased and untrustworthy. How can you be sure that you've really gotten started? Here are a few questions to help determine if you're on the right track:

- Do you make time to practice daily creativity?
- When faced with a problem, what is your reaction? Is your first thought: "I can't do this / I can't handle this" or "What can I do about this?"
- Do you have an attitude of curiosity and learning?
- Are you constantly on the lookout for creativity around you?
- Do you spend more time consuming or creating?
- Do you challenge yourself by doing the uncomfortable, even frightening things to reach your dreams?
- Does your work bring value to the people and world around you?

Whether you notice it or not, you are changing.

**For good or ill, your every action determines
what sort of change is taking place in you.**

If you set your course beforehand and continue to make corrections toward your goals, you will reach the destinations of your choosing. I say destinations because there will always be somewhere new to go, and your imagination can take you there.

Each new journey can lead to another: bigger, better, and greater than the one before. Each project, job, friendship, experience, and stage of life can help you grow and improve, if you allow it.

The temptation after every great victory is to settle down in your plush recliner, build a nice little fortress of the familiar, and hit the snooze button on life. Friends, that's as sure a way as any to stop living.

There's nothing wrong with a breather, but you've still got places to go and new ways to grow. After all, you've still got a lot to learn.

CHAPTER 33

Learn

A good friend of mine, Lonny, has a phrase he likes to repeat often:

Always be teachable.

These are good words to live by. Here's another, often refuted phrase I'll bet you've heard before: "You can't teach an old dog new tricks."

Regardless of how easy it is for aged canines to learn, there is some truth to this: the older a person becomes, the harder it is for them to learn new things.

Part of the reason for this is simply biological. The mind just isn't what it used to be—the older it grows, the less processing speed and storage capacity it retains. It's an unfortunate part of life we will all deal with if we live long enough.

But there is another component to this: older people tend to get set in their ways. They've formed ideas and opinions that, like concrete, become more solid and unchangeable the longer they sit undisturbed.

While it may be more challenging to learn the older you become, it is far from impossible. So if you want to keep learning, you have to stay teachable. It's an attitude you must cultivate today so you'll continue learning tomorrow.

It sounds simple enough, and in many ways it is. Strangely enough, one barrier to remaining teachable comes from learning. When we learn a lot, we can become proud. We don't like to admit that there is still much we don't know.

Eventually, we can get to a point where we think we know everything there is to know about a subject. The result? We form incorrect views, ones that become difficult to correct later on.

And why do we need to keep learning? Change, of course.

New and better practices are constantly being discovered. New studies reveal inefficiency in old methods.

Be it foreign aid, dieting, clothes washing, fishing, or programming—we've made significant improvements in all these areas over the past decade. Even the information and technology from just ten years ago in these areas has become outdated.

I recently read a book about how, because of the changes in our culture and past flaws we've previously ignored, the old styles of parenting are not as effective on youth today and thus we need to learn and adopt new methods. On a personal level, we suffer when we don't accept change and aren't open to learning from (or even making) new discoveries. What's worse, society at large suffers.

I would like to supplement Lonny's phrase with another:

Keep learning.

If you hold these two in balance—be teachable and keep learning—you will not lack creative growth in your life. If you want your creative knowledge to grow by boundless leaps, adopt a humble attitude that allows you to recognize an opportunity to learn from any person and any situation.

Even when you're around people you dislike or in unfavorable circumstances, there is a lesson to be learned—if nothing more than an example of what not to do or how to avoid such things in the future.

But learning is more than just the intake of information. There is a point at which we go beyond our capacity to take in useful information. Even a vacuum cleaner has to get emptied from time to time before it just sucks at sucking.

This is one of our great challenges today, in the age of mass information. Information overload is a very real thing. It's overwhelming and quickly becomes stress inducing.

In a nod to *The Rime of the Ancient Mariner*, we drown in a different sort of ocean where there is

Info, info, everywhere,
Yet no one stops to think.

I had a neighbor who had a very serious hoarding problem. Her car was completely packed with trash, with just enough space for her to sit and look out the front and side windows. The few times she opened her garage, all I could see was a wall of trash. I'd never entered her house, but I'd heard it was made of narrow walkways between heaping trash piles.

It got so bad, she was ordered by the city to clean it up or the place would be condemned. Soon after, some neighbors and I pitched in to help clean her yard. Even the news showed up to the event—not that they helped much.

One of our neighbors, a kind gentleman, spent much time consoling her through the process. The whole time, she sat there bawling. While we tossed out moldy newspapers, broken dishware, and tattered clothes, she pleaded with us not to throw it into the dumpster—attempting to convince us how each and every one of those items was of great value. And this woman owned an apartment complex—she was not wanting for money.

It was hard to watch, harder even to be part of it.

We know how to collect heaps of information, but how valuable is it really? Unless we make some use of it, not very.

Information without application quickly becomes garbage.

Part of becoming teachable is learning how to be a good learner—odd as that sounds.

Derek Doepker, who I've mentioned before, breaks learning down into two categories: passive and experimental. Passive learning is more along the lines of research—reading a book like this one, for example.

Experimental learning is learning through doing. Depending on the subject, you may need to do more of one type than another, but both are essential.

If you don't study, you won't know where to start, or you'll end up learning things the hard way. There are centuries of knowledge on any given subject at your disposal. Why not use it or at least spend some time with an expert?

Once you've had your beak in a book for a while, set it down and go put your knowledge to use. What good is a library of knowledge if you don't put it to practice?

The ability to learn requires both attitude and action. Take time to study well, be open to new thoughts and ideas, then go out and put your new discoveries to the test.

Did I mention there's a special reward for all your learning and trying, besides just getting better at something? You also get better at getting better. You gain confidence

CHAPTER 34

Confidence

If there were a magic pill to make you feel confident every time you set out to do something new, would you take it? I probably would, provided it had no negative side effects (like it made you really gassy or something).

As far as I know, no such pill exists, or at least it isn't yet legal. Although, if you already are gassy, there are some non-magical pills that could help you. That aside, how do we gain the confidence we need to begin?

Confidence is the second component in the creative pursuit and goes hand in hand with the climactic moment. When the hero at last overcomes whatever foe stood in their way, they not only do so with confidence, but they also gain confidence through their moment of triumph.

Confidence builds on itself—the more you have, the more you gain.

To begin, recognize the reasons you already have for confidence. Look back at what you've already done. It's no magic pill, but it'll do the trick.

When you take a moment to recount all your past accomplishments, you'll gain confidence. Every little success is a cause for recognition and celebration. It is a climactic victory, even if it's a very small one.

And don't go telling me you've never accomplished anything. You're reading a book right now, aren't you? It may have happened a while ago, but it took a lot of learning to become literate (unless you're some kind of baby genius). Many people around the world, and even in your own country, are illiterate.

Let me also point out that you're alive right now, so unless you've been coddled and spoon fed your whole life, you've learned how to survive in this world. Chalk those up in your list of confidence boosters, my friend, but don't stop there.

Sometimes, even after you recount all your past successes, you still don't feel any more confident. And that's all right. If I haven't made it clear yet, creativity isn't always easy—it stretches us, makes us uncomfortable, even requires us to do things we're afraid of. Often, you simply have to get started whether you feel confident or not. It's just as important as stepping out even when you're afraid.

This bears repeating: start small, and work your way up. Trying something new, something unfamiliar, doesn't always have to be a struggle. Find someone with knowledge in that area, do some of your own research, or try it with a group of people.

Set yourself up for success, and your confidence will grow.

As you do more, you gain confidence. The next creative endeavor will become a little easier to begin. In a way, creativity is that magic pill. You just don't get to take it until after you've done the first difficult task. But once you have, it gives you an extra strength boost for the next one.

Creative confidence gives you that extra push to get started and motivates you to keep going when you're tempted to stop. It's fuel for momentum.

Here's another way to look at confidence building: think of life as a role-playing game (RPG). Confidence is a stat we all start out very low in—you begin inexperienced and uncertain. Everything is new.

Then as you try new things, your level of confidence increases. Even when you fail, you can build confidence. It may not have turned out the way you planned, but it probably wasn't as bad as you expected. It's worth another attempt.

Much like a game, there are certain tasks you won't attempt until you attain the required level of confidence. You're not going to take a job as a lifeguard if you don't know how to swim, but if you've spent some time in the water, to the point other people are calling you Dolphin or McFinley, that lifeguard position is no sweat for you.

Confidence comes with learning and practice.

If someone asked me to teach a class on astrophysics tomorrow, I'd feel incapable. Even attempting to teach it would lead to sure embarrassment. I imagine that by the end, the class would feel more confused than when they'd started.

Had I a month or two of preparation and read as much as I could on the subject, that's another story. Granted, I wouldn't be the next Neil deGrasse Tyson, but I would have enough confidence to at least expound on some of the basics to the uninitiated. As you study, you naturally gain confidence in the subject—you know what you're talking about.

The best part is, once you become confident in one area, you automatically increase your confidence in other areas. You prove to yourself what you are capable of and realize you can take on new similar tasks with less difficulty. If you've learned how to operate a forklift, learning a backhoe won't seem as hard.

Keep in mind, there are also ways to kill your confidence. If you constantly dwell on what you can't do, you'll never learn, you'll never try, and thus you'll never grow in confidence. You'll be stuck spinning your wheels, like a tractor in a bog.

When you do apply yourself to a subject, you really have no option but to improve—even through failure. It gets better: confidence takes you beyond your areas of expertise. The more you prove to yourself what you are capable of, the more you'll be willing to try something in which you have no related experience.

This doesn't mean that as a skilled computer programmer, you'll automatically be an expert in kung fu (sorry *Matrix* fans), but it does mean you might give it a try. Mastery of one subject produces a willingness to take on another.

What about overconfidence? We've all seen a headstrong person leap blindly into a situation they had no business being in. It's facepalm inducing. It's a train wreck waiting to happen, and as much as train wrecks get viewers, you don't want to be the one driving that train.

This is where we must draw a distinction between confidence and pigheadedness. Confidence comes from looking at your track record and gaining an assurance in your own abilities. It leads to taking risks and discovering new opportunities. Pigheadedness comes when you refuse to learn from past failures or ignore your limitations and instead plow ahead, regardless of the warning signs. It is the opposite of being teachable.

The overconfident never learn—
they are doomed to make the same mistakes again.

Throwing yourself over and over at a cinderblock wall is not a great way to knock it down, but it can give you a solid headache.

A confident and wise person will learn from the experience of failure and make better choices going forward. They will recognize their own limits and act with them in mind.

When it comes to creativity, confidence will push you to stretch your boundaries and discover new and interesting possibilities. It's all part of embracing change.

You may be used to drawing with a pencil on paper, but have you tried painting with ink on canvas? You may be great at giving presentations in the office, but have you tried reading stories to a large group of children, giving different voices to all the characters? You may like going on little hikes around town, but have you tried kayaking a river or rock climbing?

There is always something new you can do with your current talents, some creative twist. They don't all need to be bigger, just different.

Look for opportunities in places similar to areas in which you already have confidence. Take reasonable steps. Just because you've been in the ice skating rink once doesn't mean you're ready for double black-diamond slopes.

When tended to, confidence can become a roaring fire, but even then, you still have to feed and protect it. Life is full of fire extinguishers. When you stop making use of it, your confidence dwindles. Guard your confidence, and it will keep you warm on those cold days. But don't let it get out of control, either. After all, you don't want to burn the place down.

Ultimately, confidence is a choice. The opportunity to take the easy route and play it safe will always be just a siren's call away. You might think giving in just a little here and there is no big deal, but you'd be wrong.

By hardening yourself, refusing to learn or grow, you soon become immovable—a slow but sure process of petrification, cooling off—becoming dead on the inside.

When you allow the inner change arc to take place, when you remain teachable, when you try new things and gain confidence, the fire inside grows. Fire softens metal, shaping it into something more useful. Fire also burns away impurities, making the metal stronger, more durable, and better fit for more demanding tasks.

Never let that creative flame inside you die.

When at last you've reached the climactic moment in your creative journey, your confidence will be stoked and you'll be fired up for the next step. That's a very good thing, because the story isn't over yet—we still need a resolution.

Confidence is not the certainty that you will succeed, confidence is the certainty that you will act.

~Ray Edwards

SECTION 11 REVIEW

What was all that stuff about again?

- When you embrace the true life of the creative, you change from within, but it's a continual process, not a one-time deal.
- Always be teachable and keep learning. You're never too old to learn yourself somethin' new.
- Through study and practice, you can turn information into application.
- Confidence comes from examining past accomplishments and trying new things.
- Overconfidence comes from an unrealistic view about your abilities and an unwillingness to learn. Just because you've walked a slackline between two trees in your backyard doesn't mean you're ready to ride a Harley across a wooden plank over the Niagara Falls while blindfolded. When the outcome of a risk assessment is death, you might want to think twice, or even thrice before making an attempt (you can't learn from a failure that kills you).

Interview with a Creative

JOEL KLING

Tell us about yourself.

I'm a professional dilettante. Professionally, I make videos for people and companies. That keeps the lights on. My other artistic pursuits are seemingly endless. I've directed and produced for film and TV. I've created a clothing line—which is to say, made a string of shirts. I've written and illustrated a children's book. I currently write for film and TV.

When do you find it easiest to be creative?

My mind is always drifting into "creative" territory. For me, it's harder to stay focused on a single task. I do find that when I'm jogging with good music, I am able to solve some creative problems, and new ideas always come to me.

Where do you look for inspiration?

I get really inspired by photography. Photography was an early love for me, which transitioned into film and video. Something about the still images still inspires and allows for my mind to make up a story. Music is also a huge mechanism for inspiration. The emotion packed into a well-crafted song kicks creativity into high gear for me.

What forms of creativity do you most appreciate or enjoy?

Personally, I have a love/hate relationship with writing. I write for TV, and there are times where that is straight-up painful! But when approached with discipline (easier said than done), there is huge satisfaction in completing a work.

In the world, I appreciate virtually all forms of creativity, from culinary experts putting together an amazing dish, to unrecognized genius spray painting their work on boxcars. Again, photography is a real joy for me.

When has a creative approach helped you accomplish something impactful?
I guess I don't distinguish "creative" versus "not creative." Does this make sense? I think if one is approaching a problem, or trying to accomplish something impactful, all thoughts toward that goal are creative.

What is one practice you would recommend to help someone be more creative?
Creativity doesn't always look creative. Most of the time it looks and feels like work. And it should. I've read in countless books that discipline is ninety-nine percent of it. A practice I would recommend (but don't always do myself) is to sit and do the work. Even if you don't feel like it. Trust me—the juices will start flowing. If they don't, put on your headphones, crank some tunes, and go for a run.

Where can people find you or your work online?
https://vimeo.com/album/1863511
www.Klingcreative.com
https://www.tumblr.com/blog/otisnotices

Section 12 - Consistency

Mountain

You step out from the dark cave into the warmth of the sun—tired, dirty, and bruised, but very much alive.

The sound of a bird chirping merrily fills your ears. You inhale as a fresh breeze passes over you, a welcome relief from the stale air of the chilly cave. The gentle wind carries the wholly pleasant smell of home cooking.

You look around and learn you are at the edge of a quaint village, the mountain's peak just beyond. On the peak sits a thin silver structure gleaming in the light of the morning sun—not quite a building, but something you recall from a vision.

As the birds continue their song, you realize one of them sounds peculiar. It seems to be belting out an avian rendition of "She'll Be Coming 'Round the Mountain" but off-key. With a flourish, I step out from behind a rock pile, remove my hat and bow low.

All traces of my former illness have vanished. "You made it! I mean, I knew you would." When I rise again and don my hat, a broad smile crosses my face. "I've brought someone."

Timble also moves out from behind the rocks, along with three others like her.

You worry this may be some sort of trap, but she runs up and gives you a tight hug around the leg. "I'm sorry, so sorry..." She can barely speak. Tears stream down her face. "Thank you," she says at last, staring so deep into your eyes that it gets a little uncomfortable.

As you examine Timble up close, you see she has all but shed her former appearance. Her horns are gone, as well as her slimy complexion. Her skin has taken on a silvery quality, and though still short, she is sleek and beautiful. The gold ring remains in her nose, but it looks more like jewelry than a mark of slavery.

"Welcome to Peak Town," I say, making a broad gesture with my arms. "We'll venture farther up soon, but I imagine you'd like to pause for refreshments. The folks here are uniquely hospitable."

As we make our way through the village, the residents—other creatures like Timble—stop what they are doing and turn to bow their heads toward you in what appears to be reverence.

"Word's gotten out about what you've done. I reckon all of Peak Town is mighty grateful for your service." I wave to some of the residents, then turn to you with a wink. "Now don't let it get to your head."

We enter a cozy house in which we must duck to get inside and, once in, can barely stand up straight. A delicious feast lies before us: roasted meats, steamed breads, sweet jellies, the freshest produce you've yet seen, and an assortment of chocolates—at least seven platefuls.

You are presented with a new outfit (your current attire is tattered and covered in ash). It has earthy tones and stitching that resembles the patterns you've seen on the old stone ruins. After changing in another room, you discover the garments not only fit you perfectly, but feel as smooth as silk.

At last we all sit around the large table to eat and converse. Only then do you realize just how famished you had become. That aside, it is the most delicious meal you have ever tasted, even though some of the flavors are foreign to you.

I stand up to speak and bump my head, then wince and sit back down again. "I imagine you have more than a few questions. You may be surprised to hear it has been three days since I last saw you. We were all worried, Timble especially. She returned to the throne room with help from her village. They carried me here, where I was given some much-needed nourishment and medical attention. A fear infection like mine is serious, but not untreatable, especially in good company. In fact, Timble here wouldn't leave my side until I had fully healed. A true friend that one is."

Timble's cheeks flush a light green.

"Speaking of company," I continue, "it turns out Timble and her kindred are the Dwelfin—the great builders of legend."

The other Dwelfin appear to be in a similar process of transformation as Timble. They are all roughly knee high, but otherwise vary widely in skin tone and stature. Some are bright colored, some darker, some limber, and some muscular or round. Each seems unique and interesting in their own way, but you would not consider any of them ugly.

"These people have long been under the dragon's control," I continue, "but now, at last, are freed. All thanks to you." I tip my hat, and the Dwelfin erupt in cheers and applause.

"You have all but reversed the curse upon them, and as you see, they are very grateful. I know they are eager to help you, as they have me. Speaking of which, remember those tentacles I'd developed? Turns out they were something of a problem, but look what they did." I raise my hands, and two mechanical appendages sprout from behind my shoulders. One grabs a mug and lifts it to my mouth. The other snatches a plate, flips it in the air, catches it, then spins it on the table. "Not bad, huh?"

A pair of Dwelfin laugh and pat one another on the back.

"They are very talented, these people, but they need someone with an imagination. And a good heart, one that won't lead them astray." I glance at my empty wrist, "I think it's time we head on up, to the top!" I stand dramatically, and this time my head breaks straight through the ceiling. The Dwelfin nearly lose themselves in laughter, which is music to your ears.

We leave the village and the other Dwelfin behind. Only Timble joins us on the short trail up to the peak. It is a clear day, and that blanket of cloud that once hung over the mountain has dissipated, allowing for a stunning view of the world below.

We pause just before the top, and I turn to lay a hand on your shoulder. "I have to apologize again for the way I've behaved. I may be a guide, but I'm far from perfect. No one is immune to fear's poison. I realize that now. It's a strong drink, but it goes down much too easy. I thought I had the better of it, but I was wrong."

I sniff the air and stare out on the vast lands below us. "There are a lot of folks out there who still need our help."

We turn and continue toward a wide, round tower that looks like it was carved from the mountain itself. "Do you know where we are?" I ask. "Yes, I told you this was Mount Dread, but it is really Mount Triumph. Perhaps it is both."

I pause when we reach the tower. A set of stairs wraps around it, leading to the top. "I wish I could tell you the dragon was gone, that everything is made right again, but he will return. I even caught a glimpse of him scurrying among the rocks as we left town. He may be small and pathetic now, but he's a sneaky devil."

I continue to talk as we ascend the stairs. "You will discover many other beasts of great power besides him. Pride, Greed, Hate, to name a few. There will always be a battle, as long as you draw breath, but your creativity remains one of your strongest weapons. Never forget that. Never forget where you have come from. Never forget who you are. Anyways, I've yammered on long enough. We're here at last."

The top of the tower is a wide, paved surface—a launchpad. In its center stands a silver rocket, dazzling in the sunlight. In some ways, it reminds you of Timble. You ask her if she built it, and she nods, "But not alone."

"Real beauty, ain't she?" I marvel. "Her name is Possibility."

We admire it for a moment, then you turn to ask what you're supposed to do.

"Well, now there's only one thing left to do. Fly!"

You stare up at the rocket in silence. Can you really fly such a marvelous vehicle?

I pat your back. "Oh, don't worry. Timble knows how to pilot the craft. I imagine she'll show you. But you alone can provide the fuel: imagination. Where will you go? That's for you to decide, but might I suggest the good people of Plateau Town could use your aid. It'll be under Black Coat control by now. Their master may be gone, but it doesn't mean they won't give you trouble. And if anyone can figure out how to end the stone curse—even reverse it—I know it's you. Heck, you might even convince a Black Coat or two to help, who knows. They say the sky's the limit, but with Possibility, I doubt it's true."

Timble runs ahead and scampers up a ladder leaned against the rocket. You follow behind but stop at the first rung when you realize I haven't moved.

"I'm sorry. I just—shoot, I hate this part. You see, I'm not coming with. No, it's not that I don't like ya or anything. Truth is, well, there's something else I didn't mention. You're an Endless Creative, sure enough, but you aren't the only one. Now I'm off to find the others, to help them on the journey. I've been thinking the forest might be a good place to find new recruits. The Dwelfin are even working on a new createamobile for me. You understand, don't you? I knew you would."

You hear me sniffle. "Hey, let's don't cry now. Like as not, we'll cross paths again. So long, my friend, and thanks for everything. Heaven knows I couldn't have done it without you."

You offer a warm goodbye, then climb inside the rocket. The door glides shut behind you with a *whiz*. Outside a port window you see me wiping my eyes, probably just some dust kicked up by the engines.

I lift my hat off with one of my new robotic arms and bow with a flourish.

You lean back in your seat and the hologram of a map appears, hovering in front of you. This time, all the locations and their labels are filled in. As you examine it, you realize the map shows more than what each place currently is. It has an overlay—a glimpse of what could be. Or are you the one doing that?

The engines roar to life, and you fall back into your chair as the ship lifts from the ground.

Timble places a hand on your armrest, wide eyed and more than a little excited. "Where to, Captain?"

You are a novelist, and the story you are inventing, with its rich plot and imaginative palette of distinct and believable characters, is your life.

~Jeff Olson, *The Slight Edge*

CHAPTER 35

Resolution

As the fictional story comes to a close, your story is just getting started. You have the tools and the know-how to approach anything with a creative mindset, to apply a creative process as you work, to pursue creativity as a lifelong commitment. There are just a few things left I'd like to leave you with before we part ways: one final aspect of the pursuit and, at last, what it means to be an endless creative.

The resolution or dénouement of a story exists to ease readers out of the climactic tension and to let them enjoy the payoff—the emotional reward—that follows everything they and the protagonist endured. Though they have read about someone else, each reader takes on the story as part of their own.

Isn't that part of why we love stories so much? They take us to new places, let us do things outside our normal experiences, allow us to see through the eyes of another.

In some small way, we become the characters we read about.

So it is with creativity: as you share your creative endeavors with the world, your work becomes part of someone else's life—it shapes them. It's powerful stuff.

One way or another, every novel comes to an end. Not every tale ends happily, but every ending ought to be a satisfying one, a closure that makes sense in the context of the story. Characters reap the rewards of their actions, and readers are left to muse over the results, to consider each character's successes and failures in light of their own lives.

In the hero's journey, the resolution is the return home, a circle back to where the hero first got started. It's a great way to show who they have become compared to the person they were when they first set foot outside the door of their own normal world.

As part of your creative journey, you will return again to familiar places and familiar faces, but you will be different—you will have something new and spectacular to share. You will, with your newly acquired creative powers, be a force for change in the world you once knew.

To be a creative does not necessarily mean leaving the world you are in, but instead seeing the world you are in with new eyes—to see the world as it is, not as it seems—a world full of possibility. Not a dead-end but a doorway, a life of wonder and possibility instead of fear and failure.

I hope that gets you stirred up like a batch of slow-cooked chili. Now, before we get too saucy, there are a few things to keep in mind about resolutions and the creative pursuit—the sour cream to your spice, if you will.

First, there is an end result, a final state, to which the creative pursuit leads.

Every road you take leads somewhere.

If you follow the creative path, it will lead to newness and change, both for you and the world around you. However, to reach such a result requires resolve—a dead-set purpose. Only those who are resolute reach the resolution they seek.

Next, though every story resolves in one way or another, it also leads to something else: a continuation. The completion of a creative task or project will lead to the opportunity for another. Even your own life will impact innumerable others', based on how you live it. It's the circle of life, baby.

Last, not every story ends well. There is a very real danger you may stray from the path and end up somewhere other than where you first were headed. You may actually be in hot pursuit of a negative outcome.

Look at the lives marked by poor decision after poor decision and where they lead. Do you think those people intended to end in such a place? Would they have made the same choices had they known the resolution they were setting up for themselves?

How do we avoid the same fate? How do we keep our feet from wandering off the right path? We must be consistent.

CHAPTER 36

Consistent

We come, at last, to the third aspect of the creative pursuit: consistency. It's not just a word to describe how your cake or pudding turned out. Though it could indicate how a person turned out; what they're made of. Something with a strong consistency is solid. Likewise a consistent person is a solid one—not flimsy, gelatinous, or gooey.

Consistency today is highly underrated. The sort of people our society often looks up to are those with remarkable skills, exceptional intellect, or stunning physical appearance. Last I checked, talent shows and major awards ceremonies don't pass out trophies for being reliable. Yet, I'd take a reliable person by my side over someone with any or all of those other qualities who don't have an ounce of reliability.

Though it seems consistency has fallen low on the list of desirable character traits by popular opinion, it remains one of the most important to possess—especially for creatives.

If you want others to value your creativity, be true to your word.

When you're dependable, when you display follow-through, people will naturally have more respect for who you are and what you do. Consistency makes you believable and able to be trusted.

Sadly, creatives have the reputation of being the opposite of consistent. They're thought of as spontaneous, sporadic, unpredictable, and unreliable—flakier than Frosted Flakes, and without the frosting.

Those perceptions may often be false, but they came from somewhere.

Let's be honest—there are many creatives who have, by word and action, earned such labels. I'm willing to share the blame here.

So why is consistency such a big deal? As long as you do great work, shouldn't that be enough? As long as your final product is a creative one, why does anything else matter?

The end result is important—no question—but the way you get there and the sort of person you are in the process is just as important, if not more so.

If your boss or family member or friend or whoever can't expect you to do what you say you will in the time you say you'll do it, anything you offer becomes greatly devalued—no matter how much creative mastery has gone into it.

Anyone can talk a big game.

Some people are pros at it, but if those words don't hold truth, they become weightless—hot air ready to drift away under the lightest gust of wind.

Rather than boast, let your work (and manner of work) speak for itself: show up when you say you will, and be honest about yourself and your own capabilities. Remember: show, don't tell; avoid overconfidence.

When you are consistent, it won't matter if you aren't the hottest thing on the market or the best in show. It's a whole lot better, and longer lasting, than all that glitz and glam. You'll give value to your audience, and ultimately, to yourself. What purpose is creativity if not for that very thing?

Creativity, at its best, is an act of service, a blessing— it gives value to others and to the creator.

Shane Claiborne of The Simple Way wrote, "Everybody wants a revolution, but nobody wants to do the dishes."

We all want to be part of something big, something world-changing, but we're unwilling to do the little menial things to get there. A consistent creative realizes it takes small things, things others won't notice, to achieve big results.

Even if you're the most creative person in the world, what good is that if you can't show up to work on time and ready to do the job (even if you work at home), if you won't help out your spouse with some chores, and if you aren't there for your kid's big tournament?

You can't please everyone—'tis true—and I don't recommend trying, but the most important people in your life deserve your very best. If you don't put time and effort into the things that matter and the people that matter, it cheapens your creativity. This isn't a show, a performance to delight your audience while the real you remains hidden in the shadows behind the curtain. Consistency comes from doing the right thing regularly—becoming the right kind of person.

This doesn't mean you must be perfect, without mistakes. Life happens. We miss deadlines, we forget, we don't always know what is important to others, and sometimes we're just plain selfish. Mistakes and wrong choices are a normal part of the learning process.

Ultimately, consistency is grounded in character—the standards you hold yourself to. Only you can decide what those are. Might I suggest you aim high? A person of noble character isn't perfect, but they know when they're off track. For someone lacking in character, anything goes. This leads to wildly unpredictable results, and not for the better.

Have you seen the high jump at the Olympics? What happens after someone has cleared the bar? They raise it. Do the same thing for yourself: keep raising the bar, because there is always room for improvement.

Consistency matters, not just for how others view you, but how you view yourself.

If you don't stick to your own self-appointed tasks, habits, goals, or dreams, you begin to doubt your own abilities. Your confidence wanes. You give credence to the nagging voice inside your head, the one saying you can't do it and you aren't cut out for this creative business. When you actually do the things you tell yourself you will, you're also telling that voice to shut its big, fat mouth.

As Steven Pressfield often advises, it's time to act like a professional. Professionalism isn't just about getting paid—it's the mindset of a master, someone who values their work, who honors their field of expertise with the way they do business. This means showing up and doing the work even when it's hard and even when you don't feel like it. This is no less true for the creative professional.

Only you know who you really are deep down inside, and until you start living on the inside the way you claim to be on the outside, you'll never trust yourself. Consistency leads to integrity (who you are when no one is looking). Integrity builds confidence, and with confidence, you gain courage to move on. They're all connected like a super-combo chain in a fighting game, each one making you stronger and more capable.

Consistent creatives are not drifters. They are willing to make those small but important course corrections on the journey, to keep them on the right path. If a ship's captain wants to reach their intended destination, they must make corrections in response to the wind and the wave's push and pull against the vessel.

Remember, to pursue something means to follow it. In order to do that, you must make sure the object you're following is still in your sights after every step, or else you will drift further away, making it harder to return to the trail. This means keeping both eyes fixed clearly on the goal at all times. In other words: focus.

CHAPTER 37

Focused

That's right. It's time to F-O-C-U-S: Follow One Course Until Successful.

I'm not sure if she's the one who invented the acronym, but I originally saw this in an email from Rebecca Matter, president of American Writers & Artists Inc. When I first saw it in the heading of the email, I knew it was a keeper.

I'll be the first to admit, acronyms can come off as contrived or hokey. Government agencies, space programs, and youth groups all go out of their way to come up with clever ones, but they are still a great way to memorize important principles.

In a world filled with endless distractions, focus is crucial. FOCUS (yes, I'm shouting it) is more important now than ever before.

What's so great about focus? For starters, it gets you where you're headed faster. It also keeps you from tripping up (or down) on the way there. I'm reminded of when my one-year-old daughter was learning the mastery of stairs, both ascending and descending them.

As you may know, one-year-olds are not experts on focus—it takes little to distract them. This becomes very obvious (and problematic) when they are climbing stairs. It takes continual coaxing to get them to make it all the way to the top without a lot of stops on the way. It takes even more diligence to teach them how to safely go down, one step at a time, without leaning too far forward and falling head-over-diaper.

How many projects have you begun only to see them fall off the tracks because you lost focus? In other words, you didn't stay the course.

You got sidetracked. You aren't alone. I've got a metric busload of them (*busload* was an autocorrect, but I've decided to keep it, for obvious reasons).

It's painful to look back on the junkyard of scrap projects we've left in our wake, but every project you are able to finish is another feather in your bird hat. Why do you own a bird hat? Don't ask me. It's *your* hat, after all.

There is something powerful, sacred even, about maintaining focus—being single-minded, about seeing a thing through.

Everyone can benefit from focus, but why is it so hard? Could it be our goals aren't clear enough, or we don't want them badly enough? Are our priorities a little off? Or have all those advertisements and temptations gotten the better of us? Whatever the case, it's time to zero in, to batten down the hatches, to rustle up the chickens, to…you get the idea. It's time to pick a course and follow it until successful.

Imagine you're a pilot with dreams of traveling the world. Well, if you've got an aircraft, fuel, and the right skills, you can. What if you're on the way to London when, halfway through, you decide you'd rather go to Australia? You change course and start going there. But then, two hours away, you decide Tokyo might hold more interest as a first stop, so you redirect once more. What'll happen if you keep this up? You won't get anywhere and will soon be out of fuel and on a one-way trip into the Big Blue.

An airplane can only go to one place at a time. You are no different.

Every time you switch gears, you're exhausting resources while not really getting anywhere. Pick your destination and go. If something changes on the way (say the airport is closed for dangerous weather), so be it. You make a change of plans and stick to your new destination. Whatever happens, you've got to land somewhere. You can't fly around forever.

If you don't pick a destination, circumstance will find one for you. It might be the bottom of the deep-blue sea. Even drifters eventually land somewhere. It just isn't the place they intended to go.

This practice of focus works just as much in daily life as it does for projects with a longer timeline. We might get halfway through an online article, jump to Facebook to check if someone has liked our post, hop on our email, switch to our favorite game app for a few turns—all while we were in the middle of getting dressed for the day.

**Replace the frantic attempt at multitasking
with direct and purposeful movement.**

Pick one thing and do it until it's done, then you can move on to the next. If you don't have time for it, you shouldn't start to begin with. There are a host of methods you can use to become more focused, but here's a practical one you can start this very moment: scheduling.

As career coach Michael Hyatt says, "What gets scheduled is what gets done." When you schedule, you set aside a particular amount of time to do a particular thing. If you don't schedule and instead wait for the right time to present itself, ninety-nine times out of one hundred, it won't happen.

Scheduling forces you to prioritize. It requires you to make a conscious decision about how to spend your time—it facilitates focus. This doesn't mean you have to always be on the clock—most clocks aren't strong enough to stand on anyhow—and you can always schedule some free time.

When you don't schedule, you're at the mercy of any circumstance or distraction to come your way. Without a schedule, you'll spend your hours on things that seem important (and may actually be) but aren't the *most* important.

When you schedule, you plan to be productive on a consistent basis.

As you set aside the time you need to work on creative projects, they get completed. Who doesn't feel good about that?

Let's look at the last part of the acronym: successful. This might be a sticking point for some. How do you guarantee everything you start will end in success? Is that even possible? In short: no.

It's silly to expect the impossible of ourselves. Do we absolutely have to finish everything we start? Sure would be nice, but we don't live in a perfect world. Things happen outside our control, or they just don't go the way we planned. We must remain open to change, willing to adapt or even abandon a project when it no longer seems feasible, when the benefit does not outweigh the cost.

I do suggest you follow the course you've set until you reach a natural end—a conclusion. Every good book comes to a conclusion, even if it isn't a happy one. It's clear when the story has ended, and it would make no sense for anything more to be written in that particular narrative.

So it is with any undertaking—stick to it until you have a darn good reason to let it go. When the time does come to either put the task aside or drop it altogether, you must instead find something equally exciting and worthy of your time (if not more so). Otherwise, you'll just be stuck grieving your losses.

Don't carry abandoned projects around like Jacob Marley's chains. Keep your eyes on what's ahead. Be like the pilot who keeps their attention on the next destination, not the past one.

The key here is eliminating distractions and moving with FOCUS (sorry about all the shouting, really). Pick one thing and stick to it until you reach the end, whatever it may be. If you do, you'll be surprised at the progress you make, the places you go, and the person you become in the process.

CHAPTER 38

Accomplishment

Eventually, a life of focus becomes a life of accomplishment.

Sitting on one side of the fence, peering over at the rolling green fields of accomplishment on the other side can be tough.

We begin with big hopes and dreams. Then the rubber meets the road, and your internal motivator, that little voice that says you can do it, gets more quiet until you can barely hear it. You wonder if you've made a mistake, if creativity really is your gig, if you shouldn't have just left it for the professionals and played it safe.

I get it. I feel the same way on a weekly, sometimes daily, even hourly basis. Very often, the more important a creative goal is, the harder it is to see it through to the end. But, believe me on this, the end will come. When it finally does, enjoy it.

As Tim, a life coach and friend once told me, "You're setting big milestones, things you've never done before. They're worth celebrating in ways you never have before."

**There is nothing wrong with making a
big deal about your accomplishments.**

Take time to recognize how far you've come as well as honor the people who helped you get there. Such events can be the stuff of memories, the things you look back on with fondness throughout your life.

Whether big or small, there is no limit to the ways you can celebrate. What is it you love to do and who could you bring along? You could get a new game you've been wanting and invite friends over to play or you could go on a cross-country road trip with your buddies. What sorts of activities are available in your town? Take someone out to a ballgame, golfing (frisbee or regular), wine tasting, or even a high tea ceremony. Explore the great outdoors and go kayaking, rock climbing, or whale watching.

One particularly memorable celebratory outing our family had was at Organ Stop Pizza, which features an amazing theater pipe organ with its own name, The Mighty Wurlitzer. Both the instrument and the musician were a thing to behold.

The sweet thing about such celebrations isn't just the way they denote your creative achievements, but also how they can be sources of inspiration in themselves, leading to further accomplishments down the road.

After you've basked in the warm glow of accomplishment, you'll get the itch, the desire to press on, to try something else, to take what you've learned and go the extra mile. Don't ignore such feelings.

As important as it is to pause, celebrate, and reflect on what you've done, it's even more important to plan out what's next on the horizon. The temptation to just kick back and rest on your laurels (or whatever sort of plant-based crown you've acquired) is all too great. Remember, success isn't a one-time thing—it's a lifestyle. Hang your plaque on the wall and get a move on.

I've hinted at this, but let me say it outright: it's easy to define ourselves by what we've done or haven't done, by where we've succeeded and where we've failed. If we let them, our past accomplishments or intended future accomplishments can become who we are, how we see ourselves.

When you live that way, your life quickly becomes nothing more than a résumé. And someone else will always have a better one.

You are more than the things you've done or plan to do. You are more than your experience. Being a creative is not about your accomplishments, great or small—it is about who you are as a person, how you view yourself and the world. It is the reasons behind your actions, the internal choices you've made based on your experiences, that truly define you.

Doing great things is good. Being a great person is best.

People can be highly creative, but for all the wrong reasons. Someone may have enormous experience in their field, the highest accolades from those in authority, the love and appreciation of the masses, and yet, be empty on the inside. They may even use their creative abilities to the harm of others. We see both examples in cultural icons whose public lives look wonderful until some tragedy in their personal lives comes to the spotlight. I hesitate to give examples, but Michael Jackson and Harvey Weinstein come to mind.

And celebrity suicides, awfully, have become a common occurrence. The deaths of Robin Williams, Kate Spade, and Anthony Bourdain were both shocking and tragic. Thankfully, there are also many who have emerged victorious from their own nadir, their personal dark night of the soul, such as Winona Ryder, Russell Brand, and Robert Downey Jr.

I bring these up not to criticize, but simply to show that "having it all" is not enough nor will it ever be. A life of fulfillment is more than fame and fortune.

It's easy to judge celebrities, to feel that because we know who they are we understand them. But we all struggle with the same challenge. We all have trouble recognizing the difference between our wants and needs and choosing the right one.

Even without the allures of fame and fortune, it is easy to lose yourself for the sake of accomplishment, to become something you never thought you were, something less than you are, to become internally inconsistent, to suffer alone. On the other hand, it's difficult to stay true to yourself, true to others, to become better than you once were, to reach out for help. It's so easy to lose sight of what truly matters.

It might not always be apparent, but at all times, we are headed one direction or another. You're going up or down—there is no plateau—and it's wise to stop a downward spiral before you crash at the bottom.

As you take creativity by the reins and steer it where you want to go, consider whether the fastest or even most popular route is the best. Maybe it's time to do something entirely weird and unconventional, even if it doesn't make any sense, because such an approach is more true—and more you—than the advice you're getting from everyone else.

Andy Weir, author of *The Martian*, is a great example of this. His book's success is, in a large part, due to his unconventional approach. As he wrote the book, he would put chapters up on his website for anyone to read. Since the fictional book about a man stranded on Mars has a lot of grounding in science, it garnered the attention of specialists such as chemists and engineers. Weir took the advice and knowledge they offered and continued to improve his story.

When finished, he put the whole story up for free. Fans requested he put it on Amazon for ease of download, so he published it for the lowest price possible, ninety nine cents. In three months, he'd sold 35,000 copies.

I don't think Weir had some ingenious marketing plan in mind with *The Martian*, or even an expectation of success. He just wanted to write a good story about a topic he had a lot of interest in and then share it with the world.

The Martian was actually Weir's third book. He considered his first book to be so bad that he destroyed every copy (save one his mother kept, bless her heart). His second was continually rejected by agents and publishers. Even after he'd given up on the goal of becoming a full-time author, Weir didn't stop writing.

The journey of the creative is one of self-discovery. In many ways, a great accomplishment can reveal what you aren't as much as what you are. It can show you what others think you should be and how much you believe them. But endless creativity requires you to be true first to yourself before anyone else.

On the creative path, there are many highs and lows—times of fulfillment and times of disappointment. At any point, you can pause and consider where you're heading and what sort of person you'll have to become to get there.

Consider your motives. Contemplate your methods. Count the cost.

The way you begin can be just as important as how you end. In truth, the way you start will determine where you end up. A good start is hard and a good end is harder because it requires constant redirection to stay on course. It takes a consistent plan. Plan to end well.

In *Baby Wise*, a book about raising children (a creative endeavor indeed), the authors give this advice, "Begin as you mean to go." Let those words sink in. Let them make an impression like a handprint on wet cement.

Start—and continue—with the end in mind.

Here are a few things to think about concerning the creative pursuit:

- Is your work sustainable? Will it last? Is it something you can commit to?
- Do the results you desire reflect the person you wish to be?
- If you had everything you want now, what would you do next?
- How could getting what you want affect others?
- Do you have realistic expectations of yourself?
- Does your creative pursuit drive you to become a better, healthier person?

Some of the above questions can be difficult to determine on your own. We aren't the best judges when it comes to our own internal development.

Internal change happens under the surface—it's invisible, at least to ourselves. This is why I highly recommend mentors or peers with whom you can share your big life goals and how you plan to reach them.

Find people who know you well and can assess whether you're taking a healthy or unhealthy approach to creativity. Find other creatives who have gone a ways down the road you're on, who have gotten where you wish to be while still maintaining consistency and integrity.

**Find people who do what they love
and who help others while doing it.**

Look for such people, and you will find endless creatives—those who are a constant source of positive change, of growth, who are wellsprings of newness, who not only do great things but do them for good reasons, regardless of how much recognition they may receive.

I've already mentioned quite a few of these people in my own life. My friends Michael, Ben, Lonny, and Dave have all been great mentors to me in different ways, though their backgrounds and careers differ widely. My coworkers Eric and Jimmy constantly inspire me toward creative thought and action. My life coach Tim has been a wonderful friend and continues to keep me on track in all aspects of life. My close friend David, one of the best thinkers I know, has been a continual sounding board for creative ideas in my life and infuses creativity and care into every aspect of his own work and personal life.

There are also professionals with whom I have only surface level relationships, but I still consider them to be teachers and guides of great personal importance to me. These include K. M. Weiland, David Farland, Ray Edwards, and Mike Foster, among others. The money and time I've spent on their resources and lessons has more than paid for itself. They pour their lives and heart into their work and it shows.

Indeed, everyone I've interviewed in this book has influenced me in a significant way and I'm sure I've played some important role in the lives of every person I've just listed. That's how it works; creatives inspire creatives.

I don't think it's hard to find endless creatives, but it may require some effort. Certainly, no one's perfect. I'm not asking you to find perfect people or to be the perfect person. If you think that's what creativity is about, endless or otherwise, you've missed the point of this book entirely.

I'm asking you to find people who are life-giving, whose work makes the world a better place, folks who, whether directly or indirectly, can help you do the same. We desperately need such people in our lives. When we learn from their examples, we discover how to embrace the life of the endless creatives for ourselves.

In the next chapter, we'll spend some time looking at people who have actively lived the life of the endless creative and how you can do the same.

Connect today to all your tomorrows. It matters.
                    ~Gary Keller, from *The ONE Thing*

SECTION 12 REVIEW

Here it all is again, but with fewer words:

- Every story resolves, but it also leads to something else. The resolution you reach shows who you have become along the journey.
- Consistency doesn't mean you need to be predictable, just reliable.
- Consistency matters, not just for how others view you, but how you view yourself.
- The fastest route to accomplishment comes when you FOCUS— follow one course until successful.
- If you want to make sure something gets done, schedule it.
- Enjoy your accomplishments, but don't let them hold you back.
- The way you begin is just as important as how you end.
- What you accomplish is not as important as who you are.
- Find people in your life whom you admire to help you on the journey—people who have already gone down the road you want to be on.
- Resting on your laurels is one way to ruin what could otherwise be a perfectly good houseplant.

Interview with a Creative

JAMES SCHATTAUER

Tell us about yourself.
I am a children's recording artist and musician for special events. I have been playing guitar, writing songs, and performing for over thirty-five years.

When do you find it easiest to be creative?
When I have lots of time to devote to a project. I understand why artists have studios, so that they can get away from distractions and focus on their work.

Sometimes having a deadline or specific reason to create something is helpful in getting the creative juices flowing to complete a project.

Where do you look for inspiration?
Other artists inspire me, beauty in nature, and paying attention to my dream life. I sometimes get ideas and musical notions when I am completely at rest, meditating or about ready to fall asleep.

Creative thoughts, notions, and musical ideas come to me in the gaps of life: driving in a car, walking the dog, flopping on the couch for a chill break or in my night dreams and daydreams.

What forms of creativity do you most appreciate or enjoy?
Creating music in a recording studio with other capable musicians is

some of the best creative fun I have ever had! I also enjoy improvisation (see interplay.org) where music, story, or dance is created in the moment, along the lines of *Whose Line is it Anyway?*.

When has a creative approach helped you accomplish something impactful?

I remember being asked to write a curriculum for a children's workbook and was inspired by listening to great music while I created the text. The creativity that went into the music seemed to ignite my own creativity in formulating ideas for the curriculum.

I have also experienced that throwing myself into what I am feeling passionate about doing, without thinking, at first, what the outcome will be has created unanticipated connections with other people and places that ultimately supported and shaped a positive outcome.

What is one practice you would recommend to help someone be more creative?

Free association journaling by the *Artist's Way* method produced magical results in my creative life! I also believe that my practices in improvisational classes have kept my creative juices flowing.

Where can people find you or your work?

www.jamesschattauer.com

EPILOGUE

Endless

You are an artist and your heart is your masterpiece.
~Ryan O'Neal, lyrics from "I'll Keep You Safe"

CHAPTER 39

Endless

Yes, our fictional story is done, but your story—the real one—is only just revving up its engine, ready to go tearing off down the highway. But before you put pedal to metal and kick up a dust cloud in your wake, let's make sure you've got the right fuel in the tank, the kind that keeps you on course and moving smoothly (no, I'm not talking about laxatives).

At this point, you may be wondering a few things: Why is there more after the resolution? What do I mean specifically when I mention the endless creative? Why do I think you should be one? What does such a life look like? When is this book going to end?

Think of this as a bonus section to address those very questions, except that last one—that will be obvious soon enough.

First, something we must address, which I'm positive you discovered long before reading this book.

Just because it's creative doesn't make it good.

I'm talking about both senses of good—quality and morality. Things of high creative content can still fall short in the quality department. In the other sense, a person may be a creative genius yet also incredibly wicked (they make for great storybook villains and awful real-life villains).

I'm no art critic, but I find most art pieces intended only to shock or offend to be of significantly lower quality. Sure, they may be effective and even culturally significant, but can you really say an installation composed of urine-filled glasses or trash piles is on the same level as the Mona Lisa or Michelangelo's David?

In *Perfume,* both the novel and film, Jean-Baptiste Grenouille is born with a remarkable sense of smell. This makes him an exceptional perfumer. However, he also murders young women in an attempt to capture their scent and create the perfect perfume. The premise is a tad far-fetched, but there you have it. Though Grenouille is eventually successful in his quest and creates what is essentially a mind-controlling scent, in the end it does not leave him satisfied. He is consumed by the masses (yes, you read that correctly) after dousing himself in his own perfume. Such is the way of villainy.

The use of creativity, while important, does not automatically make something or someone right. Not every display of creativity is an endless one.

Where does that leave us? Should you toss the creative out like the two-year-old Beef Stroganoff you just found in the back of the fridge? Nay! Well, yes, toss the Stroganoff out, for goodness' sake, but hold on to creativity.

Creativity is a tool—a very important one.

Like any tool, it can be misused or abused. When you want to drive some nails into a piece of wood, a hammer works better than most other things. If you haven't used a hammer before, you have a much higher chance of bending the nail or smashing your thumb in the process.

You could even hit someone else with a hammer, should you be so inclined (you meanie), but neither of those things negate the hammer's usefulness. A nail gun is even more efficient, and also more dangerous in the hands of the incompetent or nefarious.

Creativity is a power tool if ever there was one. As Spider-Man's good old Uncle Ben taught us, power and responsibility go hand-in-web.

Like any tool, creativity is useful, but it takes skill to learn how to use it well. Also, like many tools, it can be used as a weapon. It takes a healthy respect of the tool—an understanding and appreciation of its power—to use it correctly and effectively.

You may, through the same creative process we've covered, find clever ways to trick people, to poison their minds (or their food), to take from others and give nothing back, but such an act would be a misuse of creativity—an abuse.

Such actions would be in direct opposition of endless creativity. They are not endless; instead they lead to dead ends. They're wrong, self-serving, do not promote newness or growth, but instead lead to decay. They don't allow creativity to flourish through others, but stifle it by hurting others.

Ultimately, a misuse of creativity is self-defeating.

As the healer, through the act of healing others, becomes more whole so also the attacker, in damaging others, loses part of themselves in the process.

There is creativity and then there is endless creativity. Creativity on its own is a fine thing, but the motive behind it and the outcome it produces deserve our consideration.

Creativity is neutral—neither good nor bad in itself—but endless creativity is the highest form of creative achievement.

When you employ endless creativity, you are using it the way it was intended. It's the cream of the crop, the wheat without the chaff, the pinnacle of mount perfect, the gold medal on the blue ribbon, the bee's knees and elbows, the warm, gooey center of the brownie, the cherry on top of a three-story, caramel-covered, chocolate-chip-coated—okay, I've got to stop. I'm really hungry now.

In other words, endless creativity is the best of the best of the best. It is good in itself and promotes goodness.

As we saw in the fictional narrative and locations the hero passed through, endless creativity causes the best sort of change—it makes us look at everything in a different light. When we live with endless creativity, we make a shift from Worry to Inspiration, from Indecision to Determination, from Doubt to Progress, from Defeat to Hope, from Despair to Confidence, from Failure to Success, from Fear to Courage, and from Dread to Triumph. It is an eye-opening journey, one that leads us to realize our potential, to let Possibility take us to new heights.

At the beginning of the book, I covered some marks of creativity.

Now let's look at endless creativity, what distinguishes it from regular old run-of-the-mill creativity. Think of these as the crowning achievements.

Endless Creativity…
- Adds value
- Provides ease or clarity
- Requires sacrifice
- Is beautiful
- Benefits others
- Is meaningful
- Is memorable
- Stirs emotion
- Makes an impact
- Connects
- Remains fearless
- Brings joy
- Is true

Let's see how these play out in real life:

Adds value: Michelangelo's statue of David started out as a giant block of marble. The marble was valuable before he began to chisel away at it, but it was worth a whole lot more once he finished. Before, I'm sure you could put a price on the marble. Now, it's priceless. It's not always easy to know how much value your creativity will bring, but you can make sure it gives more than it takes.

Provides ease or clarity: Whether it's those trash-grabbers with the pincher claw at the end so you don't have to bend down or an app that helps you learn a new language through fun games and cultural immersion, there are many creative products that turn the difficult and complex into something doable and feasible.

As every construction worker half their salt knows, why work harder when you can work smarter? Usually I hear this after spending far too much time and effort trying to cut a thick tree branch off with a hand saw when I should have been using a chainsaw.

Such innovations greatly improve our quality of life because, let's face it, we're not in the stone age anymore. We have dishwashers and washing machines for good reason!

Requires sacrifice: Have you heard the story of Dick Hoyt and his son, Rick? Dick has pushed his son, a quadriplegic, through over one thousand races, including marathons and Iron Mans. After their first race together, Rick told his father, "Dad, when I'm running, it feels like I'm not handicapped."

If that doesn't move you to tears, go watch some of their races online. Dick's dedication to his son is a creative act—who else had thought to do such a thing before? It's awe inspiring to see not only a father's dedication through extreme physical exertion but also his son's delight as he's towed, biked, and carried through each race.

What if we used creativity in such a way, not only for our kin but for others in our lives, to take them further than could have ever gone alone?

Is beautiful: But isn't beauty in the eye of the beholder? Isn't it subjective? To an extent, yes. But there are many things we can all agree are beautiful—a colorful sunset, for example.

Beauty is more than opinion—it's a mark of endless creativity. Whether it's the interior of a cathedral with light pouring through stained-glass windows, the perfectly arranged bouquet of flowers, Beethoven's *Moonlight Sonata*, or the epic computer-generated scenery and effects from movies like *Interstellar*, *Avatar*, and *Lord of the Rings*, we cannot help but to be filled with awe and wonder at the beauty they hold.

Much like a mosaic made from bits of shattered stone and glass, even broken things can be made beautiful. When you live in endless creativity, you reveal your own inner beauty, despite, or even because of, your own brokenness. You may even, like a stained-glass window, allow the light of endless creativity to shine through you, revealing the beauty in others.

Benefits others: This could mean a whole host of things, such as meeting the needs of others, showing them appreciation, or giving them dignity. Earlier, I mentioned Seiichi Miyake's tenji block, which has helped many visually impaired pedestrians safely navigate public spaces.

One of my favorite companies (the people who run it are also fantastic) is Bought Beautifully. They partner with other organizations across the globe to provide fair wages, safe conditions, and dignified employment to people in need. This usually equates to education and business opportunities for people who have been living in extreme poverty, disadvantage communities, or were trapped in slavery. And their products are top notch! Check out their online store at boughtbeautifully.org

Have you heard of the Fowlers? They're a family from Atlanta who turned a canceled wedding into an elaborate meal for the homeless.

When the remarkably popular mobile game *Pokemon Go* had just come out, my friend's son passed out refreshments to traveling players as an act of goodwill. Though others followed suit, he was one of the first I'd heard to come up with the idea. He even made the local news.

When it comes to benefiting someone else, consider how an unlikely hobby, connection, or event of yours could be used to make a positive change in the life of another person.

Is meaningful: Actress and singer Caitlin Crosby found a new way to look at an item that had often been discarded when no longer in use: old keys. After meeting and talking with Rob and Cera, a couple living on the streets who made jewelry, she began The Giving Keys, a company that employs the homeless to engrave keys with single words of inspiration. Those who purchase keys are encouraged to pass on their key to someone who also needs a word of encouragement in their life. As this company demonstrates, meaning can be found and made from the most unlikely places.

Is memorable: If you're like me (and if you are, I'm sorry), you may hear the dulcet tones of Nat King Cole singing *Unforgettable*. No? It's just me then.

Our minds serve as a natural filter, marking the things we find meaningful or important to be remembered again and again. It may be you have a favorite poem you often recall (mine would be "Up-Hill," by Christina Rossetti), a verse you repeat often, words of encouragement you hold near, a scene from a film, a striking painting, or photograph that you often bring view in your mind's eye. Memorable works of creativity truly are endless—they continue on in our hearts and heads long after we've encountered them.

Stirs emotion: The video game titled *That Dragon, Cancer* delves into a father's experience of loss as his young son suffers from and eventually succumbs to cancer. It is honest, haunting, and heartrending, yet hopeful and, because all of those things, stirring. It serves as a unique way to experience something very painful (through a video game, of all things).

Though we can't always predict what emotional impact our creativity will have on others, we should aim for something that touches the very soul and center of the audience. That only happens when it comes out of the deep emotions of the creator.

There's more to creativity than just making people emotional, but if our work produces no reaction, it's hard to imagine why anyone would care about it.

Makes an impact: Photographer Jeremy Cowart has made a habit of using his artistic skill toward remarkable ends. He traveled to Rwanda for a documentary and took photos of genocide survivors standing beside someone who'd killed their family members, a person they now have forgiven, often posing at the very scene of the crime.

He is a big part of The Purpose Hotel, a place where staying in a room will get a child sponsored, paying for internet will help fight human trafficking, and every product is made by or helps people in need.

But you don't have to cross an ocean to make an impact. Kristal Bush, a former social worker, owns a company that provides easy and affordable transport for people who wish to visit the incarcerated. She says, "I feel like I was born into it."

Think of what experiences or abilities you have and how they might change the world for others, whether they're on the opposite end of the globe or just down the street.

Connects: In many ways, we are more connected to other people than we have ever been in the history of humankind. Thanks to advances in technology, especially the internet, we can reach anyone just about anywhere on the planet. Yet, despite all that, so many still feel very alone—one study showing half of Americans, mostly younger people, feel lonely.

Without deep, meaningful relationships, without the feeling that someone really understands and accepts you, loneliness persists. And loneliness has been linked to some nasty things like addiction and early death. Creativity, however, can help build the essential bridge that links us together.

Author Michaelbrent Collings suffers from major depressive disorder along with suicidal tendencies. Suicide has become a growing epidemic, and a tragic one at that. Michaelbrent seeks to help others who face the same challenges, by posting about his daily triumphs and struggles on his Patreon page. By doing this, he hopes to make allies and become an ally in what he calls his war on suicide.

Remains fearless: Not unafraid, mind you. Endless creativity exhibits boldness in the face of fear. Corrie ten Boom recounts in her book *The Hiding Place* how her family had a wall with a secret entrance built into their house to help Jews hide during the Holocaust. She and her family eventually were found out and taken to concentration camps.

After her release, in honor of her sister's vision, she opened a house to offer healing and forgiveness to former Nazis. That takes some real guts.

There are people like Harriet Tubman, who ran the Underground Railroad to help others escape slavery and fought for women's suffrage. Though her work was dangerous and fiercely opposed by many, she continued on. Such acts of creative fearlessness make for stories of true heroism.

Brings joy: In his book *Surprised by Joy*, C.S. Lewis recalls how his brother's miniature toy garden had once stirred in him a feeling of joy—not happiness or pleasure, but something deeper. He called it an "enormous bliss," and "an unsatisfied desire which is itself more desirable than any other satisfaction," something that could not again be fabricated, but only discovered.

Maybe we don't all define joy in exactly the same terms, but the feeling is unmistakable. Joy may be elusive, but, once realized, is more than worth the pursuit.

In a handwritten letter to one of his readers, Lewis compares joy to security with these words: "It jumps under one's ribs and tickles down one's back and makes one forget meals and keeps one (delightedly) sleepless o' nights. It shocks one awake when the other puts one to sleep."

Will your creative dreams ultimately bring joy to yourself and others? I've talked to many an author who, simply by talking about their work, can light up a whole room. There is an excitement, a blissful satisfaction that comes when a creative's work is in line with their deepest and truest desires. When that happens, it creates an inspiration that spreads like wildfire.

Is true: Though a work be one of fiction, there is a line between one that is honest and one that is not. Looking back at some of the older Disney movies, we see some things being portrayed that don't line up with reality.

No, I don't mean the fairies, talking furniture, or mermaids. There are subtle and not-so-subtle messages like this: once you find the right guy and get married, life continues as happily ever after. In reality, marriage is often a struggle, a commitment of continual sacrifice, even for the match made in heaven.

How about this one: all you have to do is believe in yourself and your dreams will come true. It's still not even clear to me what that means exactly, but there are a good many people who battle addictions or conditions like depression, and I guarantee the way out of their difficulty involves much more than self-belief. I'm not saying there's nothing to be gained from those stories—nor am I bashing Disney, they've given us just as many incredible and honest tales—but they portray things we realize now are simply not true.

Every story we tell will have some flaws, some things that are off the mark, because we, the storytellers, have flaws of our own. However, with each new creative work, regardless of how many flying carpets, dragons, or unicorns it has, it's important to examine how real it is, to determine to the best of our ability whether its message lines up with reality.

Jon Foreman of the band Switchfoot has a great statement about the expression of truth in art: "Fitting in is not a high enough goal to make of your life or your art…for us as a band, [we have] a much bigger goal, which is: How do we express timeless, transient truth that will open the windows and the doors of the soul, so people will look at a bigger horizon than what the mirror has to offer?"

Like Foreman, we must consider what view our creative work offers to others. Is it a window of truth to a greater world or just a well-packaged bundle of half-truths to make a quick buck?

These are but a few examples, and this list is far from exhaustive. You may notice overlap in the examples given above. This shouldn't be a surprise: what is beautiful stirs up emotion, what is meaningful is often true, and acts that benefit others often require sacrifice.

These different attributes can be so closely linked they all seem like the same thing and, at times, are. Not every work of endless creativity has all these qualities. However, they make up the core of endless creativity.

You may be wondering, why endless creativity and not some other kind? Creativity, in its purest and best form, is endless. Though the act from which it sprung may end, its effects echo on and on, shooting out across the universe like light from a pulsating star.

Never underestimate how far a little bit of creativity can go.

Every great creative achievement was built on many, many smaller, almost unnoticeable ones. Michelangelo may have painted the ceiling of the Sistine Chapel by himself, but how many hands went into building that chapel? How many hours did his parents put into raising him or his instructor into teaching him how to paint? Where did his brushes or supplies come from? Many people who received no great recognition were part of an incredible final product.

To be clear, if you're only in it for recognition, you will be disappointed. Not because you'll never get any, but because it takes a long time and a lot of work to get noticed and, also, when you do get it, you won't be satisfied. You can't make yourself the chief end of your own creativity. It must pass on through you; otherwise it dies.

If you let creativity be its own reward, you will appreciate the value of creativity for what it is, and from that appreciation you will continue to create more and better things—things that will live on and on.

The process is truly endless, as are the results.

CHAPTER 40

Love

Though creativity be endless, the end of this book is nigh upon us. But first, let's talk about value again and how important it is to endless creativity. Namely this:

Things of greatest value are the things that last.

By this rule, endless creativity is of inestimable value because it lasts forever. This, if nowhere else, is where we may have differing outlooks. I'm of the belief that people continue on after their physical passing. I believe in the existence of the soul.

Others (and perhaps you) believe we're all headed toward a final and inevitable end—of life, the earth, the sun, energy, the universe, and pretty much everything. This often leads to nihilism: a belief in meaninglessness. After all, how can anything matter if it's all going to be gone one day?

While I do believe the earth itself will come to some form of an end, I also have a hope that it, like people, will be made new—a rebirth, much like the one from the hero's journey. I see purpose, not meaninglessness, in what we do and how we live because those things will impact an eternity—one we can only begin to imagine.

Even if we may not agree on where we're heading, I hope you will consider this: If there is even a remote possibility that people continue on in some capacity, should we not pour our time, energy, and especially our creativity into them? Are you willing to open your eyes and see the inherent value of every human being—yes, even though there are billions of them and some are remarkably flawed?

Can you accept each and every one of them, like yourself, has a purpose, a reason for being here on this planet with you? Are you willing to view the worth of people in light of your own self-worth?

While we can't help everyone, or even most people, shouldn't we do the most we can to help the ones we're able to? Shouldn't we employ endless creativity toward something of endless value? Only you can answer those questions for yourself, but as for me, it is a resounding, propounding, and astounding "YES!"

Endless creativity is a high calling—no one has it down pat (it's an expression, but if your name is Pat, then yes, I'm still talking to you). Not everything we do will meet the qualifications of endless creativity. It's a learning process, yet this is what we should aim for: the highest mark.

The closer we get to endless creativity, the better we'll do next time. The principles laid out in this book, if followed, can guide you on that path. Let's look at the three steps of the creative journey one more time.

The creative approach:
1. Observe
2. Question
3. Respond

The creative process:
1. Inspiration
2. Imagination
3. Innovation

The creative pursuit:
1. Courage
2. Confidence
3. Consistency

Think about it this way: when you become observant, when you question, when you respond, it creates an example for the people around you to do the same. When you're inspired, it inspires others. When you take steps of courage, it sets a path for others to follow.

Like the water cycle, there are different phases of creativity, but they feed into one another endlessly. Do you see it?

The creative river runs on and on, long after you and I are gone.

The best things are the ones that last the longest, that stand the test of time. The lives we now have won't last forever. We will change, we will pass on, but the changes we've made on the world will continue to impact generations to come. If you don't think future generations need our help, look around for a hot second.

In your own personal life, I'm sure there's no shortage of things that could be improved: finances, work relationships, family relationships, physical health, emotional health, direction in life, or maybe your shoes just don't fit like they used to. However big or small your problem, there is a creative solution waiting to be found (or it's just time to get a new pair of shoes—if so, I hope you choose some snazzy ones).

We live in a troubled and troubling world, one filled with problems—things like the refugee crisis, human trafficking, racial injustice, terrorism, drug abuse, domestic abuse, shootings, inequality, infectious diseases, poverty, addiction, famine, drought, political corruption, suicide, mass incarceration, natural disasters, wars, and so on. Such things keep me up at night. These issues hit us all in different ways, but it's hard not to feel hopeless when matters like those are the deluge of the daily news. There's no denying it: the world has some serious needs. People with problems abound.

It could be your ears have gone dull and you don't pay much attention to the bad news anymore. It's not your problem, right? You've got enough things to deal with. Besides, one person can hardly begin to fix problems like those, so why try? But what happens when they come knocking on our own door? After all, a problem left alone only grows.

**The world may be dark, but the work
of the endless creative brings light.**

We can run and hide from the problems, pretend they don't exist, or we can do something about them. In the face of trouble, we need endless creatives who will stand with faith and hope, believing their actions can and will make a better world.

It's time for each of us to step up, to be the creatives the world needs, the ones we were made to be. As with any major movement, it starts with one person taking a stand. Just one endless creative can make the difference between a snowflake and an avalanche. I'm talking about you!

The need is great—it's nigh unfathomable. But the solution is not impossible.

There remains one missing ingredient if we hope to meet the needs around us, if we hope to overcome the darkness. In order to have any lasting impact, to make even the smallest change in ourselves and in the world, there is something we must learn to do.

Love.

That's right. I said it. We have to learn how to love. Not in a fluffy-pluffy, goochie-coochie, wuvey-dovey way, like how I feel about pie or puppies. It's not a love based on good vibes, flights of fancy, or moments of great passion. It is a love that grows, steady and sure, from something real, deep, and lasting—an endless and unquenchable love. Such a love empowers the endless creative to be more, to rise up, to change.

For the creative, love is the most powerful and essential fuel.

To be creative is to love both the work you're doing and the ones you're doing it for. It is the source of our motivation. It gets you up out of bed on days when you feel like crap, it makes you spend a ton of money on a flight to meet with people in another country who don't look or live like you, and it gives you the courage to stand up and speak even when you're terrified.

As Dienekes, the Spartan warrior and teacher from *Gates of Fire* learned, "The opposite of fear is love."

We spoke of finding courage in the face of fear, of meeting your fears head on. But without the motivating drive of love, it can't be done. As written in 1 John 4:18, "There is no fear in love, but perfect love casts out fear" (English Standard Version).

Love pushes us on, toward change, into the uncomfortable. It enables us to take steps into the unknown. It opens our eyes to empathy, to not only see the hurt of others, but to identify with it, to be stirred up to action on their behalf. As Bob Goff demonstrates in *Love Does*, love is what leads us to action.

To hope is to expect a better future.
To love is to make a better future.

Real world-changing creativity comes when we are able to love change, love others, love our work, and to love ourselves this way. It's a love that gives more than it takes, suffers harm but does not return it, forgives over and over, and doesn't give up no matter the odds. As we do this, we learn to love life itself. In this way, we truly live.

One of the hardest lessons I've learned in life is that I can't make a person love me. On the flip side, there is no single person whom I cannot love. Family provides us with one of the best opportunities to practice this. No matter how they treat you or how you feel about them, they're still your family. Time and again you will be given the choice to give love or hold it back.

Because of my parents' divorce and my own marriage, I now have six parents. In a way, each has loved me—some to a greater extent than others. Try as I might, I can't increase their love for me. In fact, the more I try, the worse I feel. But I can choose how much I will love each of them.

The harder it is to love someone,
the greater the opportunity to choose love.

And love is just that—a choice. Creativity also is a choice. No one can make you quit, and no one can make you stop loving. In all the many things you do throughout the day—the little actions you take—you either demonstrate or deny love, just as you demonstrate or deny creativity.

I see this love perfected in the person of Christ. He spent most of his time caring for the outcasts of society, the downtrodden. Be it women, children, the sick, the lame, foreigners, prostitutes, or tax collectors— Jesus loved them all and desired the best for them.

He caused change in their lives. He gave them value. He upheld justice in an unjust world. When he was attacked and persecuted for his actions, he did not fight back but instead forgave the people who caused him harm while they were throwing everything they had at him. I find his life remarkable.

In the stories he told, the relationships he formed, and the way he treated people, Jesus did what no one expected—he challenged the old way of thinking and loved people with incredible boldness. His whole life was a demonstration of endless creativity.

Of course, there are other examples: Mother Theresas, teachers, soldiers, firefighters, doctors, counselors, musicians, farmers, parents, sanitation workers, or vagabonds who give themselves up for a greater cause, who lay their own lives down to lift up another. This is the heart of the endless creative.

Think about those in your own life who share the same heart. Look to them for guidance. Learn from them. Become like them.

True love is about caring for people so much it hurts—so is the life of the creative. When we live a life driven by love, our creativity shines brightest.

CHAPTER 41

Purpose

And now, my creative cohort, the time has come—the final crescendo.

Endless creativity is, ultimately, a call to purpose.

All right, this is where I get honest with you. Not that I haven't been, but it's time to get real—I mean really real. I've dropped a few hints, but let me say it plainly: being creative is not your purpose.

Creativity isn't going to make all your problems go away, and it's definitely not going to fix everything that's wrong in the world. It won't, in itself, fulfill you or give you true purpose. Even if you could eliminate all your problems (or the problems of the world) with creativity, more problems would arise to replace them.

If your problems were suddenly eradicated, you'd just be left asking, "Now what?"

I don't believe a world without problems is possible. Even if it were, I don't think I'd want to live there. Here's why:

Problems provide meaning.

Creativity is a path, a journey that is never complete—it isn't a destination. It can aid you in solving problems, discovering joy, and finding purpose.

If you'll allow, creativity plays a very big role in that process, but it's not the be-all-end-all. It ain't the answer to life, the universe, and everything (which is forty-two, according to Douglas Adams). However, by using the creative approach, you will ask the right questions, ones that lead to such an answer.

Creativity is an excellent launchpad. It might be the fuel and the rocket, but it's not the reason we go in the first place. Spaceships are great because of where they can take you—to visit the stars or, at least, the planets and such in between (the stars are too hot to visit, after all).

You begin with creativity, you continue with creativity, but you don't stop there. Creativity is its own reward, but it also demands a purpose, a reason for being, an end goal.

Life itself requires purpose. Otherwise, what's the point? Everyone has one—whether or not they know what it is. If you don't yet know yours, what better time than now to begin the search?

Purpose can seem like such a weighty and intimidating word, but it's fairly simple.

You live out your purpose when you use your unique passions and abilities to make a positive difference in the lives of others.

Purpose is living out your creative calling. It means changing the world in a way that only you can. This could be big or small—it may impact many people or just a few (maybe one). Your purpose may change over time, and while you will have one overarching purpose, there will be smaller ones as well.

In the TV series *Merlin*, the titular character is Arthur's guide and protector. He is the only one who possesses the compassion, insight, and magical talent required to fulfill this task. This is his purpose. He influences many other people as well, but really he's got just one person, one calling in his life. Like a host of other heroes, he resists the call at first, but eventually he embraces it.

As Gary Keller writes in *The ONE Thing*,

Purpose provides the ultimate glue that can help you stick to the path you've set. When what you do matches your purpose, your life just feels in rhythm, and the path you beat with your feet seems to match the sound in your head and heart.

Unlike Merlin, you probably don't have an ancient dragon locked away under your castle just waiting to tell you your purpose. So you'll have to find it another way.

Take a creative approach. You'll have to conduct your own round of observation, question, and response, but here are a few to help you get started:

- What are my unique interests, and what do I enjoy about them?
- Which things do I care most about—what moves me?
- What talents do I possess?
- Where do I have the most experience?
- What resources do I have?
- How can I use my interests, talents, experience, and resources to do something great?
- What is my story—the details of my life in which I find meaning?
- How might I use what I have and who I am to add value to others?
- What sort of people do I find myself drawn to or most identify with?
- What are some of the common struggles in my community?
- Who can I help today?

Did you know Leo Tolstoy, regarded as one of the greatest authors of all time, struggled with purpose and meaning? In his book *A Confession*, he spells out his struggles with a series of questions:

"What will come of what I am doing today or shall do tomorrow? What will come of my whole life?"

"Why should I live, why wish for anything, or do anything?"

"Is there any meaning in my life that the inevitable death awaiting me does not destroy?"

Even after a major existential crisis in his later years, Tolstoy clung to a purpose he'd adopted much earlier and had even written down in his journal as a twenty-one-year-old. For Tolstoy, it was about living to make things better, especially when it came to others.

You may not be Tolstoy (and that's just fine—I'm not either), but you can make a change in this world for the better.

It's not about having a specific set of skills or talents, how many resources you have, your good looks or intelligence, or even a certain personality. All those may help in one way or another or they may be an obstacle, but the lack of them does not hinder your creative abilities, just as the possession of them does not guarantee creativity. Every person has something to give, something unique to bring to the table. You are no exception.

You were born a creative, a world changer, but it's your choice to live it out. Unless you do, there will always be something missing in your life—an ache. Your creativity will be hollow and your joy just out of arm's reach.

And everyone else will be missing out too.

The world is waiting—crying out—for you to live your calling (they just don't know it's you they need).

But where do you begin? Start with where you are and who you are right now.

Look at the things you're working on at present. Do they lead to a specific goal? Do they further your own journey? Do they help make the world just a little bit better for you and others? Whether you're hard at work or taking some time to relax and recover, look for the reason behind what you're doing.

When your actions have a purpose,
they lead to the discovery of purpose.

Causing change is fine, but it's about more than just that. It's the reason behind the change and where that change leads.

If your only goal is to bring change, you will be frustrated. Change always comes, it doesn't need to be forced, and not all change leads to improvement.

Instead, begin by serving, by offering what you have in the form of help. That is the most powerful and natural way to cause change—to find a need and meet it.

A true calling is formed in the context of community.

As for me, my calling is to bring hope to others by revealing the wonder of God through stories. It's what I'm passionate about. It's the thing that makes me feel alive. In whatever action I take, big or small, I can hold it up to my calling and see if I'm on track. If I'm not operating with others in mind, I'm drifting from the target.

Finding your calling doesn't mean you need to have things all figured out first. It doesn't mean you need to have all the answers. Actually, it's better that you don't—it means you'll be more open to new possibilities. All you need is something to give.

Maybe you don't feel like you have anything to give the world. I promise that you do. Give them your story.

Everyone has a story to share and only *you* can tell yours. Others may offer advice or show you examples of what makes a better life, but your story is yours alone to tell. Each part matters. With every creative act, you write another page in your ongoing story. It isn't you, but it is an expression of who you are.

**Let your creativity be part of the bigger story,
a story without an end.**

As I said, this isn't a self-help book. It's an invitation—a journey into something beyond yourself. It is a call to bring value, live with purpose, and, ultimately, to love.

To live such a life, you will have to make the hardest choice.

Much like the hero from the hero's journey, you must allow your old self to die, and, in doing so, be reborn. As dramatic as that sounds, it's just as much a mundane activity. Dying to self is a daily process. For some, it's so common that it's easy to overlook. It is the choice of self-denial.

As Julia Cameron observes, "The creative process is a process of surrender, not control." True creativity requires all of you—a giving up of your whole self.

You may not feel like you have much to give, but all you have, all you are, whether much or little, is exactly enough.

You are enough.

Your calling is about you, but it's not *all* about you.

The life of the giver, the one who does not hold back, causes the greatest change. It means becoming a living sacrifice, a stepping stone, a shoulder to stand upon, a path to something better.

The beauty of it is when you give yourself, it isn't a loss. You get something much better in return. You become something better. This is the freedom that comes from self-denial, from creativity itself—you learn how to get out of your own way.

That's when the real magic begins.

A hero is someone who has given his or her life to something bigger than oneself.

~Joseph Campbell

FINAL REVIEW

If you've somehow forgotten everything you read up to this point (perhaps from a large bump to the head), I hope you will remember these few things:

- You were made to be and are a creative if you believe it and live it. Every child is born creative—it's just a matter of keeping in practice.
- You don't have to be an artist to be creative. One requires skill in a certain area; the other is an overall mindset.
- The more difficult a problem, the greater the need for a creative solution.
- To be a creative is to accept and promote change, to be part of something new.
- Creativity isn't always easy, but it's worth the effort.
- Take the creative approach through observation, question, and response.
- Follow the creative process through inspiration, imagination, and innovation.
- Pursue a life of creativity with courage, confidence, and consistency.
- The truest and best form of creativity is the kind that lasts: endless creativity.
- Our creative works ought to benefit others as well as ourselves—this is how they live on.
- Love is the greatest fuel for creativity: love for others, for yourself, and for the work.
- Creativity is the journey, not the destination—one that leads to the discovery of purpose.

If, heaven forbid, someone makes you take a test on this, there is your cheat sheet.

CLOSING WORDS

Thank you for reading this book, or at least flipping to the end and reading this page—if you did, why not go back and read the rest? It's totally worth it—believe me.

If you got something out of reading this, I'd sure appreciate a review. It would mean the world to me, the galaxy even. Not the universe though—I mean it is just a review, and I have to draw the line somewhere.

There remains much to be said of creativity, and this book barely enters the atmosphere of such a planet-sized topic. But I've got to end somewhere, so I'll wrap this up with just a few closing thoughts.

A life of creative surrender, service, and sacrifice can seem disheartening and lonely at times. You may feel as if you've given your all and still come up empty. You may feel abandoned—that no one understands or cares. As real as feelings are, they don't make it so.

I believe loneliness and the depression it can cause to be one of the greatest problems of our time. Even though technology has connected us in so many new and exciting ways, it has also fostered lifestyles of isolation.

The truth is you aren't alone and you don't have to go solo. It's not your job to save the whole world by yourself.

Creatives inspire creatives. If you follow the path of the endless creative, if you look for opportunities to form relationships, you will soon find others keeping pace beside you.

Friendship requires effort, but the steps of the creative journey can lead you there. In this age of connectivity, it isn't hard to find like-minded people who will encourage, guide, and cheer you on, giving you the strength for the next step, reminding you who you are and why you're here.

Surround yourself with creatives and you will learn how to be your most creative self.

Yes, you can be the start of a movement, but a movement doesn't happen without a big crowd of support. Find your crowd, find the mentors who can help, the peers who understand your goals, and the mentees you can lead (no, I didn't say manatees, but I hear they need help too).

To that end, I hope you'll check out my website: www.creativeandbeyond.com

You'll find a profusion of posts and resources aimed at helping creatives on their journey. Besides that, you can always reach out to me through the contact form if you'd like to talk. Whether the topic be light or heavy, my digital door is always open, and I'm itching to hear your thoughts (or maybe it's the poison ivy I just walked through).

As you prepare to set this book down, I hope you're left with an unquenchable excitement. Quite frankly, I'm excited for you—I can't possibly hold it back. I can't wait to see what you make, to find out how you are changed and how you change the world.

Here's the one final piece of encouragement I'd like you to remember: make time for daily creativity and don't let anyone, not even yourself, convince you it isn't worth it.

When you welcome the creative into your life, when it becomes a close companion, you will find a reward greater than riches, you will find fulfillment because you will be on the road to living your true calling.

I hope this story has inspired you, and, even more, I hope someday to read your story and be inspired.

Well, what are you waiting for? Get out there and be the endless creative you are. We're all counting on you to do just that.

Creatively yours,
A. P. Lambert

Let them call you a failure, incapable, hopeless, useless, incompe-
tent, wrong, a lost cause—you'll be in good company, with some
of the greatest people to have lived. But if they ever call you un-
creative, consider it your chance to prove them wrong, about that
and everything else.

~A. P. Lambert

~ SDG ~

ACKNOWLEDGEMENTS

There are so many voices and influences that go into the creation of a book, it's impossible to fit them on a page or two, even if I could bring them all to mind. Even so, there have been many fine people in my life who have not only helped me to grow as a creative, but have contributed in very tangible ways to the creation of this book.

First and foremost, I'd like to thank my wife, Britt, for tirelessly encouraging me throughout my many, varied creative pursuits. You're the fire that keeps me going, especially on those days when just giving up seems particularly appealing.

My loving parents (all six of them) and the fantastic ones we've adopted along the way (all four of them), for the parts you've played in shaping both my life and this book. You have given and continue to give me worthwhile things to write about—I treasure each and every one of you.

Abigail and the rest of the team at Hearts Unleashed for believing in this work and for your essential role in making this book a reality. Your excitement is infectious, I love it! And a special shout out to Val for your editorial work. Your polish really made this thing shine. I appreciate your honest and sincere approach.

Dori Harrell, the book's first editor. Thank you for the focus, wisdom, clarity, and professionalism you brought to this book. Your confidence played a major part in helping me believe in it myself.

Susan Harring, for all your hard work making this book look superb!

My buddies at The Forge, Andrew and Bob, for always picking me back up, providing some of my favorite conversations, and for giving me great things to aspire to.

Landon, a solid friend and a pretty decent pastor too. I appreciate you.

Tim, for your coaching, for always being interested in what I'm up to, and just for being a good chap to spend some time with.

My good friend David, one of the best thinkers I know. Thanks for asking the right sort of questions and for just being there. Hey man, when are we going to write a book together?

ABOUT THE AUTHOR

Aaron (AP) Lambert is a creative professional who helps other creatives achieve more and find purpose in their work.

Ever since his youth in Southern California, the creative force has been a major part of his life. Whether it was drawing pages full of alien creatures and their habitats, writing stories about the future, or crafting games from paper and cardboard, he was passionate about inventing new worlds for others to explore.

During high school, after discovering a free level editor for one of his favorite computer games, he joined an online community of dedicated fans who created and released their own missions for anyone to play. During that time, he learned the value of creative support (both given and received) and the power of storytelling through the experience of a game.

Aaron studied Media Arts and Animation at The Art Institute of California in San Diego, receiving his bachelor's degree in 2005. Since then, he's worked for over sixteen years in the animation and entertainment industry.

He's worked on hundreds of video game titles including Gears of War, Left 4 Dead, Dead Space, Uncharted, Call of Duty, Injustice, Mortal Kombat, Rogue Company, and Resident Evil. He's also worked on some films like Invictus, Tron Legacy, Ant-Man and the Wasp, and Spiderman: Far From Home. Not to mention a few commercials (like that first Kia Soul commercial with the dancing hamsters and the robots), and even an animated YouTube channel.

While he's explored many creative pursuits, he still holds a special love for stories—whether he's telling his kids a tale about a hot dog named Frank who washed up on a beach or working in his day job animating characters for games and films.

Aaron also enjoys hiking, foosball, board game nights, Smash Bros tournaments, and hanging out at the local brewery or coffee shop with a few good friends. He lives in Northern Arizona with his amazing wife, four incredible kids, fourteen adventurous chickens (but who's counting?), and a dog named Zalu, who loves people as much as a canine possibly can.

While he spends much of his time writing or designing games, he usually has a few other projects in the hopper.

You can find out more about what he's been up to at: www.creativeandbeyond.com

CPSIA information can be obtained
at www.ICGtesting.com
Printed in the USA
BVHW080404110323
660179BV00013B/611